For the Love of Guinea
(Three months in an African diamond exploration camp - 1980)

by

Darcy Joy Williamson

Cover painting by Stephen Aifegha

Dedicated to Fred, without whom

I would never have known Guinea

Edited by Brent Davy

ISBN: 9798321943601

Imprint: Independently published

Table of Contents

Introduction:

By the time I had reached the age of thirty, my life had been akin to a branch blown into a fast-flowing stream. It would float freely for a time before getting hung up on a pile of debris or captured in an eddy where it spun in circles until storms rose the water high enough to again serge downstream. The journey was meant to take me to open water. But again, and again my life became snagged, beached, and caught in eddies.

There are many challenges in the river of life. We are pushed along by its current, hoping to be carried by the flow, making plans, making choices, wanting control. Yet, how many plans worked out as we had expected? How many choices had we believed to be right, turned out wrong? And how much control does one really have? Spending three months in a West African diamond exploration camp in 1980, answered many of these questions. At the end of the adventure, I returned home a changed person.

PART 1 – BEFORE GUINEA

Fred and I met in the early summer of 1979. We were introduced by the mother of a friend of mine. She and Fred's mother had purchased a small house together in the nearby town of Donnelly, Idaho, as a summer get-away. I was a thirty-year-old divorcee with a nine-year-old son, Wayde, living in an apartment in my parent's home in McCall, Idaho. We had just returned from a forty-five-day book-sales trip.

At the time of Fred and my meeting, I had authored two books, *How to Prepare Common Wild Foods* (1976) and *School at Home, an Alternative to the Public School System* (1979), both published by Maverick Publications in Bend, Oregon. Originally, *How to Prepare Common Wild Foods* had been self-published. Since reading Euell Gibbons' 1962 book, *Stalking the Wild Asparagus*, I had been harvesting and preparing wild food to include in a cookbook. I knew nothing about book marketing in the beginning, just that the concept of a cookbook using wild food was a viable topic. Taking out a loan from a local bank, using a piece of land my grandmother had gifted me as collateral, I published 5,000 copies of *How to Prepare Common Wild Foods*. My friends, Jack and Betty, flew me to Bend, Oregon in their Cessna 180 to deliver the manuscript to Maverick Publications. The book was printed in an 8-1/2 by 11 inch format at the cost of one dollar each, delivered. Once printed, the owner, Ken Asher, personally delivered the books to McCall, Idaho via a U-Haul trailer. My mother and father had cleaned out a large coat closet in the foyer of their home for storage of the books.

Pandemonium erupted when my parents and I saw boxes upon boxes of books crammed in the back of the U-Haul. Obviously, we had had no idea what amount of space storing 5,000 copies of an 8-1/2 by 11-inch publication would require! The printer was eager to get the books unloaded. He had friends in Boise where he had planned to overnight before his return to Bend. The mass of printed material would fill my parents' living room three boxes deep! I frantically phoned a friend who lived in an old farmhouse with multiple rooms. Did he have a room that I could rent for storage? He informed me that he was planning on putting the house on the market, but the books could be stored in an unused ground floor bedroom for the time being. Fortunately, the U-Haul was able to be backed up to an outside window where the boxes were passed through, one by one, and stacked floor to ceiling, filling much of the room.

A major challenge lay ahead – getting the massive number of books sold before my friend put his house on the market.

A week later I hooked my small two-bed tent trailer to my green 1966 Rambler Ambassador station wagon, loaded the back with a dozen cases of books, tossed my son's home-schooling books on the back seat and he and I set off on our first book sales trip. First stop was Boise, Idaho. At the time, I was comfortable with my own company, but shy and awkward when dealing with people I didn't know. Walking into a bookstore and asking someone to buy my book tied my stomach in knots. Writing and publishing the book was easy. Promoting and selling it was the hardest part of the business and regretfully I was unprepared.

I left Wayde at a café a few doors down from the bookstore to enjoy a bowl of ice cream. Carrying an armload of books, I stood nervously outside The Book Shop entrance on Boise's Main Street. My heart was racing, and I felt a touch of nausea. Taking a deep breath, I entered the store and spotted a business-like woman over by the cookbook section acting as though she was surveying the stock rather than looking for a book to purchase.

Mistakenly assuming that the person was associated with the shop, I approached her, and nervously stood there.

“May I help you?” She asked.

“Would you like to purchase some books on wild food?” I blurted.

She sized me up, then glanced at the stack of books cradled in my arms and said, “No. Not really. I was looking for a good book on Italian cuisine. Have you any suggestions?”

“No. Not really.” I answered awkwardly, before backing away and looking frantically around the store. A young woman had just walked behind the check-out desk and was totaling up a customer’s sales. I anxiously waited for her to finish before timidly approaching the counter.

“Yes?” She asked, looking up.

“I have written these books. I mean, this book.” I said, handing her the top copy from my pile.

She stood there and thoughtfully examined some of the pages and actually read through one of the recipes. This isn’t so difficult, I thought to myself.

Then she said, “Well, I just work here. I don’t do any of the buying. You need to see Jean. She’s down the hallway located at the back of the shop…first door to the right.”

I entered panic mode as I slowly made my way down the hallway. Inside an open doorway was a small woman wearing owlish glasses, sitting behind an over-sized desk shuffling through paperwork. I was on the verge of losing my nerve when she glanced up.

"What do you want?" She asked, in a slightly irritated voice.

That did it. I burst into tears. "You don't want to buy my books, do you?"

Startled, she motioned for me to enter the small office and held out her hand. I stepped forward and handed her a copy of my book, then backed away toward the door.

That first 5,000 copies of my publication had a plain white back cover. No artwork or introduction about what the book contained, no price – just stark white naked. Jean studied the book, frowning as she glanced at the blank back cover, but noted that the book had a copyright page complete with a library of congress number. Nodding, she examined the table of contents, then some of the recipes and illustrations.

Finally, she looked up and said, "This is a very good book! Very timely. What's retail?"

"Retail?" I asked.

"The price people pay for the book."

Strangely, I hadn't thought that far ahead. How much should the book sell for?

Jean was staring at me, obviously realizing how uninformed I was about the bookselling business.

"Six ninety-five." She finally said. "I could sell a lot of this title at six ninety-five."

I nodded in agreement.

"What's the wholesale price?" She continued.

When I didn't offer up an answer, she said, "Forty percent. That is standard. I purchase the books at a forty percent discount and sell them for six ninety-five. I'll start with two dozen. I'll have a check ready when you come back with the books."

I had only eight books with me which I hurriedly handed to Jean before heading back to my car. I still remember the thrill of that first sale. It was an incredibly bright August afternoon. Rushing past the café, I gave a thumbs-up to my son sitting there with his empty bowl. Impatiently waiting for the streetlight to change, shifting from foot to foot, I dashed across the street to the parking lot to retrieve the books. In my excitement, I managed to lock my keys in the car. Jean sent me back with a check and a wire coat hanger, with which my son managed to unlock the door.

Jean became a mentor, and in years following she held numerous book-signing events featuring my newly released titles.

I sold 5,000 copies of *How to Prepare Common Wild Foods* within a year. The bank loan had been paid off, and five thousand dollars set aside for the printing of a second edition. I had worn out my Rambler station wagon and retired my tent trailer, upgrading to a yellow 1970 Chevy pick-up truck to tow a 1966, 16-foot Aristocrat Lo-Liner trailer.

Upon returning to Bend to purchase another 5,000 copies of the book, Ken Asher offered to be the publisher of the wild food book, as well as my next proposed book, *School at Home, An Alternative to the Public School System.*

Since my self-published first edition had had successful sales, my contract with Maverick allowed me to distribute my own books, not only collecting royalties but distributor fees as well. Royalty was ten percent of the wholesale price of books sold. The distributor fees were ten percent of the retail price, allowing me to make enough money to support my son and myself by doing two forty-five day book sales trips a year. Five hundred copies of future publications would be printed at a time and stored in Maverick Publication's warehouse. No more frantic searches for book storage!

Spring tours took me through parts of Idaho, Montana, and Wyoming. The autumn tours covered much of Oregon and Washington. Each tour would take me to new towns in each region, expanding my market. Aside from bookstores, sales were also made to libraries, health food stores, and outdoor equipment shops. This was when the book market wasn't dominated by big corporations and a time when managers of the rapidly expanding chain, B. Dalton Booksellers, could still purchase from local authors. Independent bookstores still flourished. There were usually one or two local bookstores in most of the towns I visited. Much of my time between book sales trips was occupied packaging and mailing book orders from established accounts.

When Fred and I met, I had been dating several male friends but was not seeking permanent relationships. Dates usually consisted of going to the local bars to have a few beers and dancing to rock n' roll and country music bands. There were occasional afternoons lounging in the area's abundant hot springs and infrequent evening dinners at local restaurants.

Fred was a geologist who had recently returned from Guinea, West Africa, where he was employed by a diamond exploration company, DDX of New York. The company shut down operations during the region's rainy season. Fred was thirty-four years old, about six feet tall, and clean shaven with a military-style haircut. One of the things that endeared him to me was he had a glass eye, which didn't always track smoothly. My dad had lost an eye during WWII. I don't remember how Fred had lost his.

Dating Fred was exciting! He wasn't into dancing or hanging out in bars sipping beer. He, as I, enjoyed exploring the out-of-doors. I found Fred's geological background fascinating. He delighted both Wayde and me with geographical facts about the Idaho Batholith when we took a road trip up the Main Salmon River in central Idaho.

Wayde & Fred in Joseph

During the three weeks of his visit, we also went hiking into backcountry lakes, boating on Payette Lakes, and canoeing along the upper north fork of the Payette River. But the most fun we three had was taking the Chevy and Aristocrat trailer to Joseph, Oregon. We camped for two nights and took the Wallowa Lake tram over 8,000 feet to the peak of Mount Howard. There are markers pointing to three states, Oregon, of course, but also Idaho and Washington. We hiked along the two miles of trail, Fred pointing out geological features and I, naming wildflowers still in full bloom in the high alpine meadow.

In McCall, we spent many evenings with my parents at their home along the Payette River. They both enjoyed Fred as he kept conversations lively and full of interest. Too soon, Fred had to return to California. We kept in touch with phone calls and long, romantic letters. Fred was to return to his work in Guinea toward the middle of January (1980) to one of the DDX's camps located near Kérouané, Kissidougou, and Macenta, where the main diamond deposits in the West African country were located. DDX had a three-year exploration contract.

DDX was a subsidiary of DDI, a U.S. company with offices in New York and France, the operator for the joint venture between DDI, HWI, COGEMA and the Guinea government. This joint adventure was financed by these three foreign companies. The Guinean government, who owned the mineral rights, contributed the land which was to be mined.

The joint venture had a three year term, ending in July 1981, to explore promising areas within the 40,000 kilometers permit in Upper Guinea. After that date a local Guinean company would be formed to proceed with mining and further prospecting if the exploration results had been economically attractive.

I had planned to leave on November 26th for my autumn book sales trip. The focus was parts of Oregon, mainly the coastal area, and Washington, as far as Seattle. Wayde and I would be spending Christmas on the road and returning home via La Grande, Oregon, to spend New Years Eve with my brother and sister-in-law. I expected to be home by the late evening of January 1st. After conferring with my son about the possibility of asking Fred to join us on the autumn book sales trip, he excitedly agreed.

Wayde liked Fred. Fred didn't exclude him from the adventures he and I shared. Whether it was a picnic lunch, a hike to Josephine Lake, or swimming in Burgdorf Hot Springs, we went as a threesome.

My travel trailer was small and had one double bed at the back where I slept during our trips. The dining table folded down into a bed for Wayde. Having Fred traveling with us would complicate things, as the bed would be shared. My son quickly volunteered to sleep in the front seat of the pickup with a bedroll. Wayde was enthused about the possibility of having him join us.

Fred quickly accepted our invitation. He took a flight to Boise, where Wayde and I picked him up at the airport November 26th to begin my forty-five day bookselling tour.

The following includes information taken from edited diary entries dating November 26, 1979, through January 1, 1980.

November 26th – The open Chevy pick-up bed was loaded with twenty cases of tightly tarped books to prevent moisture damage. I had arrived in Boise a day earlier to cover my current accounts there, including The Book Shop. I was able to have a pleasant but short visit with Jean Wilson.

At the airport, Wayde recognized Fred at once and ran to him. I had a less enthusiastic approach, feeling a bit shy. We hugged, and Fred, sensing my unease, kissed me on the cheek rather than the lips. Once Fred had settled his things in the trailer, we headed toward Baker City, Oregon, hoping to make an afternoon stop at

Betty's Books, a new store that Jean Wilson had told me about, owned by Betty Kuhl.

Betty was welcoming and made a sizable purchase. Fred and Wayde went to the pickup to get the books while Betty proudly showed me around her new bookstore.

From Baker City we proceeded along Highway 7 to connect with Highway 26, pulling off on a side road to camp a short distance north of Prairie City. Fred had arrived for the trip with a handful of road maps covering Oregon and Washington, which he used to follow our route and point out geological features along the way. He wanted to spend time sightseeing, which I could see might become a problem. Even though I had no itinerary, enough books had to be sold during the five weeks to bring in the needed income to carry Wayde and me through winter.

The plan had been to overnight at John Day, but Fred was intent on visiting the Dewitt Museum in Prairie City, so there would be no early morning start. According to the information Fred had, the museum was in the building that had once been the western terminus depot of the Sumpter Valley Railroad. Fred was keenly interested in railroad history. In fact, as I was soon to learn, Fred had a charming, childlike enthusiasm for many things, historical, as well as geological.

I was feeling more relaxed with Fred. Our night together rekindled our romantic attraction to one another. We had a leisurely morning which included breakfast in a small Prairie City café. Normally, I would have prepared breakfast in the trailer, but this being the first full day of the sales trip, I decided to splurge. At 10:00 A.M. we arrived at the museum, which was located a couple of blocks from downtown, only to discover that it was closed on Tuesdays. Fred was very disappointed. I, on the other hand, was glad to get on with the business of the day.

I made a couple of small book sales traveling through John Day. After making nearly five hundred dollars in sales to my established accounts in Bend, I stopped at Maverick Publications to pick up several more cartons of books and to introduce Fred to Ken Asher and his wife Shirley. The Ashers took us out to dinner that evening, after which I drove to the outskirts of Sisters, Oregon to camp.

November 28th – December 12th After restocking my Sisters, Oregon accounts with books, we continued along Highway 242, spending two days covering my Springfield and Eugene accounts. Then we traveled along Interstate 5, making sales in towns along the way and engaging in sightseeing detours. After making sales in Roseburg, Fred convinced me to backtrack a few miles to Road 138, then travel the unimproved road sixty miles to see Toketee Falls and then on to Crater Lake. Toketee Falls was located a short distance off Road 138, along Forest Road 34. I had missed the turn-off onto the forest road and had to find a place to turn around a few miles along Road 138 to backtrack. At that point, I was wanting to bypass the waterfall excursion and continue to Crater Lake. Fred and Wayde convinced me otherwise. After missing the "No Trailers in Parking Lot" sign, I had to maneuver the truck and trailer back out of the tight parking lot to find a place wide enough along the forest road to tuck in. We walked a quarter of a mile back to the parking lot and trailhead.

I was feeling tense but, walking up the rustic, broad, stone stairway through the old growth forest began to relax me. The Christmas tree scent of Douglas fir, mingling with the faint spicy aroma of Western red cedar was calming. Red Belted Polypore mushrooms hung hoof-like from deceased Douglas fir, while Turkey Tail mushrooms – shades of brown, tan, and blues – fanned in multiple layers across fallen, decaying big leaf maples. The sun, shining through the branches of Pacific Yew, some still speckled with bright red berries, cast lacy patterns along the pathway. The roar of the nearby falls fractured the forest serenity, growing louder as we navigated up nearly two hundred steps to the viewing platform. There, the North Umpqua River plunged through a narrow basalt gorge, forming a two-tiered waterfall, one dropping forty feet, the other eighty. The scene was breathtaking. The sheer beauty caused tears to well up as I hugged Fred tightly. He had insisted on seeing Toketee Falls and I had been reluctant, almost missing this enchanting place.

Between Toketee Falls and Crater Lake, the Chevy's engine overheated. We had to pull off the road three times for the engine to cool down before reaching the lake. These were the times that I would dub my yellow Chevy, yellow Lemon. We camped for two nights in Crater Lake National Park. Fred had his maps spread out across the trailer's table, selecting places for our next adventures. This exploring fervor of his resulted in our first argument about time spent in pursuits other than bookselling. I found that I was no match in disagreements with Fred and ended up backing down.

December 13th -- 18th I had not previously visited Medford on my book sales trips. However, I did manage to make four small sales. After visiting my accounts in Grants Pass, we took the Redwood Highway to Crecent City, joined up with Highway 101 and traveled north back into Oregon from California and up the Oregon coast. We reached Coos Bay on the 16th day of December, now well into our third week of the five-week tour. I found Fred's enthusiasm for adventure and exploring new places to be both fun and exasperating. He had wanted to make stops at nearly every park and attraction along the way. Fred and Wayde had a great time exploring together. I enjoyed the adventures too, but also had a feeling of restlessness and "getting on our way". We had visited nearly every roadside attraction between Grant's Pass and Coos Bay. The positive thing for me during these roadside stops was that most parks and attractions had gift shops. Gift shop owners and managers eagerly scooped up my wild food cookbooks. This presented a big boost in sales in a market I had not previously discovered. I phoned Ken Asher asking him to ship four more boxes of *How to Prepare Common Wild Foods* to general delivery in Florence, to be picked up on our way through…hopefully by the 19th. Currently, there was still a good inventory of books, but I wanted to be certain there would be enough stock to cover my Washington accounts.

Since our arrival in Coos Bay was on a Sunday when few shops were open, we camped at Sunset Bay State Park and spent the early part of the day walking the beach under cloudy skies, hoping to find sand dollars. Toward mid-afternoon it was raining too hard to continue our outdoor pursuits. There had previously been some gentle rain during the trip but nothing significant. Now, I began worrying about the tarped books sitting in the back of the pickup, fearing the downpour could pool around the tarps and dampness seep in and warp the books. Fred went to take a hot shower at the campground facilities to warm up and get into some dry clothes. Meanwhile, Wayde and I climbed into the back of the pickup amidst the downpour and started hauling the heavy boxes of books into the trailer, piling them three boxes deep along the floor. Boxes were piled two high on the seat cushions on one side of the table and partly on the opposite cushion, leaving just enough space for Wayde to sit while doing his schoolwork. Book boxes were also piled four deep in the small closet-like toilet area. The refrigerator was barely accessible, and boxes of books had to be leaned across to access the sink and stove.

Wayde changed into dry clothes in the pickup cab while I managed to do the same in the trailer. Fred dashed in, his head and upper body sheltered beneath his jacket, warm and dry from his long hot shower. Leaning over boxes of books, I made a fresh halibut dinner served with lemon sauce, fresh green salad, and steamed rice. For lack of space, the three of us ate our meal on the bed. Fred seemed oblivious of the fact that his lack of involvement in helping to move the books to a dry and safe place had irked and disappointed me. I was also a bit stressed to be running way behind schedule, needing to have the trip finished in time to spend New Years Eve in La Grande. I had to remind myself that for Fred, this trip was a vacation. For me, it was a vital means of income.

The rain had stopped by morning and the sun was showing. After the three of us moved the boxes of books from the trailer to the back of the truck and secured them under the tarps, I left the trailer at the campground and did my sales route around the Coos Bay area. Wayde was to work at catching up on his home schooling. Fred, too, stayed behind to explore more of the state park. Sales went well, taking most of the day to visit and restock my established accounts and adding two new – a health food store and a gift shop. After reclaiming the trailer, we traveled up the coast as far as the Oregon Dunes National Recreation Area, camping the night at Honeyman State Park. That evening Wayde and Fred were busy pouring over maps, concentrating on the sand dunes, our first planned stop in the morning.

Fred bought us passes on the guided dune buggy rides. He took his binoculars in hopes of seeing a Western Plover but didn't spot any. A few miles south of Florence, we followed a beach access road where I dropped Fred and Wayde by the south jetty to explore. After unhitching the trailer in the large parking lot there, I headed to Florence in the Chevy to pick up the books Maverick Publications had mailed. While in town, I managed to visit my three accounts, restocking two. The manager wasn't at the third business, a souvenir shop located in the old part of town by the Siuslaw River. The shop was out of the wild food books, so I planned to revisit it the following day when it opened at ten in the morning.

In 1971, when Wayde was a year old, his dad and I had lived in Florence for seven months before moving to Biddeford, Maine. I remembered a place at the north jetty where there wasn't an official campground, but an area where camping was allowed. I picked up Wayde and Fred, hooked up the trailer and moved to the north jetty. I had purchased freshly cooked crabs while in town, along with a cabbage, which I made into coleslaw. After dinner the three of us walked to the beach. We found small keyhole limpet shells, some periwinkles, and a few sand dollars. As the sun was setting, we reluctantly made our way back to the trailer. It had been a wonderful day and I felt very close to Fred. Our love continues to grow as our understanding of one another deepens.

December 19th – 22nd It was now Thursday, the 19th. New Years Eve was just twelve days away. As we headed north toward Newport, Wayde and Fred had already planned to stop at the Sea Lion Caves, then spend an hour or so at Agate Point looking for stones. I realized that at the rate we were traveling, there would be no time to cover my accounts in Washington along Interstate 5 between Portland and Seattle. Coming to that realization, the stress that I had been feeling eased. I had, after all, made numerous new accounts and sales at the roadside attractions and park gift shops. I expected strong sales along this stretch of the

Oregon coast and inland through Corvallis before returning to Seaside and working north to Astoria. Portland would take two days to cover accounts, then a day's travel east to La Grande. We'd spend the planned New Years Eve with my brother and sister-in-law, Fred would make his late-night January 1st flight out of Boise, back to California, and Wayde and I would be back in McCall that evening. I'd be okay financially.

We parked in a wide spot along the highway, looking down at the Sea Lion Caves, then walked the short distance down the driveway to the entrance. Visitors were funneled through a gift shop first, where passes to the attraction were sold. Fred took one look at the gift shop and disappeared. He came back with half a dozen wild food books and quickly had them sold. The manager insisted that I autograph the books. Two immediately sold to visitors in the gift shop before we took the elevator down into the big natural cavern to view the sea lions. Fred couldn't help grinning at having successfully made his first book sales.

It was still slightly "off season", but we had been told that there were nearly eighty huge mammals lounging around in the cave. Their cacophony echoed off the cavern walls. They barked, growled, mooed, and swayed. The pungent scent of sea water mingled with musky sea lion scent filled the salty air. The three of us delighted in the sight, sound, and even the smell of them!

Further down Highway 101 we came to Agate Point, not far from Yachats. I left Wayde and Fred hunting for agates where a creek met the ocean and went on to Yachats to cover one account there – a nice sale of a dozen books. When I returned to Agate Point, both Wayde and Fred were disappointed in not having found agates.

I was able to make sales to two accounts in Waldport before closing time. We then headed east along Hwy 20 toward Corvallis, pulling onto a forested side road to sleep. I prepared a simple supper of grilled cheese sandwiches and canned tomato soup before tucking in for the night.

I had eight accounts to visit in Corvallis. Fridays are usually good for sales. However, this day's sales were lower than average due, I believe, to being so close to Christmas. I sold more of my new home-schooling books than the wild food cookbooks, which surprised me. We traveled back to the coast where I made sales at three accounts each in Newport and Lincoln City. After eating at a hamburger joint in Lincoln City, I drove us up the coast toward Oceanside where we camped at the Cape Lookout State Park. Fred saw people digging for clams at low tide and went to investigate.

In the morning, I left Fred and Wayde at the camp while I visited my accounts in the Tillamook area. Wayde needed to catch up on his studies and Fred had left early for the beach. Saturdays are usually not good for sales, but I did better than I had expected! I purchased marshmallows, Hershey bars, and graham crackers, plus some hotdogs, lettuce, and potatoes for our dinner.

When I arrived back at the trailer around 4:30, both Wayde and Fred were gone. I whittled some sticks for cooking hotdogs and marshmallows, started a fire in the firebox, wrapped the potatoes in foil and set them along the edges of the forming coals. I had considered setting the outside picnic table for dinner. But the air had grown chilly and rain clouds were skulking across the sky. I abandoned the outside picnic table and set the small inside table with plates and silverware, instead. We could cook outside, but "dine" in the comfort of the trailer. I started the propane heater.

It was growing dark when I heard Wayde calling, "Mom! Mom! Look what Fred's got!"

Wayde was muddy up to his waist. Here came Fred, equally muddy, with my plastic waste basket nearly overflowing with razor clams. Neither were dressed for late December! They both looked frozen to the core.

"You two wait out here…go stand by the fire." I directed as I entered the trailer and filled my largest cooking pan with water to put on the stove to heat up. Then I rummaged around in Fred's backpack for dry clothing. I dug out Wayde's dry clothes from the storage area beneath the table bench. Rain began to patter on the aluminum roof. Fred and Wayde shed their wet clothes and quickly donned the dry clothing before entering the trailer, where they finished cleaning up with the warm water I had heated. So much for hotdogs and S'mores over a campfire. I boiled the hotdogs and finished baking the potatoes in the oven. We used whittled sticks to roast marshmallows over the flames produced by the gas stove burners. As we ate the sticky treats, Fred and Wayde entertained themselves with tales of how Fred borrowed a shovel from one of the other campers and stalked the wily razor clams. Meanwhile, I sat there wondering what I was going to do with all those clams.

December 23rd – 25th We arrived at Seaside mid-morning on Sunday the 23rd. Attempting to make sales on a Sunday almost always results in a fruitless endeavor. Additionally, Monday, the day before Christmas would not be a good day for sales. Shop owners are already in "sales mode" marking down their inventory. So, I decided that the day would be leisurely spent in Seaside, then we would move north to Fort Steven State Park and camp there through Christmas.

We visited the Seaside Museum with its tanks of jailed sea life and walked the Seaside Promenade – "the Prom". Stopping at Legg's Pharmacy we purchased some marked-down Christmas items, a string of miniature lights, some small glass tree ornaments, tinsel, and a package of little candy canes. Then we walked down the street and had dinner at Cathay Garden, a Chinese restaurant, before heading north along Highway 101. Enroute Fred had me stop along the side of the road near a wooded area. He and Wayde snuck through the dark with a flashlight and handsaw, searching for a little tree, and came back with a three-foot Western Red Cedar sapling. It was dark by the time we drove fifteen miles up the coast to Fort Steven State Park and selected a campsite at the south loop.

Christmas Eve's morning weather was misty and cold. I was heating tea water when Wayde came in from the pick-up cab.

"Would you please take this waste basket to the spigot at the end of the cul-de-sac and rinse these razor clams, fill the basket up with fresh water and bring it back here?" I asked.

Wayde gave me one of his "Aw, Mom…" looks, but went about the task. By the time he returned I had scrambled eggs, sausage and toast set out on the table. After the three of us had finished breakfast and I had the morning's dishes washed, dried, and put away, I curled up on the bed contently, Colleen McCullough's novel, *The Thorn Birds*, in hand. Fred slouched beside me reading a tattered copy of *Fire in the Earth; the story of the diamond.* We had planned on exploring some of the park's historical sites after lunch.

Wayde, however, was restless and started asking questions, interrupting our reading.

"Where's the cannons? Are there cannons? Did any of the Japanese get killed when they tried to attack the fort? Did things get burned up? Is there a lighthouse? How deep is the ocean around here..."

Fred got up, put on his raincoat, and handed Wayde his.

"Time to explore some of the old artillery gun batteries", Fred said. Wayde hastily put on his raincoat.

I had over three hours of peace and relaxation. I was on my third cup of coffee. Where were they? It was raining out – a steady drizzle. I dumped the clams into the little trailer sink and poured cold water over them to rinse away any remaining sand. Then I filled my large cast iron skillet with a single layer of clams, pushed snuggly together. In a small saucepan I melted butter, added ample cloves of freshly minced garlic, then set the pan aside. I put on my rain jacket and gloves to brave the cold drizzle, which was now falling at a slant, due to the wind. I pulled a plastic bag from my pocket and, with gloved hands, filled the bag with pinched off fresh stinging nettle tips. Over by the water spigot I found a lush patch of sheep sorrel. I stuffed a few handfuls of that into my jacket pocket.

Back at the trailer I rinsed the stinging nettle tips and placed them in a saucepan with only the water clinging to their leaves. With scissors I finely snipped the rinsed sheep sorrel into a small bowl and placed the bowl into the refrigerator.

Now five hours had passed since Wayde and Fred had taken off to explore. The entirety of Fort Stevens Park was over 4,000 acres. What if they had gotten lost? Where was the nearest phone booth? Should I unhook the trailer and go in search of the two? I decided to wait another thirty minutes before entering a full-blown panic…and here they came, laughing, out-of-breath, red-faced from the cold, and soaking wet, again.

I didn't have to ask where they had been, Wayde was more than eager to tell me. After they had visited the old Artillery site, they decided to hike down to the end of the Clatsop Spit where Fred thought they might spot some plovers. Sadly, they saw none.

"Then coming back," Fred laughed, "We couldn't remember where we had parked."

"So, we walked and walked and walked until we saw the yellow pick-up and the trailer. Then we ran like crazy people!" Wayde added, excitedly.

I was too relieved to be upset with them. It was such a large campground that I could have easily done the same thing myself. I sprinkled olive oil over the razor clams, turned the burner to medium-high and covered the skillet with the cast iron lid so that I wouldn't have to witness the dying clams pop open. Meanwhile I steamed the nettles in a covered saucepan until they were wilted. I divided the nettles onto three plates. Uncovering the skillet, I doused the opened clams with the butter and garlic mixture, before placing them on the beds of steamed nettles. The snipped sheep sorrel was lavishly sprinkled over each plate to give the dinner a lemony tartness. The baked razor clams were such a hit that I quickly cooked up two more skillets worth, saving just enough of the clams for tomorrow's Christmas day chowder.

After the dinner dishes were cleaned and put away, we set the tree up on the dining table. The little tree's trunk was firmly pushed into a coffee can filled with sand. Lights were wound among the branches, then small glass balls and candy canes were hung. Strands of tinsel were liberally strewn overall, then the lights were plugged in. The three of us sat in silence, sipping spiced cider, and admiring the beautiful little Christmas tree.

Finally, Wayde asked, “Can I get Fred’s and my package from the cupboard above your bed to put by the tree?”

“You snooped!” I accused.

“Don’t I always?” Wayde laughed.

Christmas morning, I woke up early and climbed across the still sleeping Fred. Quietly, I lit the oven and removed the frozen, unbaked, store-bought cinnamon rolls from the tiny freezer compartment. I set the kettle on the burner to heat water for instant hot chocolate and grabbed the bag of marshmallows from the small pantry. Then I plugged in the little Christmas tree and sat down at the table with a satisfied sigh, gazing at the colorful string of miniature lights. The small cedar tree gave off a soft woodsy scent. The packages wouldn’t fit under such a tiny tree, so the tape recorder for Wayde sat on the windowsill, wrapped in bright red paper with a big green bow. The gift that I had purchased for Fred, leather slippers with fleece lining, sat beside it, similarly wrapped. Tucked beneath the tree was a small packet wrapped in newspaper, tied with twine.

Wayde came in with a swoosh of chilled air and a slamming of the trailer door, startling Fred awake. I made each of us a mug of hot chocolate, topped with marshmallows, as the cinnamon rolls finished baking. The air was spicily scented.

Wayde was thrilled with his tape recorder. Fred seemed pleased with the slippers. Then Fred slid the newspaper wrapped package out from under the tree and handed it to me. I grinned as I unwrapped it, noticing that it held several handwritten index cards.

First Card: Good for one oil change – I will even buy the oil.

Second Card: Good for one dinner at the restaurant of your choice.

Third Card: Good for one Chevy wash and wax.

Fourth Card: Good for one homecooked meal compliments of chef Fred.

Fifth Card: Will you marry me? I will be good to you.

I sat in shocked silence. I glanced at Wayde, who sat across the table from me.

"What?" he asked, puzzled.

"I just proposed to your mother," Fred answered.

"Mom!" Wayde exclaimed.

"I want you and Wayde to come to Guinea. I will buy your plane tickets to Senegal. We'll get married in Dakar before we go into Conakry. It will be better for all of us to have you as my wife, rather than a single woman, when we enter camp. I love you. I want us to be together. The three of us, as family." Fred said.

Guinea is a small country that lays on the great bulge of West Africa. It is bordered by the Atlantic Ocean, Guinea-Bissau, Senegal, Mali, the Ivory Coast, Liberia, and Seirra Leone.

I looked at Fred, then back to Wayde, who sat there with a pleading expression.

"I need to be alone for a bit," I said. "I'll be in the truck. Just give me some time to think." I exited the trailer.

I sat shivering as I climbed into the pickup cab. I wrapped myself in Wayde's bedroll, still warm from his sleep. It wasn't that it was that chilly in the cab. I think that I was in shock, somewhat. The proposal had been unexpected. I needed to think things through. I had been in love and married before. More than once. Nothing had worked out. It wasn't from lack of trying.

I loved Fred. But was it enough? Fred was different from other men I had known. Smart…to the point of being brilliant. A self-sufficient and financially secure bachelor. Opinionated. Used to having his way. Would I be lost to his dominance or was I strong enough to hold my own?

And there was Wayde. There was something special between Fred and Wayde. Fred enjoyed being with my son. He was kind to the boy, but could be firm, as well. A bond had quickly formed between the two. Not that Wayde hadn't had opportunities to connect with other men. He had had a stepfather who had officially adopted him. However, as Wayde grew older, the battle between the two became more volatile.

"Take your kid and get out!" I had been told. So, I did.

Africa. How much would the opportunity to go to Africa play in an acceptance? Africa had always been in my heart; from the time I was a very young girl. It was the place I had always longed to be. It wasn't about elephants and giraffes. It had always been about something else. What that something was, at that time, I could not comprehend.

And Fred. Obviously, he had spent time thinking about this proposal of marriage. He had things already laid out. When and where we were to meet in Africa. And to marry. And why it was a good idea to wed before entering the camp in Guinea. It wasn't a spontaneous thought…something to tuck under a Christmas tree at the last minute. Was it?

Yes, I loved Fred. But was it enough? Was love ever enough?

I exited the truck, took a deep, cleansing breath and opened the trailer door. The hot chocolate mugs were empty, the cinnamon rolls consumed, and a pair of expectant eyes were turned my way.

"Yes," I said. "Yes, Fred, I will marry you."

December 26th – 31st We left the park early Wednesday morning and headed toward Astoria, where Fred treated us to breakfast at a little café while we waited for local businesses to open. Book sales were very good in Astoria, so it was a busy morning and early afternoon. We traveled along Hwy 30 toward Portland, making a couple of sales, restocking my accounts in Rainier. I wanted to reach OMSI (Oregon Museum of Science and Industry) before closing. Hwy 30 connected to 26 and we arrived at Washington Park two hours before OSMI closed. Wayde and Fred headed to the exhibit halls while I went to the combination gift and book shop. We were to meet at the big walk-in heart in an hour, then go together to the planetarium. I was a half-hour late, but Fred and Wayde had plenty to occupy themselves with the hands-on displays. I had restocked the wild food cookbooks, twenty-four copies! And the shop purchased a dozen home schooling books. This had been my biggest single sale of the trip. We backtracked about five miles up Hwy 30 to a wide pull-off along the river to spend the night.

I had previously been granted permission to leave the trailer at the far edge of the OMSI parking lot during the daylight hours of the 27th and 28th while I covered my accounts in Portland. The little trailer was supplied with breakfast and lunch fixings for Wayde and Fred, who assured me that there was enough to explore at OMSI and the Portland Zoo to occupy them for two days.

Thursday's sales went well. I'm not comfortable with large city driving and frustrated myself by getting misplaced a couple of times by going in a direction away from where I had intended to be. I covered my accounts in Portland and Vancouver, emptying three cartons of books. The wild food books were selling three for every home-schooling book. I returned to the OMSI parking lot around 5:30 and pulled the trailer back to the place where we had spent the previous night. The guys had had a great day but hadn't been to explore the zoo, yet. They planned to spend the following day there while I covered accounts in Beaverton, Tigard, Oswego Lake, and Gresham.

Sales on the 28th were on par with the previous day. This had been my last full sales day of the trip. There were a few places to stop on my way to La Grande, but not large accounts. I was able to get back to the trailer a little before six. Fred and Wayde were ready. They had things put away in the trailer so that all I needed to do was hitch up and drive off. We crossed the Columbia River into Washington, connecting with Hwy. 14. We had pizza in Stevenson and spent the night in a large pullout alongside the river. The following morning, we crossed back across the Columbia and had breakfast at The Dalles, before heading east along Interstate 84.

About twenty miles west of Pendleton, I spotted flashing lights in my sideview mirror. I glanced at the speedometer; I was traveling a few miles-per-hour below the posted speed limit. I put my signal on and pulled off the first place along the highway that would safely fit my pickup and trailer. I rolled down the window and retrieved my information from the glove box to hand to the state trooper.

Then the passenger door opened. Fred and Wayde exited the pickup.

The trooper was explaining that I had been pulled over because the side mirrors on my pickup weren't adequate; I needed mirrors that extended further out. The trooper was amicable…but not for long.

Fred had approached from around the hood of the pick-up.

"What do you mean, the mirrors aren't adequate? She saw your lights, right? She pulled over right away, correct? Obviously, she could see clearly enough, don't you think!"

And there was Wayde, standing beside Fred with his tape recorder, the microphone pointed up toward the now, highly irritated trooper.

"Get back in the vehicle!" The trooper ordered the two.

My heart sank. Thinking that the likely warning ticket would now certainly be a full-blown traffic ticket. And I was correct.

Fred was smug. Wayde was proud that he had gotten the whole confrontation recorded on his tape recorder. He had evidence, should the case go to court! And me? The one with the ticket?

"Children!" I thought. "I've been traveling with children!"

At Pendleton I made two sales, then we headed up the steep "Deadman's Pass" through the Blue Mountains toward La Grande, Oregon. At the top of the pass, we pulled into a roadside camping area. The campground was closed for the winter, but there was a plowed area where I parked to spend the night.

After a leisurely morning, we arrived at my brother and sister-in-law's home in La Grande. Wayde was excited to have time with his cousins and the three took off to town to go to the arcade. Fred relaxed into easy conversation with my brother, Gregg, while Veronica and I prepared lunch before settling into a four-way cribbage game. The three kids returned on schedule and occupied themselves in my nephew's room playing games.

Veronica had planned on roasted chicken for dinner with green beans. I made mashed potatoes and put together a green salad. It felt good to be in the kitchen with my sister-in-law while my brother and Fred watched TV in the living room. Veronica wanted to know everything about Fred and how the engagement had come about after such a short time of us being together. And how I felt about taking my young son to Africa. She was a more protective mother than I was…maternal to the core. I foresaw Africa as an adventure for Wayde, whereas she foresaw danger and the likelihood of misadventures. She had been right, of course.

January 1, morning 1980 – We left La Grande around 8:00 in the morning. Fred had a late evening flight out of Boise, but the weather was wicked, so we wanted to get an early start. The wind was up, and the blowing snow was creating white-out conditions. My brother had been up early and had hot coffee and donuts waiting when we came in from the trailer to say goodbye.

There is a mountain pass about twenty miles south of La Grande. I had been over it a few times with the pickup pulling the trailer. Having navigated the steep "Deadman's Pass" between Pendleton and La Grande two days earlier, I didn't give this insignificant pass a second thought. However, as I was shifting gears down as the grade steepened, the gears seemed to be sticking. This had happened a few times previously on the trip. Fred had topped up the transmission fluid outside of Pendleton as a precaution before heading up "Deadman's Pass".

Just as we reached the top of the pass, there was the smell of burnt engine fluid. When I went to shift into higher gear, there was no response. I managed to get the pickup and trailer eased off to the side of the road. Fred got out of the vehicle and lifted the hood. I quickly followed. The wind was howling through the mountain pass, whipping the falling snow into a white-out frenzy. Both pickup and trailer shuttered under its force. The sharp acrid smell from beneath the hood confirmed my fear – the transmission was toast.

Fred went into high gear. He slammed down the hood, and Wayde and I followed him into the trailer. As Fred was picking up his stuff and cramming it into his backpack, he was giving me orders.

"Get the propane heater going. I don't know how long you and Wayde will be here before help comes. I'll call your brother when I get a ride to Baker City and let him know where you are. I'll meet you in Senegal at the Dakar airport on March 17th. I should be on my two-week break from camp then. Before I leave for Guinea, I'll get a letter off with plane tickets for you and Wayde, plus any additional details. Apply for Guinea visas right away. It will take some time. If you can't get visas before it's time to leave, just go. We'll sort it out when you get to Africa. And pack light. Don't bring a bunch of unnecessary stuff."

Fred gave me a quick kiss and was gone. I left the shelter of the trailer and watched as he walked down the edge of the freeway, thumb out, and like a ghost, disappear into the swirling white maelstrom of snow.

PART 2 – PREPARING FOR GUINEA

The following includes information taken from edited diary entries dating January 1, 1980, through March 14, 1980.

January 1, afternoon, 1980 – After Fred had left, I started the propane heater. Within thirty minutes the trailer had warmed up nicely. The kettle was put on the stove for tea, even though neither Wayde nor I cared for it. Fred had been the tea drinker. We sat at the table in silence staring at our filled cups, watching tea slosh onto the table with each passing semi-truck.

Within two hours, Gregg showed up in his old van. First, he had to tow my Chevy back to La Grande. There was concern about leaving the trailer unattended at the side of the road, but the Chevy needed steering and brake action during towing. Wayde rode with my brother as I guided the towed vehicle twenty miles back to my brother's house. My sister-in-law took Wayde into the house to fix him something to eat while my brother and I went back for the trailer. Gregg had brought two different balls for the hitch, not knowing which size would fit. He was always thinking ahead. Fortunately, the one on the trailer easily connected with the one on his van.

My brother is a man of few words. He tends to be a listener, rather than a talker. Perhaps that is why he has the wisdom that he has. Gregg's wife Veronica is a talker and keeps conversations flowing and entertaining – the perfect pairing with one so content to just listen. The drive between the pass and La Grande was silent most of the way.

The first thing that Gregg said to me was, "I know a good mechanic. Not too expensive."

We continued in silence for ten miles or so before he spoke again.

"So, Fred just left you and Wayde stranded there." Not a question. A statement.

I spoke up for Fred, "He had a plane to catch."

Another few miles passed before Gregg commented, "Tickets can be cancelled."

January 2nd – The next day my brother called the mechanic. We towed the Chevy pickup to the man's garage. After a few minutes checking under the hood, the mechanic verified what was already suspected. He said he'd have to locate a rebuilt transmission and find out how long it would take to receive it before he could estimate how long it would take to install it. Also, he had work to get done ahead of working on the Chevy. The mechanic guessed that it would most likely be between ten days and two weeks.

While in La Grande waiting for my truck to be repaired, I applied for a passport. Wayde didn't need one since he was a minor traveling with me, but it had been suggested that there be a copy of my son's birth certificate to present, as well.

Fred had said that the two of us needed to travel light. I knew that I could fit a lot of items in a large backpack and carry my guitar. Wayde was strong enough to carry a medium-sized backpack with his basics. There could be a light piece of luggage that could be pack with extra clothing and toiletries. But Wayde's schoolbooks would be very heavy and cumbersome to take to Africa.

There was a serious discussion with Wayde about his homework. My proposal was that he work extra hours on his schoolwork and finish before we left for Africa in mid-March. That would put a lot of pressure on him, as his curriculum through Calverts Homeschool Program out of Baltimore, Maryland, was demanding. However, I also knew that it took Wayde an average of three hours to complete a day's lesson. If he doubled up two days a week and did three hours of school one weekend day each week, he would have his school year finished by early March. If not, the guitar would be left behind, and his books would be taken instead. He was seriously considering the proposition, but there was still hesitation, so I added an incentive.

"In Guinea, you will likely make friends with children in villages near camp. If we didn't have a bunch of books to carry, you could have a small case with gifts to give to the children." I suggest.

Wayde liked that idea and committed to finishing his schoolwork before we traveled to Africa.

Next, work began on obtaining visas to enter Senegal and Guinea. I spent countless hours at the La Grande public library researching ways to acquire visas. I found that I didn't need a visa to enter Senegal if remaining there less than ninety days. Normally a visa could be requested through a country's embassy, but I could find no embassy listed in Guinea.

However, there was a reference to Ambassade de la Republique de Guinee; 2112, Leroy Place, N.W.; Washington D.C., to which a letter was sent requesting six visa application forms, three to be sent to my brother's address in La Grande, and three to my parent's address in McCall. Postage stamps were included with my request.

I did find that Guinea, a country closed to outside visitors, required an invitation from a government official, or a business, to have the possibility of being granted a visa. The government official or business would also need to assume financial responsibility for the guest. The official requirements were copied down. I knew that getting the visa would not be a simple task. What I didn't know was that getting my son and myself into Guinea would be nearly impossible.

Visa Requirements for The Republic of Guinea

A visa is issued only for business purposes.

The applicant or his employer must send a letter stating purposes, region, contacts, and nature of contracts within the Republic of Guinea.

A period of 10 to 15 days is necessary for procedures.

When we receive approval from Conakry, we then contact the applicant.

The following items are to be sent to us after approval:

Passport
10 dollars
3 photos
3 application forms

The application forms can be obtained at the Embassy and must be filled out.

If the applicant is invited by a member of the Government of Guinea, copy of invitation must be forwarded to the Embassy, and the visa can be issued at once.

Visas for tourists are not issued.

Mr. Francoise Lampietti, Managing Director of DDX, was written, asking if he would assist me in obtaining a visa to enter Guinea as the wife of one of his geologists on the 1980 Guinean diamond exploration.

I also wrote a request directly to Guinea's President, Sekou Toure, asking him to grant me permission to enter his country with my ten-year-old son to be with my husband, currently working as a geologist with DDX in diamond exploration in Upper Guinea.

An appeal to Guinea's first lady, Hadja Andrée Touré was sent. She, being a married woman, also with a son, could possibly relate to a woman who wanted to be at her husband's side, to make life easier for him in an unfamiliar country.

Once the letters were sent, all I could do was wait.

While at my brother's waiting for my transmission to be fixed, the three forms from Ambassade de la Republique de Guinee, in Washington D.C. had reached me in La Grande. The forms couldn't be filled out until my passport had arrived, which was to be mailed to my parent's address in McCall.

The truck's transmission was installed and ready to go nearly three weeks later. The mechanic had worked until late on Saturday the 19th. Gregg drove me over to pick it up. The total was a little over three hundred dollars.

My brother helped me hook the trailer up to the pickup for an early departure Sunday morning. That evening, I took Gregg, Veronica, young niece, and nephew out to dinner. I was so grateful for their hospitality. How could I ever repay them?

January 20th – Dawn was just beginning to brighten the sky. The trailer's propane heater was turned off. My son was awakened. As he dressed, I went into my brother and sister-in-law's house to say goodbye. A light skiff of snow had fallen during the night. Freezing temperatures had sculpted it into paper thin ice crystals that glittered when captured in the glow of my flashlight. Gregg gave me a big hug and handed me a large mug of coffee to start me on my way.

The roads were icy, and it took seven hours to make the four-hour drive. When we turned off Hwy. 95 and headed up Hwy. 55, just ten miles from home, we waited in a line of traffic for nearly two hours. There had been several slide-offs up Goose Creek Canyon. It took sanding and tow trucks, coming in from both ends, to untangle the mess.

While waiting for the canyon to get cleared I told Wayde that when we got to McCall, I wanted to be the one to tell my parents of Fred's and my engagement. When we reached McCall, Mom and Dad gave us enthusiastic greetings. Mom was just finishing preparing dinner – meatloaf, mashed potatoes, and peas. Wayde had had a hamburger and French fries when we had stopped in Weiser to fill up on gas and wasn't hungry. I took my son's backpack, guitar, and my suitcase upstairs to the apartment, then joined my parents at the dinner table. Wayde excused himself to unpack and get settled in his room.

I sat down at the table and reached for the catsup to douse my meatloaf.

“How’d the trip go, Hon?” Mom asked, as she took a sip of wine.

“Fred and I got engaged Christmas,” I answered.

My dad looked up from his plate, put down his fork and turned so that he could look directly at me. “You don’t have to marry every man that puts his shoes under your bed, you know.” Then he took a sip of his whiskey and leaned back.

“Bob!” Mom scolded.

Then turning to me she asked., “When would you plan to get married?”

“Late March, in Africa.”

“The plot thickens,” Dad said, taking another sip of whiskey. “You always said you wanted to go to Africa. You taking the kid?”

“Yes.” I answered.

“Good. He needs to see how the rest of the world lives.” Dad drained his glass, stood to leave the table, then paused to ruffle my hair. I felt the love travel down his arm.

As Mom and I cleared the table and washed the dishes, she said, “It’s always harder on your dad when you’re not near.”

“I know.”

Before going upstairs to the apartment, Mom handed me a stack of mail. Once in my room it was sorted through. The passport had arrived, as well as the duplicates of the form requested from Ambassade de la Republique de Guinee. And there was a letter packet from Fred!

Enclosed in Fred's letter packet were two roundtrip Apex tickets to Dakar via Pan Am. The return trip had to be within ninety days – therefore we would need to return by the 16th of June or face penalties. Also included was a five-page printout "*Memo Concerning DDX Operations in Guinea*" and a four-page printout, "*Background Notes Guinea, Department of State, September 1978.*"

Fred's letter was brief and to the point. He was looking forward to reuniting with Wayde and me. He will meet us at the Dakar-Yoff International Airport on the morning of March 17th. The three of us will leave for Conakry on the 27th. He signed his letter, "Love, Fred."

Also included in the packet was a list of items that I was to bring with me. Fred asked for two hundred dollars in traveler's checks, four tubes of super glue, ten 2 oz. tubes of Deet lotion, vegetable seeds for a small kitchen garden, 2 dozen cup hooks, and enough malaria pills to last the three of us four months.

I decided that it would be a good idea to sprout some seeds for added nutrition, so radish and alfalfa seeds were added to the list. Also, on my personal list, I will be taking a nice shirt and tie for Wayde, and a simple, but elegant, dress to wear for Fred's and my marriage.

Eager to learn as much as possible about Guinea before arriving, I visited the local library the following morning and ordered: American University, "*Area Handbook for Guinea*" Washington

D.C. Government Printing Office, 1975; Hapgood. "*Africa from Independence Tomorrow.*" New York: Atheneum, 1965.

January 25th – Yesterday, a notice from Ambassade de la Republique de Guinee. The application could not be processed because it did not fit the criteria for entry into Guinea.

Today I received a short, curt letter from Francoise Lampietti. He doesn't want women in camp, married or not, especially with a child. He outlined a few details to make his point. Aside from Guinea being a harsh place due to illnesses, poisonous snakes, and parasites, both a woman and a young child would be a distraction to camp members. He did not want either of us in Guinea. Period. No further discussion.

I chewed my bottom lip, quietly sitting and thinking…digesting Mr. Lampietti's curt and to the point message. His letter did not distract me from my goal to enter Guinea. Rather, it stoked a fire and heated my determination. I resolved to prove him wrong, should I manage to get into the country.

To add to my sense of growing isolation, my parents left for a six-week vacation and won't be back until sometime in April. They are friends with two other couples. The three couples have travel trailers and go on extended trips together during the winter. This is their fourth year. The group is going to take a slow trip down to Mazatlán, Mexico to do some deep-sea fishing, explore the area, relax, and enjoy the warm weather. I am to take care of the plants and house pets including, their two dogs – Colonel Klink, a schnauzer, and Chuck, an English pointer – until I leave on March 15th. A friend of the family will then occupy the house, taking care of the dogs, plants, and Mom's assortment of tropical birds.

January 27th – Fred's mother, Valerie, sent a package. I opened and read the note accompanying it. She wrote that she was very excited about her son's and my upcoming marriage. Though we had only met a couple of times, Valarie was pleased that Fred had chosen me as her daughter-in-law. She added that Wayde was an "instant gift", bringing into the partnership a grandchild. The eight blocks of four postage stamps enclosed were to be given as gifts to Guineans who provided services. The ring was a special gift for me. It was from her personal jewelry collection. She suggested that if Fred hadn't given me an engagement ring, that I wear it on my lefthand ring finger until he replaced it with a wedding band.

I unwrapped the small gold-foil, wrapped box, and stared in awe at the ring nestled in the box's purple velvet lining. It was stunning! The ring was hand-crafted gold, sculpted in the shape of the head of an owl. The owl's eyes were small facetted rubies. Slipping it on my finger, the ring fit perfectly. I was so happy that Fred's mother was pleased with our engagement.

January 31st – It has been one month since returning home. It was a cold, clear day today – one of those brutal but beautiful days when the temperature doesn't rise above zero degrees and the sky is azure blue. Icy breezes released tiny crystals from tree boughs. Everything sparkled.

But melancholy held me tightly in its clutches…a rare occurrence for me. An unsettled twist in my gut; my mind not focusing on what needed to be done to get Wayde and myself where we needed to go. Tears brimmed, threatening to fall. Finally, I curled up with a copy of *Collected Poems of Robert Service*. It seemed fitted to the brutal cold of the day – *The Cremation of Sam McGee*.

Something startled me awake, I don't know what. The sky had darkened, and the light of the full moon shone brightly beyond my apartment window. Wayde was sound asleep in his room.

Dressed warmly in my snowsuit, I quietly went to the garage and strapped snowshoes on. The moon lit the way to the river. Ice stretched six feet on each side of the river, its lacy edges brittle at the water's edge.

Snowshoes broke through the crust along the trail obscured beneath layers of snow. After following the river to the horse corrals, Roz, my mother's white mare, nickered a greeting. Then Pawnee, my palomino, sidled up and snorted, his warm exhale turning into frozen mist. Removing the snowshoes, I brought them a bucket of oats from the barn. What will become of Pawnee when Fred and I marry? Will Roz miss him if he was to be sold and taken away?

So many questions; so many worries – it wasn't like me, at all.

February 1st – I received a letter from Fred! It was longer and written with more love than the first. Fred missed us and felt that we would fit right in with the other members in the camp. Most of the men had expressed excitement at the possibility of having a young boy joining the camp, more so than having a woman's touch around the place. Only one camp member disapproved of us being there, a man named Bill Davis. He is the camp boss.

Fred added twelve large cotton handkerchiefs and a package of 24 razor blades to his list of items that I was to bring. By the time he had written this letter he had yet to receive any of mine, which is not unusual, I suppose. Mail to the Guinea diamond exploration camp goes through the DDX office in France, before being rerouted to Africa.

February 10th – The librarian called this afternoon and said that one of the books ordered had arrived, "*Area Handbook for Guinea*". She couldn't locate a copy of the other. "*Area Handbook for Guinea*" was written just five years ago, so the information would still be accurate. Most of the day was spent reading it and making notes.

* The official language is French, due to Guinea being under French rule between 1895 and 1958. There are a variety of tribal languages, as well.
* In 1958 Sékou Touré became Guinea's first president and formed the Democratic Party of Guinea (PDG) two years later.
* Guinea is slightly smaller than the state of Oregon, 94,926 square miles.
* Formal name, Republic of Guinea
* Capitol, Conakry
* The climate is tropical and subtropical.
* Kissidougou, the largest town near camp, temperatures over the course of the season vary from 60°F to 91°F. It is rarely below 54°F or above 98°F.
* There are an estimated four and a half million people in Guinea.
* The ethnic groups include Foulah, Malinke, Soussous and fifteen smaller tribes.
* Malinke (also known as Mandingos) live in Upper Guinea, where DDX is doing exploration.
* There is ten percent literacy. Life expectancy is 41 years.
* One U.S. dollar. equals approximately twenty sylis, Guinea's currency.
* Health is poor due to malnutrition, lack of adequate sanitation and insufficient health care.
* Common Diseases include communicable, malaria, venereal diseases, and tuberculosis.

* The average annual income is the equivalent of $140.
* Natural resources are bauxite (the principal source of aluminum), iron ore, diamonds, gold, and waterpower.
* Agriculture includes rice, cassava, millet, corn, coffee, bananas, palm oil, and pineapple.
* DDX Camps A, B, and C are in Upper Guinea, the most lightly populated region in the country.

One of the most exciting things learned from the book was that the greatest west to east distance is approximately 450 miles; north to south is around 350 miles. It wouldn't take long to travel from one end of the country to the other! We could go from Conakry to camp in less than a day. We should be able to travel around the country with ease and do a lot of exploring!

February 11th – A notice was received from President Sekou Toure's office. It was simple and to the point. Visa applications denied. Now what? Fred had said that if I didn't have visas by March 17th that we were to go anyway; meet him in Dakar on the 17th and figure it out from there.

What if Wayde and I traveled all the way to Africa, but were turned back at the Guinean border?

How strong was the chance that that could occur? The messages from DDX, Ambassade de la Republique de Guinee, and President Sekou Toure were to the point and firmly stated – "No."

I hadn't heard from Guinea's first lady, Hadja Andrée Touré. That query had been a long shot, anyway.

February 12th – I had a dream last night. Wayde and I got off the airplane in Dakar and Fred was there with two camels. He was wearing army fatigues and had his face blackened. No one exiting the plane seemed to think that camels standing on the tarmac was strange.

We rode the camels to the border of Guinea. Wayde's and my faces were now blackened. We were going to sneak across the border, but the camels would draw attention to us, so we had to get rid of them. Fred wanted to eat them, but I convinced him to turn them loose and shoo them back toward Dakar. But they spun around and ran through the streets of Conakry, instead. People were chasing after them.

Awaking, my heart was pounding. How were Wayde and I going to get into Guinea?

March 1st – Wayde turned ten years old today. I made a chocolate loaf cake, fried chicken, and potato salad. Then packed up a picnic basket and we headed for Riggins and the Salmon River, leaving the snow behind for a day.

Riggins is just sixty miles north of McCall (5,000 feet), but at a much lower elevation, (1,800 feet). While there were still six feet of snow in McCall, there would be buttercups and green grass in Riggins. But best of all, there were sandy beaches along the river. I took a blanket for lounging and to spread out the picnic lunch.

It was Saturday and there were several McCall families escaping the mountain snow and enjoying the first large beach heading up the Main Salmon River. Children were playing "Fox and Geese". Wayde quickly joined in the fun. The paths had been made in the sand in the shape of a spoked wheel. One child was a fox, and the remaining children, geese. The players must stay on the paths made in the sand. The center (hub of the wheel) is the safety zone, but only two players (geese) can be in the center at one time. The fox must try to catch a goose. Once one is caught, the goose becomes a fox. It's a simple game, but the children were having a great time playing it. Do the children in Guinea play similar games?

The sky had been overcast, but no accompanied wind. The sun came out for a brief time, but it had been enough sun to warm the top layers of sand. I took my shoes and socks off and buried my toes in the warm damp sand and gazed across the river at the mountains rising sharply upward. Pale green patches of spring growth decorated pockets of earth scattered amid the rocky cliffs.

I felt a sharp pang, missing Fred, remembering our summer trip up this river, and learning about Idaho's Batholith. Suddenly the doubts about going to Africa without visas were no longer an obstacle. I had written Fred that Wayde and I would be at the airport in Dakar on the 17th of March. Fred had previously written to me that he would be there waiting for us. One step at a time. Keep moving forward.

March 7th – It was a bright sunny afternoon as Wayde, and I went to Boise. He had completed his Calverts Homeschooling Program. On our way out of town we had dropped the final packet of exams in the mail to Calverts. We were on a shopping expedition! The first stop was Bon Marche on West Idaho Street.

Wayde went to look at shirts and neckties in the boys' department, while I shopped in the women's. After trying on numerous dresses, I found them too hot for the African climate, too formal, too white, too colorful, too everything but just right. As the salesgirl lugged the armload of dresses from the fitting room, she said over her shoulder, “Maybe a skirt and top would be more suitable?”

And she was right! A flowy, maxi-length, full-circle skirt in a very pale dusty blue hue was purchased. The fabric was a light-weight linen, cotton blend. So perfect! It could be worn with white sandals or even barefoot, for a beach ceremony. Yes! I could visualize me standing barefoot on the broad sandy beach, skirt lightly billowing in the breeze, holding a single gardenia blossom.

The skirt was paired with a simple, lightweight, pale dusty-blue, linen, cotton tunic top, with three-quarter sleeves, capped in lace.

In another department I located a narrow, fifty-eight-inch-long, hand-painted silk scarf in rich jewel tones of emerald, amethyst, amber and garnet. It could drape over my shoulders or be tied in a big bow around my waist, positioned at the hip.

Aside from the ensemble being perfect for a casual wedding ceremony, it could be worn to dinner parties. Would there be dinner parties in Guinea?

Wayde finally found me. He was out of breath from dashing around and looked disappointed. “I couldn’t find a ‘best man’s’ shirt. But please, Mom, don’t make me wear a tie. They look too dorky.”

“Who said that you would be “best man”? I asked.

“I just did!”

After paying for the items, I drove to Kmart to find small inexpensive toys as gifts for the village children. Wayde spotted the boy's clothing department and went to see if they had any "best man's" shirts while I perused the toy department. Within a few minutes Wayde came dashing back. He had found his "best man's" shirt!

Following him to the boy's clothing department, Wayde proudly took from the rack a red batik-style, polyester-rayon blend shirt with a large dagger-style collar and white buttons. The brand was "Boys Fashion Shirts". A variety of brightly colored medallion-like floral patterns, in hues of purple, turquoise, umber and olive were scattered over the shirt. It was on sale for under six dollars.

I smiled down at my son, reminding myself that the shirt was to be his choice, not mine.

"You've found your 'best man' shirt!" Thankfully, he had previously decided against the necktie.

We returned to the toy department where Wayde selected six Diecast Hot Wheels cars; four packages of small balloons, a dozen toy plastic parashoots with little men attached; twenty small high-bouncing balls; and two bags of marbles.

Hungry after our afternoon of shopping I drove us up to Overland to have Chinese food at the Golden Star Restaurant. We started with some egg rolls, then ordered Shrimp Chow Mein and Egg Foo Yong.

Wayde was tired and slept most of the hundred miles back to McCall. In that quiet time, I found myself daydreaming about a romantic African wedding ceremony.

March 10th – I had been hoping to receive a letter from Fred. There has been no word from him since the first of February. It's been almost six weeks.

March 13th – My friends held a "Goodbye and Good Luck Party" at Foresters, a bar in downtown McCall with live music and a large dance floor. There were about twenty people in the party group. They'd pushed tables together and ordered pitchers of Vodka Gimlets with crushed ice, my preferred mixed drink. There was also a large chocolate sheet cake with jungle-green frosting, decorated with small plastic monkeys and sprinkled with large rhinestones. Cute.

One of my regular dance partners, Dorian, swung me onto the dance floor. We had been on again and off again lovers. We danced country swing well together, winning a couple of local dance contests.

"Don't I give you enough adventure, Babe?" He said. "You don't have to go off to Africa to find it."

Crazy Jack, a well-known local character, took the next dance. He was a big man that didn't country swing, but would dance wildly, regardless of the tempo. As he fisted the air and jigged with his feet, he yelled above the throb of the band, "Ya haven't been around this Frank guy long enough to go to Africa with him. Hell, if you want to go to Africa that bad, I'll take ya."

"His name is Fred," I loudly corrected above the pulsating music. "Even if you had money to take me to Africa, Jack, you're on probation."

After three hours of country swing dancing, eating mounds of green frosted cake, and guzzling goblets of Gimlets, someone had taken me home and had gotten me into bed.

March 14th – I woke, fully dressed, with an excruciating headache and a plastic monkey tangled in my hair. The bedding had the stench of stale cigarette and cigar smoke. I undressed and staggered into the shower to stand beneath the hot spray, grateful that this would be my last wild party for a long while. At least that was the plan.

After the long, hot shower I took a couple of aspirins and went into the kitchen. There at the kitchen counter sat Wayde, eating a generous serving of last night's cake from a paper plate. After one look at my green-lipped son, I dashed to the bathroom.

Upon returning, Wayde asked, "Mom? Do you have the flu?"

He was told that it was not the flu, but a punishment called a "hangover" caused by over-indulgence during the previous night's farewell party.

The remainder of the miserable day was spent doing laundry and packing. We leave tomorrow for Boise. My knotted stomach is an accumulation of last night's farewell party, the departure for Africa, and no word from Fred.

PART 3 – ARRIVING IN AFRICA

The following includes information taken from edited diary entries dating March 15 through March 26, 1980.

March 15th – On the afternoon of March 15th my friend Eve, along with her adult son, John, and his wife, plus the couple's nine-year-old son, drove Wayde and me to Boise. McCall was experiencing one of its March blizzards. Much of the driving was through near white-out conditions. Bundled up in the back seat, the two boys beside me, I gazed out the window at the snowstorm. Though unseen beyond the white squall, I knew each meadow, creek, and forest we passed by. These places were known when spring's scattering of yellow buttercups graced the edges of receding snow; when the alfalfa fields were the color of pale, green velvet; when cattails hosted red-winged blackbirds; and hawks, rode wind currents, hunting field mice. I had been this way hundreds of times before. Was this goodbye?

Leaving for Africa

We arrived in Boise, to mild temperatures, green grass and worn-out clouds scattering across the blue background, as though fleeing the late afternoon sun. After depositing our luggage in our motel rooms, the group went to Boise Pizza, the best in town. The boys played pinball as the adults visited and sipped mugs of cold draft beer.

Eve and the boys were dropped off at the motel and we three younger adults "tore up the town", starting at Dinos and ending at Goodtime Charlies. We returned to our lodging at midnight, foot-sore from dancing and rapidly descending from beer highs.

March 16th – Seven o'clock arrived very early this morning, but we made it to the airport in plenty of time. At the airport I received two surprises. First, John presented me with a white rose corsage; the second, a friend, Larry, that I had spent time with at McCall, dancing, and drinking beer, showed up. I asked him if he was flying off somewhere. He told me that he was not, then handed me a bouquet of silk daffodils and one red silk rose.

"To brighten your grass hut," he said.

Larry was invited to walk with us to the gate, but he declined and left. I was touched by such a kind gesture from one that I hadn't known well. At the gate, Eve, a world traveler, handed me a map of J.F.K. airport in New York.

"You'll be needing this," she said as she gave me a hug, then also slipped a sterling silver linked bracelet into my hand, "and this." She continued. "Find sterling charms on your African adventure and future adventures that you are bound to have. It will provide you with a record of special places and lasting memories."

The flight from Boise to Chicago was pleasant. This had been Wayde's first time in an airplane and it had taken him awhile to settle in. A young medical student from Buffalo, New York, shared our row and visited. She was returning from her spring break, having spent it skiing in Sun Valley. Chicago had been my mother's birthplace, so I viewed it with keen interest as the plane circled for its landing. The city was windy and overcast; we had left the blue skies while flying over Montana. There was an hour layover, which barely gave us time to make our connecting flight to New York. Our seating companion during the New York flight was a young Asian man enroute to Hong Kong. He had been studying in the United States for five years to become an electronics engineer.

The J.F.K. airport was huge! I felt extremely grateful to Eve for the map. We had a four-hour layover, so lunched on burgers at one of the airport cafes and shopped for the first sterling charm for my bracelet, settling on the Statue of Liberty. We had seen the statue from the aircraft window while circling for landing. She stood, dominating Liberty Island, her torch held high – as in liberty or defiance? Or both? Map in hand, I easily navigated through the horde of people to Pan Am gate 4 for flight 188 to Dakar. As we boarded the nine-hour flight my stomach felt queasy with apprehension at leaving my home country. But topping that, I didn't know if Fred would be waiting for us at the Dakar-Yoff International Airport. I hadn't heard from him in six weeks.

Wayde watched the on-flight movie, *The Electric Cowboy*, to help pass the time. Sitting next to me was an elderly missionary heading for Kenya. He said that he was very familiar with Guinea and gave me advice and information concerning the country.

He told me that Guinea is an extremely poor country. It has a high infant mortality rate and a below average life expectancy. Diseases, especially malaria, and parasites, such as the Guinea worm, are rampart. Medical facilities are nearly nonexistent. Since 1978, under President Ahmed Sékou Touré, the country has become known as People's Revolutionary Republic of Guinea. Once in power, Sékou Touré closed the country to visitors. Therefore, there is no tourism, no hotels, or restaurants. Even in Guinea's capitol, Conakry. There is no American

Embassy, there are no missionaries…the population is around eighty percent Muslims, predominantly Sunni.

"You do have visas to get into Guinea, have you not? If not, do not go there!" He stated with authority.

I nodded my head, yes. It was a lie, and it wasn't. Yes, we had no visas.

March 17th – The plane landed; passengers lined up in the isle waiting impatiently for the heavy airplane door to be unlatched and opened. Then we filed down the shaky metal steps to the tarmac, the early morning air slapping us in the face like a warm, wet, salt-ladened rag. I had not slept for over twenty-four hours. My mind had been filled with an emotional stew of foreboding, excitement and expectation, each bonding so well together, that there were no imperceptible differences. And yet, now, standing on the tarmac as luggage was being unloaded from the plane's cargo hold, I was wide awake and alert.

We hauled our luggage to the terminal to be processed through customs. It took less than ten minutes to show my passport and Wayde's birth certificate before leaving through the terminal exit.

And there was Fred, grinning broadly!

I ran into his arms, fighting back tears. We had made it! We were in Africa and my fiancée was here to guide and protect us. This was only the second day of Fred's two-week vacation, and he told us that he had planned some special things to see and do in Senegal!

The three of us boarded a local bus which jounced toward Dakar, as we clung to a support pole, and attempted to keep the luggage from sliding to the back of the vehicle. While bouncing along, I viewed dark-skinned women vibrantly dressed in brightly colored fabrics draped and wrapped around themselves, their hair elaborately wound in matching fabric. There were young mothers carrying their babies bound in cloth and secured at their lower backs, with just the infant's head poking out. Pony drawn carts transported wares and women hunched beside the road selling produce from large woven baskets. An assortment of grass-sided huts with thatched roofs crouched in clusters.

We exited the bus at the wrong stop and had quite a walk to the Hotel Continental, located in the Commune de Médina region, where Fred had gotten us rooms. Dragging along two backpacks and two pieces of luggage, plus a guitar, was not an easy feat. Finally, Fred hired a young lad who had been following, to assist us. I realized that although Fred's French is limited, it certainly would help us find our way through Dakar.

French is also the official language of Guinea, used as communication in schools, government administrations, and the media. However, there are over twenty-four Indigenous languages spoken in Guinea, the largest being Susu, Pular, and Maninka. Maninka is the tribal language that dominates Upper Guinea, where the DDX camps are located.

Although what I have seen of Dakar thus far, is interesting, I am eager to get to the camp in Upper Guinea. Having read that the main feature of Upper Guinea lies to the east of the Fouta Djallon, a highland region in the center of the country. The area is described as a lightly wooded and tall-grassed savannah, which will better suit my African expectations. This intriguing area is broken by a long rocky spur extending east along the Mali border. The region's altitude averages a mere 1,000 feet. Hard, rusty-red, lateritic crust underlies much of the savannah. It is this hard, crusted area where Fred will be drilling for samples during DDX's diamond exploration.

During our trek to the hotel, I learned my first African lesson, and an expensive one at that. An African man approached us, and with sorrowful eyes, held out his open palm with what appeared to be three small gold nuggets. In clear English, he told us his heartbreaking story. His father lay dying, desperately ill, in another village many kilometers away. The grieving man had no travel fare and was desperate to go to his father's side. The gold nuggets had to be sold to make the journey, and in the event…here the man managed a few tears…that his father died, money to pay for his burial. Fred was suspicious. I was downright gullible. Almost immediately after the man scurried off with my fifty-dollar bill, leaving me with the three gold-colored nuggets, another African man approached with a similar story and cheaper nuggets. Regardless of my repeatedly telling him, no, I did not want to purchase his nuggets, he ruthlessly pestered me until we were safely in the hotel.

Fred paid the lad who had helped with the luggage, but before the boy left, my son held up his hand to pause the boy's departure. Wayde dug into his backpack and handed the youngster a bright red diecast Hot Wheels convertible, which the boy took, then held out his hand for another. I had to stop Wayde from obliging!

During our walk to the Hotel Continental, Fred had cautioned me that our lodgings are classified as a two-star establishment. From traveling through Oregon on my book tour with Fred, I had become aware of how frugal he was, so his choice of accommodations did not surprise me. Beginning to lag from the lack of sleep and stress of travel, I could have slept well in a large cardboard box.

The hotel was six stories tall, with an ageing whitewashed façade. Each room facing the street had a small, arched balcony with black iron railing. The Hotel Continental had the quaint, antiqued look that one would have expected of an ancient city building. Our rooms were three flights up, facing the street. Once inside, the rooms, though in need of fresh paint, were clean, and had a simple charm. There were no adornments on the walls. Bed coverings offered the only splash of color in each of the rooms…earthtone African prints, mingling with sunset hues with a river of blue and green snaking lazily across their widths.

Both rooms were ample-sized. One could step out onto the balcony to view the street below, hosting a smattering of street venders. The rooms were similar, except for the beds. Wayde's room had a double bed, while Fred's and mine had two singles. Each room had a small dresser, and two wooden straight-backed chairs. In the far corner of the rooms, behind large plastic privacy curtains, were free-standing showers, with hot running water. Overhead, a large fan forced air movement. The fan in the room Fred and I shared produced soft, rhythmic squeaks marking each rotation. There was a shared dressing room with toilet in the hallway a short distance from our rooms.

Children were playing in the street and Wayde wanted to take a packet of balloons to share with them. He was told to stay within view of the balcony and to knock and wait a few minutes before coming back to our room. He grinned his sly smile as he exited. We heard him running down the stairs, excited to make friends with the children.

Fred and I made quick use of our privacy on one of the single beds. We had had a long three-months separation. I was a bit hesitant at first, but there was not time to just ease into things. After lovemaking we quickly showered and dressed, then moved the chairs to the small balcony. We sat and watched Wayde, and the children bat the balloons into the air, attempting to keep them airborne. Occasionally one would pop, resulting in screams, followed by fits of laughter. I snuck sideways glimpses at Fred, as he sat smiling broadly at the children at play.

I knew little about this man, having met him a mere eight months ago. Soon he would be my husband and Wayde's stepfather. I wondered how he would react when seeing me in my lace-sleeved blouse and long, flowing skirt; hair curled and pinned atop my head, stray ringlets cascading around my ears. It would be the me he had never seen – lips red, lashes blackened, and eyes delicately shadowed. Cheeks with a touch of pink, in a faint, unfading blush. I felt tingles of love-spikes toward Fred, and happiness at the thought.

Wayde was called in from play and both he and I took naps on the single beds as Fred explored the nearby neighborhoods looking for a nice place to have dinner. When he returned an hour later, both Wayde and I had difficulty rising from our sleep stupors. But Fred was in a playful mood, pulling back bedcovers and threatening to douse us with cold water.

We strolled along Avenue Blaise Diagne. My stomach growled from the fragrance of roasting peanuts that clung to the hot humid air. Venders were roasting the legumes over small charcoal stoves, in sand-filled metal vessels that resembled oversized gold pans. Fred said that the treat was made with a small, roundish, red-skinned African peanut. He pulled a couple of coins from his pocket and handed them to the vender. The vender rolled three small sheets of newspaper into snow cone shapes, scooped roasted peanuts into a fine sifter and shook away the sand before dumping the hot peanuts into the three cones and handing us each one. At first, I picked at them tentatively, expecting gritty sand residue. But there was none! They were delicious!

Seemly, out of nowhere, a large African woman wearing a long, brightly colored, dashiki caftan with batwing sleeves, and matching head wrap approached. She lowered a mango-filled basket from her head, selected a large ripe mango and handed it to me. I smiled and thanked her. Then she held out her hand for payment. I glanced over at Fred.

“Would you like to have the mango?” he asked.

It was soft and fragrant with ripeness. Of course, I would like a mango. But what if I hadn’t? What if I gave it back to her? Would she be as enraged as the second gold nugget seller had been and follow us back to our lodging? These were the things that I was pondering as Fred handed her a five-franc coin. She deposited the coin in a small pouch before reaching her hand out for another. Fred shook his head, no. Giving a slight shrug, she repositioned the basket on her head and sashayed off.

We had dinner at the small indoor restaurant that Fred had found during his earlier walk. I was famished, the peanuts having only whetted my appetite. Wayde and I each ordered an entrée called Poulet Yassa – fresh lime juice marinated chicken, which was then grilled before being smothered with caramelized onions. The dish was served with rice.

Fred had Lamb Mafe. The ingredients are simmered together for a long while, mingling their flavors, and served with rice. Fred and I shared our meals. The Mafe was delicious, but aside from some chunks of lamb, I couldn't tell what the other ingredients had been. Whatever they were, the slow cooking mingled them together to form an unforgettable piquant sauce with a hint of peanuts. Or was that a lingering flavor from the sand roasted peanuts I had eaten earlier?

Wayde was so exhausted that he could barely finish his meal…an oddity for my son, who had a grown man's appetite. Fred carried the giggling boy back to the hotel, slung over his shoulder.

March 18th – We slept late, then had breakfast brought up. The Hotel Continental provided a complimentary petit dejeuner consisting of bread, butter, coffee, and warm milk. I slathered the creamy, ripe mango on our bread. After breakfast we headed for the market.

The market consisted of small stalls crammed together, some in enclosures and others free-standing along the sidewalks. An African man approached me with a broad, toothy smile and slipped a long necklace, made of various large seeds, over my head.

"A gift for you! Beautiful woman," he grinned. "Now, you gift me fifty francs."

He held out his palm, his fingers repeatedly extending and curling back in a come-hither motion. I tried to give him back the necklace, but he would have none of it. He demanded his gift. Finally, I flung the necklace at him and the three of us hurried away. We continued to be pestered by street venders but were determined not to allow them to spoil our market adventure. The fish market was quite smelly; however, the vegetable market was very intriguing. I saw more strange vegetable varieties than I had ever seen before. I am hoping to learn more about them and their preparation while in Africa. We never paused long in any one place while touring the market, because when we did, we were accosted by transient venders who reminded me of a swarm of hungry mosquitoes.

It was hard to admit, but I didn't care for most of the native Senegalese people that I had encountered in Dakar. There was pushy arrogance about many of them. I had a difficult time warming up to those who treated me as though I were a walking pocketbook.

We left the market and walked toward the beach, taking a bus part of the way. While riding the bus I asked Fred if the people of Guinea were as aggressive as those in Dakar.

"Not at all," he replied. "They haven't had tourism exposure nor a cultural shift. They are gracious and accommodating. You will love them."

I breathed a sigh of relief.

At a small beach, Fred sat in the sand and read work related reports while Wayde and I explored tide pools. We discovered brittle stars, sea anemones and urchins, large black sea slugs which excreted purple slime, chitins, small fish, and numerous other oddities. I had never had more fun exploring tide pools than I did with my son.

As I was pointing out the sea life, Wayde asked, "Weren't you studying to be a marine biologist a long time ago?"

"Yes. A long time ago. But I became a mother and author, instead. Which turned out to be much more rewarding," I assured him.

As we headed back to town, we discovered that the banks had closed. Without francs, there would be no dinner. After returning to the hotel, Fred asked the clerk if she could cash a traveler's check. The clerk said that she couldn't do that, but she would be glad to loan us twenty francs until the banks open tomorrow. Suddenly, the Continental seemed very much like home!

Wayde went out onto the street to play kick-the-ball with his new friends, with strict instructions to be back in his room by dark.

Fred and I talked about our future. He had yet to inform me as to when and where we would wed. I didn't want to force the subject, so let it ride. The topic discussed was more in line with what roles I could assume once we arrived in camp. What was I willing to do, and not. I let him know that I was willing to help make life in camp easier in any way that I could. But wouldn't know what needed to be done until arriving at camp and assessing the situation.

I felt close to Fred, but I am not totally at ease. He seemed more withdrawn than I'd remembered him to be, and more prone to worry. Hopefully, we will resolve this soon. I know that it will take some time to readjust to one another. And giving ourselves time to do so is as it should be.

The three of us enjoyed dinner at a small café eight blocks from the hotel. It was 9:00 P.M. when we returned to our rooms. Wayde went to his room. Fred and I relaxed in ours. I was surprised that my feet weren't tired from all the miles that we had covered today. Instead, they are ready to go again tomorrow.

I was a little disturbed at Fred's explanation as to why we sleep in two single beds, while Wayde sleeps in a double one. Fred told me that it costs two francs more to have a room with two singles. There was only one room with a double bed available. He was, therefore, forced to take one room with two singles. Since a room with single beds was more expensive, it was Fred's reasoning that that was the room we should have. Hmm?

March 19th – This morning, we rose early. Since all markets close from noon until three, Fred figured we had best get some chores done in the morning. Our petit dejeuner arrived, and I smeared our bread with what was left of the mango.

Our first order of business took us to the post office to mail letters. We proceeded to the bank where we cashed some of the traveler's checks I had brought, then on to Air France to book Wayde's and my flight to Conakry. We shall keep our fingers crossed as to whether we'll be able to get visas. Fred assures me that he has people in Conakry working on getting my son and me into Guinea. Since Guinea is a closed country, it was not going to be easy.

Wayde had stayed at the hotel during our chores, playing street games with his friends. We returned to find him distraught over the demands of a young beggar who claimed he needed money for food. However, Wayde didn't give into his compassion and kept his francs in his pocket.

After a brief rest we headed for Hann Forest and Zoological Park via bus. Again, the bus journey was colorful and interesting as I caught glimpses of people, housing, and markets. Hann Park was fascinating! I saw my first baobab tree. It resembled a tree growing upside down, roots in the air! We walked through various gardens – coconut groves, towering eucalyptus, banana trees, many citrus varieties, most unknown to me. The weeping paperbark trees were in bloom. Their white, bottlebrush-like blossoms filled the air with a musty, rather than sweet, fragrance.

Wayde was far more interested in the zoo, rather than the botanical gardens. There we viewed crocodiles, lions, reptiles, dingoes, camels, birds, and a wide variety of primates. Wayde got grabbed by a monkey when venturing too close to the cage, causing a riot of laughter from the small crowd of spectators. We tossed peanuts to warthogs, monkeys, and alligators...the alligators were not impressed.

My son announced that he would like a chimpanzee for a camp pet. I, on the other hand, was fond of a mongoose which begged to be scratched. Fred had decided that he would like a miniature deer, which was quite affectionate. But when a Secretary bird took a liking to Fred and showed off by dancing around and leaping in the air spread-winged, we all decided one would be a delight to have around a bush camp. None of us favored boa constrictors, mambas, or smelly hyenas.

After exploring the park, we walked to Hann Bay to view the beaches. Several individuals were sail-surfing. Locals were selling freshly caught fish. We sat in the sand awhile, then strolled along the shore before returning to the road to catch a bus back to the Continental.

We dined at an out of the way, just down the street a few feet, and around the corner café. But we had to walk seven blocks to get there – but there it was, just a few feet down the street and around the corner from where we had begun. Fred was frustrated from the search. I tried to lighten his mood by reminding him that it was going to be a very short walk back to our rooms. But his mood remained unchanged and became more aggravated when the café was out of the entrée he had ordered. The prices were right, however, and Fred grew calm as he began to feed his long neglected and growling stomach.

The most wonderful part of the day was that I felt my love for Fred deepening.

March 20th – I had become a little depressed last night, which was unlike me. Understandably, Fred had been tired and fell asleep after we'd finished our letter writing. I felt the need to be close to him. He woke up and we were able to talk. He was patient with me and wanted to understand what I was feeling. We cuddled on one of the single beds and remained in each other's arms until morning. It was wonderful to wake up with Fred close beside me.

Today we went to L'Hippocamp! It is a well-known French get-away with grass bungalows, an expansive sandy beach, and an onsite restaurant. Fred had reserved us three nights at the resort. While Fred ran a few errands, I completed our packing and had the porter help me haul our luggage downstairs to be put into storage until our return from L'Hippocamp, Sunday. I packed an overnight case with our toiletries and a single suitcase with a change of clothes for each of us, and my lightweight suede jacket in case nights were cool.

While packing for our resort stay, I had considered packing my wedding skirt and blouse, plus Wayde's "best man" shirt. However, I didn't. If Fred had planned on the two of us getting married there, he would have said something.

When Fred returned, he hailed a taxi to take us to the bus terminal. His French proved to be handy as he negotiated taxi rates. The driver had quoted Fred a price of twenty francs. Fred told the driver that he was "full of it". The driver ended up taking us to the terminal for ten francs.

The terminal was open air and crowded with the usual venders. We shared a green coconut full of cool coconut water as we waited for the bus to Somone. However, the time for its arrival and departure came and went. I spent part of the waiting time writing letters while Fred reviewed some French from his dictionary. We ended up waiting over four hours for the bus's arrival and departure.

The thirty-mile bus ride to Somone was well worth the wait. The journey took us through forests of baobabs, past horse drawn carts and herds of goats, through villages of thatched roofed huts, and orchards of mangos – ripe fruit dangling from their umbilical cords. Throughout our trip, the bus stopped to pick up and let off hordes of colorful characters.

It was nearly dark when we reached L'Hippocamp. What an enchanting place! Our hut was within twenty yards of the beach – with miles of white sand and the lulling sound of the surf. We dined almost immediately in the open cafe shaded beneath an expansive thatched roof. The open dining area looked out over the surf. The tables were set with white tablecloths and linen napkins. We feasted on appetizers of small fish filled pastries with a delicate tomato dipping sauce, followed by an entrée of grilled chicken slathered with a mixture of garlic, butter and lime, with a side of deep-fried puffs of egg batter. Ice cream arrived for dessert. We receive three meals per day, which are included with the lodging.

After dinner we returned to our hut. Wayde retired to his bed, while Fred and I strolled down to the village and watched locals dancing to the beating of drums. Most of the dancers were young and agile, springing around and flapping their arms to the rhythm. Upon returning to L'Hippocamp we relaxed with a Coca Cola at one of the bars along the beach. The salt-tinged air smelled fresh. The warm breeze carried a hint of citrus blossoms.

This has been the happiest day, yet. I am elated to be with the man I love and the beginning of a new life together.

March 21st – We slept until eleven. Wayde had risen early and gone off to explore. When he returned, he was disappointed.

"Where are the hippopotamuses?" He asked.

Fred laughed and tousled Wayde's hair. "There are no hippo's here. Hippocamp refers to a place of a mythological sea creature. You probably won't see one of those, either."

I told Wayde that I had seen a monkey in an outdoor cage by the L'Hippocamp office. He immediately went to make friends with the monkey.

Fred and I walked up the beach to the mouth of the river. While Fred swam in the freshwater channel, I sat in the sand and sifted through piles of small shell bits. Wayde joined us and went swimming with Fred, then explored the beach opposite the channel.

At two o'clock we returned to the dining room for a lunch of lightly battered fish sauteed in butter along with fresh green beans, broiled potatoes, and slices of fresh melon with salmon colored flesh. The meal was spectacular.

After the three of us had a short nap in the bungalow, Wayde stayed behind to swim in the surf and collect small seashells, while Fred and I wandered down the beach and through the village of Solomon. Some village women were pounding millet, separating the chaff from the seeds. They indicated that I should give the pounding and winnowing a try. Then Fred stepped in to attempt the task and the women went into fits of laughter at the sight of a man doing women's work.

The tide was going out and I enjoyed exploring the tide pools along the rocky stretch of beach with Fred. There were sea slugs and pretty shells, including cowries, drills, and murex. We then walked the mile back to our hut.

Wayde had spent his day swimming in the river channel and playing with a group of local children. Fred and I enjoyed a Coca Cola in the shade of a cabana bar and watched the French couples wander the beach. We were the only Americans at the resort.

Back at the bungalow we all had cold showers before dressing for dinner. Again, the food was extraordinary. First, we were served a creamy fish soup, followed by grilled lamb steaks, fried eggplant, and rich custard-filled cream puffs.

After dinner Wayde went to feed the monkey scraps he had salvaged from dinner. Fred and I relaxed in the bungalow writing in our journals. It has been a very fun day!

March 22nd – I had slept restlessly last night. Finally, I dressed and slipped out into the cool early morning air. L'Hippocamp was quiet. I walked along the beach enjoying the solitude of my own company as the wet sand squished between my toes. After my cooling beach stroll, I returned to the bungalow. Fred was up and dressed; Wayde had already gone to the restaurant for his petit dejeuner and to visit with the monkey.

Fred and I skipped breakfast. We strolled along the shore picking up shells along the way. A group of local craftsmen pestered us to purchase their wares, but we firmly declined. It was lunchtime when we returned from our walk, and we were famished. We dined on couscous, a richly sauced and spicily seasoned lamb stew, fresh green salad, followed by a silky prune custard.

After lunch we rested in the bungalow. The heat was oppressive. I napped while Fred read reports. Later, Fred wanted to go for a swim. I decided to remain at the bungalow. I sat in the quiet and pondered why it was so difficult for me to understand the emotions that I had been feeling, today. Perhaps it was the realization of being so far from home. Here, in this white and blue paradise, my thoughts were not of sandy beaches and ocean waves, but of meadows filled with blue camas; streams swollen with winter's runoff; trails winding through the coolness of fragrant Grand Fir forests; the laughter and closeness of friends. These feelings were most likely the adjustment to my new life in Africa – a pendulum swinging between the familiar and the new, before settling somewhere toward the middle.

Soon, I began to miss Fred and went in search of him. I located him by the mouth of the river. He and Wayde were warming up from their chilly swims. We sat on the warm sand for a while, then I went into the ocean to try to catch a ride on the waves. Fred and Wayde soon joined me, and we frolicked for a couple of hours body surfing.

Later the three of us wandered back up the beach to lounge in front of our bungalow. Along came the pesky locals with their wares. Fred and I struck up a barter which ended in a trade of my second-hand suede jacket for a blue tie-died, sleeveless, cotton shift, which draped mid-calf, and an embroidered dashiki top. What a trade! It had been great fun with Fred bartering in French and me refusing offers.

Fred and I shared an invigorating cold-water shower and dressed for dinner. I wore my new blue shift. Our meal was slices of roasted brahma bull – it had to be. It was so tough even the monkey couldn't chew it! But the sauteed green beans seasoned with fresh herbs and the croquets served with a light, creamy tomato sauce was excellent. The dessert was a bowl of garden-fresh strawberries, sweet and tangy.

This evening Fred and I shared a bottle of wine which left our heads spinning!

March 23rd – Last night was another restless one. Too much sun and too many hungry mosquitoes. Fred slept soundly, as I tried not to toss and turn in our shared bed. When we arose early in the morning, Wayde was already off having breakfast and feeding the monkey. He left a note explaining that he was walking to the village of Somone to purchase peanuts. The manager of the office had agreed to give the monkey some peanuts every morning while the supply lasted.

In Wayde's absence we made the best of our last morning at L'Hippocamp, feeding the sexual hunger that had been growing during the past few days. Afterward we headed for the river anticipating a refreshing swim. However, we ended up wading along the river's edge with a group of local women raking fingers through the sand for clams. We helped one woman and her young son fill their pail.

We returned to our hut. Wayde had returned from delivering the bag of peanuts to the office manager. After the cold showers the three of us packed for our departure, scheduled to take place after lunch.

Sunday lunch at L'Hippocamp is an anticipated affair. Many French visitors drive from Dakar just to partake of the weekend's feast and a few hours of beach lounging. The feast began with large chunks of broiled fish drizzled with a creamy lemon sauce, followed by thick slabs of pork roast, the layer of fat highly seasoned and crisped. There were small boiled yellow potatoes swimming in sweet cream butter, and an assortment of vegetables similarly dressed. Mounds of fried cabbage, with a spicy blend of herbs and a liberal sprinkling of salt, were placed on the tables. The large bowls of fresh salad greens, dressed with olive oil, fresh lime juice and salt catered to the French palate. Bowls of expertly peeled pink and white grapefruit segments, lightly sprinkled with sugar, were served with ice cream dappled with bits of vanilla bean.

During our trip to the bus stop, we rode in the back of a "taxi" – a rattletrap late model truck with a canvas covered bed and hard wooden benches. We waited at the bus stop as a swarm of women surrounded us, their combined sales jabber, merging into one insistent whine. Baskets of mangos balanced on their heads. Baskets of mangos rode against their hips. Baskets of mangos shoved beneath our noses. And, gratefully, here came the bus! At the last minute I grabbed a large mango, shoved a 5 franc coin into an outstretched hand and leapt onto the bus, the din still ringing in my ears.

The thirty-mile-long bus ride took nearly three hours to reach Dakar. The driver stopped at each tiny village to let a passenger or two on or off. Such stops were expected and necessary. The bus, however, was stopped numerous times by police, the problem being that the roof of the bus was overloaded with passengers and baggage, including a large fishing net caging a flock of flapping, squawking chickens. With each stop, a fine was paid.

Once the bus stopped so that the driver could amble into nearby bushes to relieve himself. Meanwhile, passengers waited, sweltering in the heat. The bus meandered into Dakar around seven. Fred hired a taxi to take us to Hotel Continental. Such a welcome sight!

We had a wonderful dinner at a Lebanese restaurant. I had tabbouleh. The tabbouleh was the best I had ever tasted. The bulgar wheat was tossed with a dense blend of fresh, diced tomato, minced parsley and mint, green and red onion all steeped in fresh lemon juice and olive oil. Fred had the paella, a bed of richly seasoned saffron rice topped with three-inch long pieces of lamb rib, halved grilled chicken thigh, butter beans, diced tomato, spicy red pepper and a sprinkling of fresh oregano. Wayde, weary of staring at the menu, ordered an omelet. We shared a dessert which consisted of a huge mango, diced, and served in a half peel shell, drizzled with a mixture of honey and fresh lime juice. For such an elegant meal, it was moderately priced.

Once back at the hotel I sent Wayde to the hallway bathroom to do his laundry in the sink. Afterward I washed Fred's and mine. The washing was hung on balconies to dry.

It had been a great day, and the best was yet to come. Our new room had a double bed!

March 24th – This morning began very well but ended badly. Fred sent me on some errands. Though I was apprehensive about trying to communicate my wants to French speaking people, I was glad for the chance to do something useful for Fred. I was determined to give the tasks my best effort, and I did. I was assigned to source approximately thirty feet of cord for making clothes lines, several dozen wooden clothes pins, and six inexpensive pocketknives as gifts for the Guinean camp workers.

Another vital acquisition on the list was a cast iron coal clothing press with a wooden handle. The heated iron is to be used to kill tumbu fly eggs that the flies deposit in damp waistbands, collars, and cuffs in clothing as it dries after being washed. The tiny larvae work their way into the flesh and hatch under the skin. The larvae are very painful to extract, and the sites of infestation may become infected. As the maggots mature, they bore out of the skin, drop to the ground, and finish their development into a mature fly.

It took me five hours, but I had accomplished each of these things, despite the language barrier. I was extremely pleased with myself. Wayde and I were both exhausted from the distance walked in the sweltering heat.

When Fred returned from his errands, I was bursting with pride. I was anticipating Fred's praise and approval, which I received until we discovered that I had mislaid the equivalent of thirty dollars! Fred was openly disappointed and angry. How could I have lost thirty dollars? I didn't have an explanation. I added and re-added the sales receipts. I had inadvertently botched the chance to prove myself useful.

Fred refused my offer to fix him some lunch, fixing it himself. This made me feel more distressed. My insides were tied in knots as I watched him eat. He wouldn't look up at me. After lunch he got up and stalked off to go sightseeing, taking Wayde with him.

I had wanted Fred to hold me for a few minutes and tell me that mistakes happen. But I really didn't expect that he would. It seems that the more I know Fred, the harder it is to express my feelings to him. Sometimes I need his strength when mine has failed. But I don't know how to ask for it. I had a good cry, then took a warm shower, and put on fresh clothes.

Fred and Wayde returned around six. I was overjoyed at seeing them. Fred seemed pleased to see me, too! I love him so much and I feel that things will work out for us.

Mike Ryan, a friend of Mr. Lampietti's, Fred's boss, phoned the hotel room. Fred had been trying to reach him to ask for assistance in sourcing some items needed for the bush camp in Guinea. Mr. Ryan said that he would send his wife over tomorrow. I am to go "shopping" with her while Fred runs some other errands. Fred and I spend a while preparing the camp list.

The three of us went to a French restaurant where I had the local specialty, Poulet Yassa. Fred and Wayde ordered an elegant sounding entrée which turned out to be fried pork chops and French fries. Wayde was pleased with his selection. I shared my Poulet Yassa with Fred.

On the way back to the hotel, we stopped by a French bakery and bought some pastries for dessert. Tonight, I again look forward to sharing the double bed with my fiancée.

March 25th – We rose around eight to get an early start. After our petit dejeuner, Fred and I walked to the bank to cash some traveler's checks. Fred went on his way to begin his errands for camp while I returned to the hotel to wait for Mike Ryan's wife, Sue.

Sue showed up shortly after ten and was quite business-like until she asked what kind of work I did. When I replied that I was an author of a cookbook and a home-schooling book, she warmed up to me. Sue began talking about a Senegalese cookbook that she had been trying to get published, *Cooking in West Africa.* We had a good visit as we shopped for the camp tools on Fred's list. I purchased a ball-cap style hat at one of the shops we passed by. It was meant to be a man's hat, but I hadn't seen anything for women aside from the head wraps. I figured that I would need some sort of head covering in the bush. It came in handy sooner than I would have anticipated.

A pesky man rushed up to Sue and me, and draped seed necklaces around our necks, saying, "Gifts for the loveliest ladies in Dakar".

Then he held out his hand and said he would like a gift of 30 francs. Instead of flinging the unwanted "gifts" at him, as I had been doing, Sue sweetly said, "We will bring you the 30 francs tomorrow."

The man smiled and reclaimed the necklaces.

"I will see you, tomorrow," he said. And walked away.

"Are you going to give him 30 francs, tomorrow?" I asked.

"Of course not! That is the accepted thing to say, here in Dakar. You are not saying, 'No', which is a word Senegalese people hate to hear. It's too final, for them. You just tell them,

'Tomorrow'. They won't believe you. But it isn't a 'no', and they accept it as a 'maybe'".

As noon rolled around, we ran into Fred in one of the tool shops. He was hunting for steel-toed canvas boots for his jumper drill workers. Sue suggested that we go to the American Embassy for lunch. Wayde and I had cheeseburgers and fries; Fred and Sue ordered a delicious-looking local dish of couscous, chickpeas, and sauce. After lunch we parted company, planning to meet again tomorrow morning at nine.

I had found Sue very interesting. She was born in London, but has lived in Africa for fifteen years, fourteen of those in Dakar. The Ryans have a fifteen-year-old daughter and a twelve-year-old son. They plan to move either to England or the United States, in June. Sue does a lot of buying for the United States Embassy and for large corporations, purchasing bulk goods for export.

After lunch, Fred, Wayde and I took the ferry boat over to Goree Island, established as a crucial hub for the slave trade in 1536. Just two years ago UNESCO (United Nations Educational, Scientific and Cultural Organization) designated Goree Island a World Heritage site to preserve its historical significance.

At the ferry terminal an Australian gentleman latched onto us. He seemed desperate for English speaking companions. Once on the island the four of us explored an old fort – WWII vintage. It was a catacomb of powder magazines and underground rooms.

There was a cannon mounted on the highest point. The sight was heart stopping. Where was the mud brick building that had once dominated that hill? I could clearly visualize it in my mind. Had I seen it in a sketch at one time? In a dream? The Australian and

I walked up the slope to the cannon. There, not far from it, were vestiges of old mud brick footings.

On the other side of the island, facing Dakar, was a partially intact fort. The tourist pamphlet stated that it had been built in the 1800s. The Australian and I caught up with Fred and Wayde. We proceeded to the museum. It consisted of the slave pens which were used to hold natives, many of them Guineans. The pens were dark little rooms with scant ventilation or light. There was a big metal door with the ocean beyond.

"The door to nowhere," I whispered.

"You've been here before?" The Australian asked.

"No," I said.

"Perhaps," I thought.

Wayde, Fred and the Australian wanted to continue exploring the slave museums. I needed to get away, so I left the three guys and walked to the small shopping square. My feet were tired, and I was feeling morose. I sat on a bench outside a local hair-styling stall.

A girl, probably in her late teens, came out of the stall carrying a chair, comb and roll of thick black thread. She persuaded me to allow her to braid my hair for the equivalent of two dollars. Another girl exited the shop and decided that she wanted to do the other side and began combing out my long brunette hair. This decision did not sit well with the first girl, and they began to quarrel, pulling me this way and that, as I clung to the bottom of the chair to remain seated. However, the first girl managed to unseat me and shoved me into the stall and into another chair.

The second girl followed. As the first girl rapidly braided my hair, wrapping each braid tightly with the thick thread, the second girl stood on the opposite side backcombing my hair to make tangles that the first girl would need to comb out. This infuriated the first girl, since she needed to get my hair done before the seven o'clock ferry arrived to take tourists back to the mainland. There was some slapping going on between the two, which drew a crowd of locals, crowding outside the stall entrance and goading the girls on. Seeing that there were only a few minutes to get the job done, since the ferry had come into view, both girls got to work, one on each side of my head, and finished in time, each receiving one dollar in payment. The gathered crowd applauded and made sounds of approval over my hairstyle.

I bolted for the closest mirror. There I stood with seven and eight inch long braids, wrapped in black thread, springing up all over my head! Truly, I was no Bo Derek! I crammed the mess under my hat and went to find Wayde and Fred at the loading dock. I found Wayde first. Fred was off looking for me. When I pulled off my hat, Wayde went into shock. I stuffed the hair back under my hat. Here came Fred. I removed the hat, and he went into a fit of hysterics. His mirth quickly cooled when I told him I had paid two dollars for my new hairstyle.

After leaving the ferry, we toured a European supermarket on our way back to the hotel, my hair concealed beneath my hat. The prices were outrageous! Milky Way candy bars sold for seventy-five cents; a small bottle of catsup, three dollars; and a can of Nestle's Quik, eighteen dollars.

I bumped Fred with my shoulder, "See," I said. "Two dollars isn't so bad for a hairstyle."

“Have it brushed out before we go to dinner, please.” He responded.

After returning to our rooms, I spent nearly an hour unraveling braids and brushing my hair while Fred showered and dressed for dinner.

At a nearby restaurant, Wayde had spaghetti, I had chunks of sauteed chicken thighs served over saffron rice. Fred, true to form, ordered some exotic, strange-sounding dish. It took us awhile to figure out what the odd-looking chunks of meat floating around in the thin gravy were. They tasted strongly of liver, but we found out that it was kidney. Yuck! I must hand it to Fred, though. He ate the whole thing.

Upon returning to the Continental, we spent the remainder of the evening doing chores. I washed the laundry in the sink and hung it on the balcony railing to dry. Fred typed a report to DDX, an account of the supplies purchased for camp.

I was keeping an eye on him, expecting him to have a negative reaction to his meal.

“Don’t you think you should be studying up on some more French? I’m certain there is a word for ‘kidney’”, I said.

He looked up from his work and replied, “I kind of liked that hairdo on you.”

March 26th – I awoke to the gleeful sounds of children -- squealing, laughing, shouting. I went to the balcony to see what had created the commotion. Small plastic parashoots with miniature dangling men were gliding to the ground. Children were leaping to grab them out of the air. Then came a barrage of small rubber balls that began hitting the road and bouncing this way and that, the giggling gaggle knocking each other over in pursuit of the prizes. Next, filled water balloons were lobbed from the balcony next to our room, creating a new wave of excitement as they hit their targets with a stinging burst of wet, or splatted on the road's hard surface. I saw Wayde beginning to open a bag of marbles.

"Wayde! Stop that! Don't drop the marbles." I yelled across to him above the excited din from below. "You go down and hand them out. Don't throw them!"

Wayde disappeared from the balcony and emerged onto the street, the excited children surrounding him. He stood, hero of the day, making certain everyone received a marble.

When he came back up, I knelt before him and asked, "Did you give everything away that you were going to save to give to the village children in Guinea?"

"Mom, these were my friends. We're leaving tomorrow. I don't even know if the kids in Guinea will like me. I know that these kids did. Now they will remember me."

Sue showed up at nine, weaving her way through the flock of children. I met her in the lobby, and we commenced our shopping expedition. By eleven-thirty we had completed the list of chores Fred had given us. We had obtained twelve enamel cups, ten cheap watches (gifts for the workers), muscle ointment, and two cartons of shotgun shells.

Sue dropped me at the hotel with plans to dine at a Vietnamese restaurant at eight this evening. Fred arrived shortly afterward, having completed his list of camp needs.

After stashing our bought goods at the hotel, Fred, Wayde and I took a bus to the craft village of Soumbédioune, located in the Madina District, to admire works of local craftsmanship and shop for a charm for my bracelet. We browsed necklaces, earrings, bags, statuettes, leather work, under glass paintings, and wooden sculptures. But I found no charms. Fred suggested that I have one of the silversmiths make one. I chose the odd-looking Senegalese swordfish that are used on some of the Senegalese francs. We scheduled a return to the craftsman's booth at 6:00 P.M. to pick up the charm.

When we returned to the booth, I was not pleased with the result and expressed my disappointment. The craftsman agreed to continue to work on it, and an hour later had produced a charm that I would be proud to wear! While waiting, Fred had purchased a hand-woven picnic basket.

There was barely enough time to rush back to the Continental and dress for dinner. The meal with the Ryans was great! They had brought their twelve-year-old son so that Wayde had someone to visit with. Sue gave me a copy of the collection of the Senegalese recipes that she had compiled and asked that I read it and give some critique. We returned to our room around 11:30 and packed our baggage. We get up at 6:30 A.M. in the morning to catch the plane to Guinea. Tomorrow we will discover whether Wayde and I have visas to enter the country.

Koundara
Saréboïdo
Guingan
Foulamôri
Kifaya
Touba
1538
Tamgué
Balaki
Gambie
Mali
Koumbia
Gaoual
Kounsitél
Yambéring
Madina Salambandé
Koumba
Dabalaré
Kogon
Wéndou Mbôrou
Tominé
Malanta
1290
Kolou
Koubia
Hamdallaï
Lélouma
Kôllé
Kâtoni
1245
Popodara
Labé
Tougué
Dabiss
Sansalé
Hérico
Sangarédi
Missira
Santou
Kakrima
Pita
Kankalabé
Kalinko
Dabali
Boké
Konsotami
Télimélé
Djallon
Bafing
Malapouya
Tiontian
Bissikrima
1036
Gongôré
Sarri
Dalaba
1421
Kavendou
Dogomet
Sangaréa
Timbo
Saramoussaya
Konkouré
Bouliwél
Kolia
Fria
Kébali
Kégnéko
Mamou
Kindoyé
Bangouya
1094
Kadiondola
1040
Douprou
Konkouré
Boffa
Linsan
Soya
Mongo
Passaya
Falessadé
Souguéta
Tanéné
Wassou
Kindia
Kolèntèn
Ouré Kaba
Maréla
Sandénia
Kaba
Madina Woula
Khorira
Mambiya
Kouriya
CONAKRY
Coyah
1124
Kolenté
Moussaya
Forécariah

CAMP C
CAMP A
Baoule Flats
CAMP B
Bounoudou
Approximate locations of Camp A & B
Siguiri
Dinguiraya
Kouroussa
Kankan
Mandiana
Faranah
Kissidougou
Kérouané
Guékédou
Macenta
Beyla
Nzérékoré
Lola
Yomou

PART 4 –EVERYTHING MOVES SLOWLY IN GUINEA

The following includes information taken from edited diary entries and letters home, dating March 27 through April 6, 1980.

March 27th -- The manager of the hotel woke us up at 6:00 A.M., but we fell back to sleep and awoke at a quarter until seven! We had to scramble to get everything together to meet the taxi at seven. The taxi ride to the airport cost ten U.S. dollars, but we were running too late to quibble about the price. Fred was worried that Wayde and I might not be able to board the plane to Conakry without visas, but there was no problem getting onto the plane. Wayde and I had the two seats in front of Fred. He sat at the window seat, trying to have a conversation in French with the Guinean man seated next to him.

During the entire flight, I felt sick to my stomach with worry. Would Wayde and I be sent back to Dakar on the return flight?

The plane touched down in Banjul, Gambia. There was over an hour delay while gas was hand-pumped into the fuel tanks. The plane had no ventilation. Sweat rolled down my forehead and dripped from my nose onto my chin. Wayde wanted water, but neither Fred nor I had thought to bring a canteen. A woman in one of the two seats across the aisle from us, fainted from the heat.

The airplane was airborne again and the air cooled. Thirty minutes later we were preparing to land at Conakry-Gbessi airport. The pilot was on the speaker warning passengers that if they didn't have a visa for Guinea to stay on the plane; if disembarking, have all the proper papers in hand. The plane

rolled to a stop, stairs were rolled to the exit, the doors opened. I grabbed Wayde's hand and followed Fred out of the plane.
There were two men waiting at the foot of the steps to greet us. Fred was smiling as they shook hands. The men were from the PDG (Democratic Party of Guinea) office and had papers for me to sign for Mr. Lampietti and PDG, stating that I assumed all responsibility for Wayde and myself while in Guinea and would not hold DDX or PDG liable for any mishaps which may befall my child or myself while in the country. PDG oversees Guinea's diamond and mining industry. I signed the papers using my name, rather than signing as Fred's bride. A look was exchanged between the two men, but they turned and walked away with the papers, seemingly satisfied.

The Democratic Party of Guinea (PDG) had originally been founded as a branch of the African Democratic Rally (RDA) in 1947, when the country was a French colonial possession. In October of 1958 the party severed its links with the RDA when Ahmed Sékou Touré, became the country's first president. During 1960, Sékou Touré declared the PDG to be the sole legal party in the country. Under a one-party state system, the PDG oversees most political and economic actions within Guinea, from checking passports and visas at the airports, issuing travel passes from one area to the other, and providing government officials (homologues) to oversee all mining projects.

Our luggage was whisked to a waiting vehicle. There were no customs, we just walked through the terminal to the waiting car. Fred introduced me to Tys, the manager of PDG's guest house, known as the Sultan House. The dwelling previously belonged to an American ambassador before President Sékou Touré closed the country to outsiders.

The house had once been grand, but now showed signs of disrepair. Paint peeled from the front façade; loose boards creaked underfoot as we crossed the porch to the front door. A large Persian rug covered the foyer's worn hardwood floor, it's once richly colored floral accents and medallion center now gray with dirt; it's wool frizzed. The bulky mahogany, leather-covered furniture in the grand room was pushed up along the walls. The room was clean, but seemingly unused. Down the hallway to the left, a large kitchen and dining area was the center point of the living quarters. Here there were signs of life.

A pot of water simmered on a four-burner Hot Point electric range, out-of-place, amid the elegance of this once regal home. A bulky Electrolux kerosene refrigerator stood next to the stove. Aside from the stove and refrigerator, there was a large expandable teak dining table hosting an odd assortment of chairs, eight in all. The only other fixture in the kitchen was a white Formica table – its surface worn from years of scouring – and four matching chairs. On two of the walls, open shelves held an assortment of canned foods and a few condiments.

The bathroom seemed a bit primitive for such a once-grand home. But, at that time, I didn't know "primitive". The bathroom had no running water. There was a toilet and a sink, plus a large scrub brush for cleaning the toilet when used. Three buckets of rust-colored water were used for flushing the toilet and washing up at the sink. The remanence of a bar of Palmolive soap slimed the once white porcelain. A clean towel hung from a hook nearby. A full-length teak mirror with beveled glass occupied the wall directly across from the toilet, giving a grandiose view of one sitting across from it.

The kitchen faced a large screened-in porch running the length of the house. The porch looked out over a well-tended garden toward the ocean; calm, curling waves breaking just beyond the garden wall. Through a small door, steps led down to the garden where paths ribboned through stands of bamboo and palms, plus an orchard of mango, papaya, and banana trees. Many fragrant flowering trees and shrubs scented the air. There was also a small greenhouse filled with ripening vegetables – tomatoes, cucumbers, squash, cabbage, carrots. A partial bag of Baugh's Animal Based Fertilizers was leaning against the end wall.

A cot had been set up on the porch for Wayde. There was a small monkey tied to a post not far from his bed. She and Wayde made friends and spent the rest of the day playing.

Fred's and my room were located directly off the kitchen. A double teak bed, with sagging boxed springs and mattress, was covered with a worn white candlewick bedspread and draped with a mosquito net suspended from the ceiling. A small nightstand stood against the wall. There were five similarly furnished sleeping rooms in the Sultan House, accessed through the living room.

Tys oversees four house boys who perform most of the daily tasks – tending the garden, doing the washing, cooking, dishing up the meals, and placing fresh flowers on the nightstand by my bed.

Fred introduced me to David McDonald, one of our camp members returning from vacation, and two men from one of the other camps, Pip (Lampietti's twenty-year-old son), and Simon, from New Zealand. Then Fred and I walked to the market.

Conakry is much hotter than Dakar had been, and the people are poorer. Along the streets and in the market, sewage runs through open ditches. Guinea is one of the world's poorest countries.

Despite its natural resources and abundant rainfall, Guinea has low life expectancy and a high rate of infant mortality.

The market offers a limited variety of goods and what's found is of inferior quality. Most dry goods are cheap plastic or rubber imports. Looking at the feet of the throng of shoppers, rubber shoes seemed to be the footwear of choice. Many booths sold clothing donated by the Salvation Army. The clothes are unloaded in bundles from ships and the government auctions the bundles off to the highest bidder. The food items were of poor quality, especially the produce.

I had been cautioned beforehand to not purchase any produce in Conakry that didn't have a rind. Limes, mangos, papayas, oranges, and pineapples were considered safe edibles, but no tomatoes, strawberries, peppers, lettuce, cabbage and similar fruits and vegetables, because crops were fertilized with human waste. The market was overcrowded and sweltering. I needed to use the public bathroom and was directed to a grass screen. Behind the screen were a couple of pits for squatting and relieving oneself. Men urinated on the screen, while women squatted. There were small squares of newspaper and paper bags for wiping. Men and women used the bathroom at the same time, there was no "men" or "women" segregation. The odors were eye-watering, and the buzz of thousands of flies deafening.

I had suffered from a headache since our layover in Gambia, so I didn't enjoy the market as much as I ordinarily may have. I look forward to returning before we head for the camp in Baoule Valley. Fred was able to find some of the things he needed to take. We also bought some bananas and juice oranges.

When we returned to the Sultan House, we sat on the porch sipping a cold soft drink called Sisi. Fred read his mail which consisted of a Valentine card I had mailed the 27th, of January, and a letter that I had mailed in early February, plus a postcard and letter from Fred's mother.

We enjoyed the cool breeze that came in off the ocean. Sweetly scented gardenia and the fragrant aroma of lemon blossoms tempered the scent of sewage. We were served a simple meal prepared by the household cook. The steward, who is fond of Fred, placed a bouquet of flowering frangipani branches in our room. Fred mentioned that the steward, Barry, collected postage stamps, so I gave him several blocks of four which Fred's mother had given me to give as gifts. Stamps in Conakry are often difficult to obtain.

Fred had errands to do and letters to write this evening after dinner. I stayed at the dining table and played poker with the guys from the two camps – A and C. I ended up with a few dollars less than I had started with, but I intend to win them back next game.

Fred and I felt very close when we retired. It is all beginning to dawn on us. At last, we are here together in Guinea. This last two and a half months getting Wayde and myself here is in the past. All the frustrations and red tape have been overcome. Tonight, I feel that whatever happens in the future it will be easier to deal with than the obstacles of the past few months.

March 28th – I woke up late this morning. The little time Fred and I had spent together was the only fulfilling event of the day. Fred had breakfast, then went to the DDX office in downtown Conakry. Fred still has four days left before his vacation ends, yet he seems to be ready to be back in camp. I suppose, even when on vacation, there is much to do before returning to work.

Fred returned for lunch, then left for Texaco. I wrote a letter to Mom and Dad. After letter writing I felt bored, so I gathered up our dirty laundry and took it outside to the wash tubs, filled one with water from a nearby bucket, and started scrubbing. But the steward quickly spotted my efforts, shook his finger at me, and took over. Finally, I ended up sorting through my suitcase and our backpacks to reorganize everything. I was uneasy today, since Wayde and I are here against company wishes. The treatment Wayde and I have received from Tys is belligerent. This afternoon, after Fred had left, I offered to help in the kitchen.

Tys rebuked my offer saying, "Stay out and away from things! The only way Fred managed to get you and the kid into this country was to threaten Lampietti that he would leave the company if Lampietti didn't help get you in. We don't want you and the boy here. It is too dangerous and too inconvenient."

For supper Tys fed us a meal of watery stew consisting of chunks of gristle, bone, and fat for flavoring, served over rice. I picked out some suspicious looking brown bits from the rice. They resembled mouse droppings, but I couldn't be certain.

On top of the hostility, Wayde has been sick all day. However, by evening he felt good enough to play poker. Fred returned shortly before dinner and visited with the other members of the camp, waiting for transportation to arrive. He introduced me to David Salsby, another member of Camp B. I sat and played a few hands of poker with Wayde, David Salsby, and Simon, while Fred read reports and caught up on his journal.

March 29th – Fred and I walked to the market again today to pick up a few bananas, oranges, and mangos, as we craved fresh food. Food at the Sultan House has been prepared from canned supplies, such as tuna and chicken. Plus, canned potatoes. Before coming to Guinea, I never knew that there were such things as canned potatoes! Our supplies are all United States brands that have been shipped over from DDXs New York supply warehouse. On the way back from the market, Fred fell ill. He began vomiting and had a fever. I helped him back to the house and got him into bed. By evening, he was feeling better and was able to eat a little dinner.

Two members of our camp, Camp A (Baoule' Valley), showed up at the Sultan House. They are beginning their two-week vacation. One of the men is Dr. Raynor Shaw, a doctor of Geology. He is heading to Dakar. The other man's name is Tony, from England. Tony is the main mechanic at camp. Tony plans to remain in Conakry during his break from Baoule' Valley. He, and a Frenchman who has flown in from Paris, are waiting for customs to release a new Poclain that was shipped here from France. The Frenchman had arrived a week ago to assist Tony in assembling the machine.

Adding the Poclain, a new piece of mining equipment purchased by DDX, is part of their 1980 Mission Statement. The company purchased a tracked Poclain excavator, shipped directly from France to Conakry. Fred seems very excited about having the hydraulic Poclain added to the diamond exploration process.

Tony said that they have a monkey in camp for Wayde. Tony and Raynor are both excited to have my son and me in camp this season. I felt a huge weight lift from my heart on hearing that news.

I would have enjoyed visiting more with Dr. Shaw and Tony, but I fell ill early this evening with a high fever, vomiting, headache, and chills. My muscles ached, especially in my legs.

March 30th – I stayed in bed most of the day sleeping. The fever has gone down, but I haven't been able to eat. Fred feels well today and is taking good care of me.

The old Mercedes truck that had brought Dr. Shaw and Tony to Conakry went back to Camp B (Bounoudou), today, taking David Salsby, Pip and Simon. Fred had wanted Wayde and me to go with the truck, too, to be left off at Camp A with David McDonald, while Fred finished dismantling the second jumper drill at the Texico yard. But I felt too ill to make the two-and-a-half-day journey.

March 31st – I felt better today, though shaky, and weak. Fred came down with the malady last night, again, but seems to be doing better this morning. I was able to eat today, but little was available. Barry, the steward, helped me cut up some pineapple for breakfast. The fruit was small and squatty compared to the pineapple common in American markets. Barry showed me how to cut it lengthwise, then run a sharp knife between the rind and the fruit. The knife sliced down the center of the flesh, then the blade made a series of crosscuts, creating lovely finger-size servings. Even the core was soft and juicy. I was told that these pineapples are one of Guinea's major agriculture exports. The fruit doesn't have stringy fiber that lodges between the teeth. It was sweet and succulent, with flavor that would shame an American grown pineapple.

For lunch Tys served each of us a half a cup of canned green beans and a small slice of bread. For dinner we were served a small dab of canned potato, topped with a spoonful of gravy, and for dessert, a small slice of papaya. Fred became irate with the meals that we had been served and Tys behavior, so he went into the kitchen and fried up some leftover shrimp and potatoes.

Tys wants everyone to either go off on their vacations or go back up-country to their camps. There is nowhere that Fred, Wayde and I would rather be than "up-country", but we must wait for the truck's return, possibly by Friday, but most likely not until Sunday. Anyway, Tys leaves tomorrow on his vacation, and everyone can hardly wait. The food has progressively gotten worse and currently the portions barely sustain us.

I met Mr. Gueye today. He is the Senior Guinean working in the DDX office, and the man responsible for Wayde and me getting into Guinea. Mr. Gueye seems a mild-mannered Guinean who speaks a little English. I saw him having a serious talk with Fred, their voices lowered. Mr. Gueye glanced at me a couple of times during their discussion, then turned his back toward me.

Fred and I retired early this evening. Fred wrote letters home, and I caught up on my diary.

March 31st late night – I went to bed early but was unable to sleep. I have been careful not to get into Fred's personal business or be pushy. It is not my general makeup to meddle with, especially when it is none of my business. But the way Mr. Gueye and Fred were talking, I had a deep gut feeling that it was my business.

Later tonight, as Fred was getting into bed, I asked him what Mr. Gueye had wanted to speak to him about. Fred said that he did not want to talk about it.

"Does it have to do with me?"

"I don't want to talk about it!" Fred was angry now.

But so was I! "Well, I do!"

Fred sat up and perched on the edge of the bed. I remained standing, my emotions surging.

“It’s about my bringing you and Wayde into the country without us being married.”

“And why was that?” I pushed.

Fred let out a long sigh. “I enjoyed being with you. I wanted an adventure with you. I thought a proposal would bring you here to Africa so that we could have that adventure together. There had been someone back home in California. We separated early last summer after being together for a couple of years. We had agreed to give it some time, and maybe try to work things out between us afterward. Then you and Wayde came along. Now, come to bed.”

Suddenly drained, I laid down beside Fred. He quickly fell asleep. I couldn’t. I was shocked by his admission. And too angry to cry.

Finally, I got up and wrote in my journal:

Moon dream was my yesterday, reality’s now stark.
Where is the man that I thought I knew?
Stranger in the daytime; stranger in the dark.
Pardon my confusion, but lover, is this you?
Caresses on the beach, kisses in the park,
Handholding as we strolled along the rue.

Moon dream was my yesterday; now it haunts.
Where is the woman that I thought was me?
Stranger to my needs; stranger to my wants,
Rather to be captured, than to remain free.

Caresses no longer sweet; kisses now they taunt,
Recalling handholding, strolling along the sea.

April 1st – This morning, I woke, having had little sleep. Physically I was feeling better, but mentally I was stressed. Fred had admitted that he had lured me to Africa under false pretenses. I felt cheated. Fred's proposal had given me little time for thought. He should have been straight with me. He should have asked me if I would go to Africa for an adventure with him and to see how well we might work together. I may have said, yes. Or, I may have said, no. This far into things I really don't know what I would have said. But Fred didn't give me that choice. As hurt as I feel, I still love him. But I no longer trust him. And I know that I never will.

I will pass myself off as his fiancée, as is his wish, during the duration of my stay here in Guinea. But when I leave here, I go as a single, unengaged woman. I will temper my bitterness, swallow my disappointment, and have that adventure in Africa.

When Fred awoke, I was up and dressed. He patted the bed and held his arms out for a hug. I went to him, and we embraced.

Then I stood and said, "You owe my son an explanation. I would appreciate you taking the time this morning to give him one."

Fred dressed and went into the screened porch area where Wayde slept.

I couldn't help wondering if I hadn't pushed Fred for answers, how long his charade would have gone on? Soon Fred came back into the bedroom.

"You need to go to Wayde. He needs you."

Wayde was crying uncontrollably. I wrapped my arms around him as he sobbed. Finally, he looked at me. “Fred isn’t going to be my dad. Was it something I said? What did I say?”

I looked at my ten-year-old son as his tears continued to fall and pulled him back into my arms. My thoughts echoed with my ex-husband’s words, “Take your kid and get out!”

Something Wayde had said escalated an already shaky relationship between his adoptive father and me. Wayde had recently turned seven years old. The three of us had walked to the corner hamburger place to have an evening meal. There was a heavy-set kid, about ten years old, scarfing up a burger.

My husband said, within the child’s hearing, “Look at that fat slob! He eats like a pig!”

To which Wayde replied, “Yeah, Dad. He eats like you.”

And it was true! So, true. I involuntarily let out a short snort. My husband stood up from the table and walked out, our meal unpaid for. I told the waitress I would be back shortly with the money and left Wayde to finish his hamburger. My husband didn’t say one thing to me when I grabbed my wallet and headed back to the restaurant. But when Wayde and I returned, he met us at the door.

“Take your kid and get out.”

My parents took us in that night, and we settled into the little guest apartment they had built above the garage. I got a job the following day at the local nursing home, as an aide.

Six weeks later my husband invited me to dinner and to have a talk. He had candles lit and placed around the living room and roses on the table. He begged to have Wayde and me return home. He had adopted Wayde when my son was four years old. Our marriage had lasted for three years, but they hadn't been easy ones. My husband was a widower and twenty years my senior. He had frequent periods of moodiness. If I displeased him, I would be given "the silent" treatment, the longest lasting an entire week. I kept his house clean and meals on time. I looked after his teen-aged children and worked to turn his place into a home. He never struck Wayde, but the verbal abuse Wayde suffered was just as bad. I refused to return, hugged my two stepchildren good-bye, and filed for divorce, taking with me my son, the aging Rambler Station wagon, and tent trailer. Plus, my unfinished manuscript, "*How to Prepare Common Wild Foods*".

I now told Wayde, "The relationship between Fred and me had nothing to do with you. It's about what isn't between us. We don't know each other well enough to be married. But Fred wanted us to be here with him. To share with him an adventure in Africa! And so, that is what the three of us are going to do. Have an adventure together, in Africa."

"Are you still going to be engaged?"

"As long as we are in Africa, yes."

"But after?"

I couldn't lie to my son. "No." I answered.

"So, I didn't say anything wrong like I did to Dad?"

“Wayde, that wasn’t your fault. I had no idea that you had felt that it was. Yes, you said something that upset your dad. But that wasn’t what ended the marriage. It had been hanging by a thread for a long time. We should have separated long before.”

At Fred’s suggestion my wedding skirt and blouse, along with Wayde’s “best man” shirt, were put into storage at the Sultan House. There was no need to take them to Camp A. Wayde and I will have something fresh to wear when we leave Africa and head home at the end of the season.

At the Sultan House the day dragged by. There is no gasoline available, so transportation is scarce. I am anxious to get away from the filth of the city and out into the savannah. Fred was at the Texico most of the day, checking out another drill. I napped some in the afternoon, then Wayde and I went for a walk as evening approached.

Walking through Conakry was like walking through a Twilight Zone – shacks and shanties crammed together; chicken, goats and children picking through the garbage lining the streets; people bathing themselves by squatting naked over a pan of water and splashing. The stench of the open sewage trenches, which emptied into the bay, permeated the neighborhoods where children played kick-the-ball with balls made of rags. Many of the huts and shacks had no doors and we could look directly into the living quarters, which were most often cramped rooms with rag bedding strewn about the floors.

But the people were kind. They smiled and gave us greetings. The openness and friendliness of the people of Conakry were starkly different from the attitude of the more citified and tourist-oriented people of Dakar, whose mannerisms and attitudes had elements of stress and entitlement. I felt my heart opening to these people of Guinea, who, although impoverished, seemed happy and grateful for what they had, little as it was.

By the time Wayde and I arrived back at the house my mood had improved. Fred had returned and Tys had left on his two-weeks' vacation.

I wondered if Tys had left us any food. I needn't have wondered. We were left cold, sliced Treet (something akin to Spam, only worse), canned beets, canned mushroom soup, bread, and rice – which we are abstaining from since becoming ill, possibly from our first meal of it. I ate very little but managed to amuse myself throughout dinner by picking baked weevils from my bread.

Fred and I stayed up late to visit with two camp members, David McDonald, and Tony. Tony was full of voodoo stories, causing me to wish that I had left my guitar at home and brought my Tarot deck, instead. David is leaving in the morning for our camp.

April 2nd – I feel better today. Fred and I talked things out last night and I am clear on where we stand. It is not where I had expected to be upon arriving in Africa, but at least now, there is some honesty.

During the morning hours we were driven around by a man from the DDX office and accomplished some things. After visiting the fuel yard where Fred procured fuel for the trip to camp, we went shopping. We bought foam pads needed for our camp beds and mosquito netting. Fred and I will be sharing a thatched hut, and Wayde will have a separate, smaller one next to ours.

After lunch and a nap, we left the Sultan House, taking local buses, ramshackle contraptions, which rattle down the packed dirt roads, crammed to capacity with people and animals. These amusing rides cost only five sylis, the equivalent of a United States quarter.

We rode to the Texico compound where Fred introduced me to Dee and Jo Ann, a middle-aged couple from Florida. They have been in Conakry since December and are leaving this evening for the United States for a two-week vacation.

Fred showed me drill #2, a used piece of equipment that he has been disassembling in preparation for transporting to our camp, against strict orders from his boss, Lampietti. Fred believes that he can obtain better gravel samples with this machine, plus he will be able to hire another Guinean worker to operate the first drill, set up near camp last year, resulting in more samples.

Wayde went swimming in the Texico swimming pool while I watched Fred wrestle with the drill. Later, I walked through the garden and lolled on the grass. Fred finally finished working on the disassembly and he and I joined Wayde in the pool. Afterwards, we took a taxi back to the Sultan House.

At dinner, Fred and I were summoned to the kitchen. In Tys absence, the cook had been instructed to cook some canned dinner. Well, he threw all the unopened cans into a pot of water and proceeded to boil them. They hadn't broken open but were all distorted and it was very difficult to get to the contents. The poor cook was scurrying around the kitchen wild-eyed and confused. Fred calmed the man by saying that the dinner he fixed was much nicer than what Tys had been feeding us.

Fred's back was hurting him from tackling the drill, so we retired early.

April 3rd – Another good day! I am beginning to feel the excitement of Guinea and gaining an understanding why men like Fred find such fascination with countries where their minds and bodies are continuously being challenged. Getting a tank of gas is a challenge; keeping a vehicle running is a challenge; going from one point to another is a challenge. Doing anything in Guinea is challenging!

One interesting thing I observed about Conakry is its electric power. One never knows when the power will fail. It can be counted on to fail at least twice a day from one hour to twelve. Most often it fails during the heat of the day and during mealtimes. When failing at mealtimes, a charcoal grill is lit, and brought into the kitchen for completing meal preparations. Meals by candlelight are common. But not necessarily romantic.

Tony received some bad news last night. The Poclain that he and the Frenchman had been waiting to be released through customs, apparently had been stolen from the shipyard dock. Since the Frenchman's only purpose for being here was to assist Tony in assembling the equipment, he has planned to return to Paris tomorrow. Tony believes that the Russian diamond miners had a couple of the machines when they were mining in the Upper Guinea area a few years ago and may have left one behind. He will also check Texico to see if an old excavator, capable of being repaired, might be in the yard there.

This afternoon Fred went back to Texico to finish dismantling the drill. While Wayde chose to stay at the Sultan House to play with the monkey, Tony and I walked back to the market to see if we could locate items still needed for the camp. We found a Russian-made hammer, but nothing else on the list.

Fred didn't show up until after lunch. I heated some canned potatoes and chicken for him and fixed a salad of tomatoes grown in the garden's greenhouse, without human fertilizer. I cleared the dishes and began washing them. Barry, the steward, came in from doing the wash and noticed that Fred had returned. He began preparing Fred's lunch. I was doing every pantomime I could think of to let him know that Fred had already eaten lunch, but Barry thought that I was just being entertaining. He put some canned potatoes in a saucepan to heat them.

I took the pan off the stove saying, "Non! Non! Fini! Mr. Fred, fini!"

Barry would put the pan back on the stove, wagging his finger at me.

Poor Barry thought that I was angry with Fred and that I did not want him to have anything to eat. Finally, I took Barry to Fred and Fred explained the situation. Once Barry understood, he thought the situation very funny, laughing while imitating my previous pantomiming.

Shortly after lunch, Mr. Gueye showed up with a Guinean government official. Since the old Mercedes truck had failed to return, as expected, and no radio communication has been able to reach the PDG office in Kissidougou to gather information, a plan was devised to rent a Land Rover to transport Fred, Wayde and me to Camp A (Baoule' Flats).

Fred bulked at this suggestion, stating that he would not leave Conakry without the drill and that the drill would need a heavy truck to haul it. The matter was discussed, and it was concluded that Mr. Gueye would attempt to rent both a truck and a Land Rover, plus procure more fuel. Mr. Gueye felt that a Land Rover was needed to transport Wayde and me, as well as our personal belongings, to camp. He believed that it would not be possible for the three of us to make the two-and-half day journey crammed in the cab of the truck. The PDG office would provide a driver for the Land Rover.

Later in the afternoon, Fred and I got a ride to Socamer market with the man who is replacing Tys during Tys's two-week absence. The replacement is a French speaking gentleman who is much more agreeable to be around. Socamer market is the one store in Guinea where European foods, such as cola, 7-up, beer, instant cocoa, and dried herbs are available. There's not much variety and the prices are unbelievably expensive. We left without making a purchase.

This evening, after supper, I read Tony's fortune using a regular deck of playing cards. It was a pleasant change from losing money at the poker table. I grinned to myself as I stretched the truth of his reading just a wee bit, adding a secret admirer and a nice chunk of money coming his way. Payback time!

Just as I was finishing up Tony's reading, the Land Rover showed up from camp. It wasn't the Mercedes truck that had been hoped for. David Salsby, who had left earlier in the week, had used the Mercedes to transport himself to Camp Bounoudou, rather than leaving it in Kissidougou, as planned, and finishing his trip in a Land Rover. The Mercedes had run into trouble enroute and was bogged down in mud somewhere along the way.

If all goes well, Wayde and I will leave in the Land Rover, and Fred will be following in a rented truck hauling the drill.

April 4th – We got up this morning hoping to see the Mercedes truck arrive, but it didn't show up. Fred went to the PDG office to see what Mr. Gueye was planning while I packed our things. Fred returned with the news that we'll be leaving tomorrow morning!

The afternoon was spent impatiently lounging around, since our chores had been completed and there was nothing to do but wait. Wayde and I did spend some time in the garden, watching lizards, banana spiders, various colorful butterflies, and the garden's pet Guinea fowl. Then Wayde returned to the porch to coddle the monkey.

Toward evening Fred and I walked down to the market for some juice oranges and mangos and decided to make some orange tapioca. Well, once in the kitchen I didn't want to stop at the tapioca, so I made oatmeal and raisin cookies, and an Italian-style pasta dish – accompanied with garlic bread. Tony joined us for dinner, as well as a last-minute guest.

As we were getting ready to eat, Mr. Gueye came by and invited us to the ballet at nine. He joined us for dinner, then Tony, Wayde, Fred and I hurriedly got dressed in clean clothing. We rode with Mr. Gueye to the event.

The ballet was held in the civic auditorium, the Palais du Peuple, a venue for special presentations, including festivals, concerts, and political events. The auditorium was built in 1967 with the financial help of the Chinese. It is an impressive high ceiling auditorium with gardens, magnificent lighting, and plush seating. Such an extravagance seems out of place amid the squalid poverty of Conakry.

I sat between Fred and Tony. Fred would whisper his translation and observation of what was occurring on stage. The ballet turned out to be a performance put on by The Pioneers, a group of youths who danced, sang, and performed speeches in dramatic fashion. The theme of the performance centered around party aims and policies. There was much singing, mainly songs praising the merits of PDG officials. Many speeches (in French) followed, also praising one-party rule. Along with Mr. Gueye, several other PDG officials were in attendance, carefully watching the performance and the audiences' reaction. For the first time since I arrived in Guinea, the country's political standing began to become clearer to me. The Democratic Party of Guinea (PDG) is basically a dictatorship, supposedly based on the will of the people, but do not tolerate political opposition. It touches all spheres of public and personal life. Party members hold every key position in towns and villages. This group of youths, The Pioneers, won favor with the observing officials and will no doubt be permitted to do other performances.

Something Tony said to me during intermission, while Fred was visiting with Mr. Gueye, startled me. He said, "There are going to be some rough times ahead for you. When you need to lean on someone for support, you can lean on me."

Are Fred and my personal problems so transparent? How much does Tony know?

It was past midnight when we returned to the Sultan House and climbed into bed.

April 5th – There was an excitement in the air as the Land Rover and rented old Russian truck were loaded! As we climbed into the Land Rover the cook bid us goodbye.

Barry, the steward, kept saying, "Madam, non! Non departee. Madam, restee!"

We drove over to the PDG office to get our "order of mission" papers. Each vehicle leaving Conakry must have papers to prove that they have business outside the city. Barricades are located along the route with armed guards assigned to check the papers. It is quite a process to obtain a permit. One does not leave the city to merely take a Sunday drive in the country, hop on over to Coyah for an impromptu picnic, or have a casual visit with friends in the nearby village of Khoriro.

At 11:00 we left in the Land Rover. The loaded truck, with David Salsby, and a half dozen workers, was still sitting at the PDG office. There were six of us in the Land Rover, plus two black kittens Wayde had adopted from somewhere. Fred, Momodu (our English-speaking Guinean driver and camp game hunter), and I rode in the front. Wayde, a homologue, and a Guinean worker, named Bongani, rode in the back.

The homologue is a government official who will observe and learn the processes of diamond exploration. There will be three different methods of diamond-bearing gravel sampling in our camp, each having a homologue present.

Once out of the city, I found the countryside to be beautiful with its tropical foliage, flowering trees, stands of wild mangos and small native villages, with round, thatched roofed huts. Fred told me that the huts were call payottes and that we would be living in one at camp.

I was apprehensive when we approached the first barricade. It consisted of an empty gas-oil barrel placed toward the center of the road, balancing a long, crooked stick. Hanging from the stick dangled a plastic bag, a tattered red rag, and an old tin can. Similar obstructions were to be encountered throughout our journey. A guard stood next to the barricade, armed with an

AK47 assault rifle and a Makarov pistol side arm, checking permits.

At several points along the route, we saw the remains of automobiles strewn along the roadside. One wreckage was two burned out autos, still fused together from their impact. This happened, our driver said, five days ago. Six people met a fiery death. Many such accidents occur along this narrow and windy road. It is not surprising, considering the condition of not only the road, but most vehicles attempting the journey. The Land Rover that we were traveling in was a case in point.

People group along the roadside attempting to purchase a ride up-country. We were too overloaded to take any passengers and saw no vehicles which weren't crammed to compacity. People were hanging from side doors, standing on bumpers, and sitting on hoods. It's a mode of life here, as well as a way for the driver to pay for gas.

There are venders who step out from the bush to sell their wares. I am told that the PDG view this as a form of black marketing by avoiding payment of the required market taxes. We bought fruit along the way and a couple of intriguing minnow traps. Our driver, Momodu, purchased bush meat –a haunch of deer – from a hunter standing along the roadside, and further on, some wooden bowls from a woman who emerged from the shadows of a stand of trees.

The journey was hot, but immensely enjoyable. I was flushed in awe as we drove up into small, forested mountains, then down, merging with vast expanses of savannah emphasized with scatterings of shea trees and baobab. We drove near several bush fires, which Momodu explained were often purposely set to clear the ground of tall grasses. Fresh, young shoots will grow for livestock feed. He said that the fires often got out of control and burned down the grass-hut villages. It was not a bad thing, he explained. Diseases are less prevalent in the savannah villages due to the fires. Villages would be established anew, leaving sickness in the ashes of the old. A thin haze hangs in the air.

Darkness came. The bush fires cast an eerie glow against the blackness of night. In the distance lightning flashed, the sky flaring brightly as we drove nearer to the threatening storm. Wind came and I sensed rain nearby. I waited eagerly for the first drops to fall. Then it came, the scent of Africa – wet, red earth mingled with the fragrance of a freshly woven grass basket.

The familiarity of the scent of rain on the savannah brought me home, the feeling deep within my soul of a long forgotten existence. Fred noticed tears in my eyes.

"Are you okay," he asked.

I nodded. Yes.

The rain was relentless, pouring in through the partially opened windows. The windows were caked with so much of the day's dust that mud slid in sheets from the encrusted glass. As swiftly as the downpour had come, it ceased. Steam rose from the road forming low hanging clouds which drifted in whiffs and swirls as the Land Rover passed.

At 11:00 we neared Kissidougou, its name meaning "a place of refuge" in Mandekan. We had traveled 590 kilometers, the equivalent of 360 miles, in twelve hours. The driver was pleased that we had made such good time! The homologue had connections near Kissidougou, so he, the Guinean worker, and Bongani were dropped off at a house on the outskirts of the city.

As we drove into Kissidougou, the horn on the Land Rover started sticking and now loudly announced our arrival at the PDG house, startling the host from a deep sleep. John Paul, a Frenchman, and his family are employed by PDG to oversee the guest house and the supply post providing food, fuel, and vehicle maintenance for mining companies, such as DDX, working the Upper Guinea Baoule Flat and Diani Basin.

The man came scurrying out of his house, swearing in French. Despite Momodu's frantic jiggling of the steering wheel, the horn was now blaring nonstop, causing Jean Paul further agitation. The obnoxious horn was finally subdued after the cables were removed from the battery. We were curtly directed to the guest house where we found a metal frame draped with an ill-fitting, musty, stained, sagging mattress. The rest of the small, wood-framed house was empty. David Salsby's folding cot was in the Land Rover. This was lucky for Wayde, but unfortunate for David Salsby, who was bouncing along in the slow-moving rented Russian truck an estimated 100 kilometers behind.

Our sheets, bedding, mosquito nets and insect repellent were all on the big Russian truck. We had to close all the windows to partially protect ourselves from the insects. The room was hot and stuffy, but we slept and slept well.

April 6th – We rose early this morning. There was still no sign of the rented Russian truck. Fred anticipated that there had been trouble and hoped that it hadn't happened too far from Kissidougou.

Fred, Wayde and I went to Jean Paul's and met his wife and two young children. The family has only been here at the PDG post for a week, but the children are already ill with dysentery from drinking the water. Their well is dry, and they are hauling water from the river, then boiling, and filtering it. Still, the children have become ill. We were invited to join the family for lunch.

Just as we settled at the table, David Salsby arrived on foot. Approximately ninety kilometers back, the truck had hit a deep rut. Both tires on the lefthand side of the vehicle had been shorn from the axels. Fred sent Momodu with the Land Rover to retrieve our personal belongings from the truck, plus whatever food and other supplies would fit in the vehicle.

David leaves for Camp B (Bounoudou) tomorrow in a borrowed PDG Land Rover. He is exhausted from his long overnight journey, much of which had to be covered on foot when he couldn't wangle a ride with one of the infrequent vehicles passing in the night – where he rode tightly crammed into an already overloaded "taxi".

Wayde swimming in the Niandan River.

During the afternoon Fred borrowed Jean Paul's Land Rover and he, Wayde, and I went to the Niandan River to fill two large water barrels for Jean Paul. The river is shallow, and the water is warm. Native women were frolicking, bathing, and washing their clothes in the river. The three of us bathed after the barrels were filled. Then a large rain cloud passed over, the brief thunder shower rinsing us clean of the brown river water and suds.

Tonight, we had planned on going into town for brochettes, a local street food made of cubes of N'Damas, a Guinean breed of beef, rubbed with palm oil, salt, and finely crushed hot pepper, then roasted over small charcoal grills. However, we were unable to locate any street venders offering the treats due to the persistent rain. We ended up eating from our supplies, having a picnic on the covered porch of the guest house, with a gas lantern for light, and rain on the roof for music. I made salmon croquets topped with a relish made of mango, lime and finely diced African red pepper…just a tiny bit of pepper, as it is the hottest pepper variety I have ever tasted. It was an exceptional way to end the day.

After we had been asleep for an hour or so, the Land Rover returned with our things and news of the Russian truck. It appears that the truck will be unable to make it into our camp because of the extent of the damage. It remains crippled along the roadside loaded with diesel fuel, drill parts and food. Now it remains uncertain whether we will be able to leave in the morning as planned. After the Land Rover was unloaded and the workers were sent on to their sleeping quarters in another area of the PDG compound, Fred and I returned to bed fully awake. The rain beat down on the roof and lightning flashed outside the now opened windows as a breeze dispersed smoke from the mosquito coil to keep the bugs at bay.

Part 5 – Life in a Diamond Exploration Camp

The following includes information taken from edited diary entries dating April 7 to June 8, 1980.

Section One
April

DDX Mission Statement – Each expatriate's mission, in whatever capacity, is to help attain the goals of the 1979 – 1980 field season program. These are:

1. Sampling by hydraulic mining in the Baoule and Diani Basins.
2. Drilling of the Baoule Flats
3. Trial of Poclain backhoe sampling
4. Reconnaissance mapping and sampling for diamonds and for gold south of Kouroussa.

April 7th Monday – Momodu stayed behind to wait for the arrival of another of our camp's Land Rovers. Fred, Wayde and I were on our way around 10:30. Jean Paul said that he would look after the crippled Russian truck and send the drill to camp on the Mercedes when it shows up. No one seems to know where that Mercedes truck is. Has it been dug out of the deep rut and moved to a nearby village? David Salsby wasn't certain which road it could be on, since there are many unestablished bush roads going this way and that. One tends to drive in the general direction, taking a side road if one way seems extra muddy or obstructed by a stranded vehicle. All roads lead to Kissidougou…in theory.

Five Guinean workers destined for our camp, had to be left behind until the Land Rover returns for them and our remaining food supplies, in a day or two.

The way toward camp was rougher today, but we had made better time since there were no check points to stop us during this stretch of our journey. We reached Kérouané at dusk, traveling nearly two hundred miles. Only thirty kilometers (18 miles) to go. It had begun to rain, and the effect of rain and the warm tropical forest created a sweet, balmy aroma.

However, the going was very rough and slow. In lower, dryer areas the Land Rover lurched past colonies of large, tapered termite mounds, some reaching five feet tall. We traveled along what I would call a non-road, the encroaching forest nearly covering the corridor, at times. The Land Rover had to be put into four-wheel drive at several points. When the driver needed to shift into four-wheel drive the first time, he had to leave the vehicle and dig mud from the front wheels to free the hubs. Afterwards, a red lever was used to make the shift.

Having been raised in Idaho at the edge of the Frank Church wilderness area, I knew what rough travel was when venturing into the back country on vintage logging roads. Guinea's back country roads put traveling Idaho's roads akin to a casual Sunday's drive! Traveling in the Land Rover over exposed boulders and through deep ruts made me ponder how a fully loaded truck could possibly maneuver through this obstacle course? It took us nearly two hours to travel that last eighteen miles from Kérouané.

David McDonald greeted us as we entered camp. Bill Davis, the camp boss, had left during the morning and we had apparently missed each other at one of the forks in the road sometime during the afternoon. I had asked David if Bill was still upset about Wayde and me coming into camp. He grimaced.

David had released Wayde's monkey, believing that it would stay around camp where there was food. It didn't. However, David is willing to share his monkey, Sange, which lives free-range in camp. Sange would no doubt provide Wayde with hours of entertainment, as well as David's puppy, Frank. David also has a lame hen, which provides the camp with a fresh egg, now and then.

Aside from David, there is a non-English speaking Frenchman, Jean Charlot, occupying camp. The others at camp this evening are Guinean. The Guinean laborers live in their own village on the savannah about two kilometers away.

Our camp, Baoule, sat on a terrace amid a scattering of Monkey Plum, Mohogany, and Afina trees. The cicadas pervasive buzzing filled the air. I wondered how a person could fall asleep with the deafening chorus.

Our payotte feels magical! The conical shape is made of sticks and long savannah grasses. The long grasses are woven together and fastened to the stick frame with thin vines to create the thatched roof. Savannah grass was also used for walls. Sticks, tied together with vines, created a lattice-like structure, then grass was woven into the framework. A crudely constructed five-shelved stand occupies space in the center of the payotte. There is a five-inch gap between the packed dirt floor and the bottom of the framework for ventilation. True to payotte customs, there is no door.

We fixed our bed on the floor with the pad that had been purchased in Conakry. Two unzipped sleeping bags were laid open on top. Then Fred produced sheets and a worn candlewick bedspread to finish making up the bed. The mosquito net was hung from a cord attached to the ceiling and draped; the edges tucked beneath the pad. Bill had left his prayer mat to use so that dirt from our floor wouldn't soil the bedding.

Wayde's payotte was a smaller version and ready for occupancy. Bill had already fixed a hammock for Wayde and draped the mosquito net.

I was sorry that I hadn't had the chance to meet Bill before he left for his vacation to thank him for all that he had done in preparation for our arrival, which included having a payotte built for Fred and me, as well as Wayde's. Previously, Fred had occupied one of the small canvas tents set up for camp members. I am looking forward to meeting Bill on his return.

I can hardly wait to see the camp in the daylight. I am anxious to begin settling in. The camp kitchen is just ten feet from our hut. This is convenient for me, as I am determined to take over most of the camp cooking.

Fred and I were elated by bedtime, feeling close and united by finally being "home". Rain came and gently fell on the thatched roof. The screeching cicadas quieted.

April 8th Tuesday – I woke up this morning and fell in love with camp all over again! Fred had already risen, strung up the clothesline between two trees behind our payotte, and headed off in one of the Land Rovers to check on his existing jumper drill. I savored the early morning sounds of birds, insects and assembling workers before jumping out of bed and setting to work, myself.

I checked out the kitchen. It is a long rectangular grass and stick structure with a thatched roof. The woven structure is solid at the back and sides, but open on the front. The approximate length is fourteen feet; the sides, ten feet. The shelter houses a long, rough wood plank table measuring ten feet long by four feet wide. A collection of enamel and ceramic cups are stacked at one end of the table as well as nine metal plates. A total of seven random stools and camp chairs are scattered around the table.

Against the back wall is a small two-burner, electric stove, for want of an electric plug in, I suppose. Two large stainless steel Berkey water filters are standing next to the stove, along with an unopened box of black Berkey filters. A small kerosene refrigerator stands against the far corner, next to an empty kerosene container.

In the left-hand corner of the kitchen is a free-standing, rough two rack plank shelf. A two-gallon aluminum pot with lid and two 2-quart aluminum pots, one with a lid, along with two medium-sized mixing bowls, balanced on the top of the shelf.

The rack below supports a medium-sized cast iron skillet, and a rusting gallon tomato sauce can, holding an assortment of metal forks and spoons. Three long rustically carved wooden stirring spoons lie alongside the can. A gallon-sized black enamel coffee pot, with missing stem and basket, also occupies the rack. On the bottom rack is a backgammon game, a cribbage board, a deck of cards, a Motorola portable cassette tape player, and a small canvas bag filled with "D" cell batteries. A single music cassette tape also occupies the rack, *Waylin & Willie*.

On the ground next to the shelf are two chipped enamel wash tubs and two, one-gallon, galvanized metal, handled pails.

I continue to explore. Last night I had been directed to the outhouse via flashlight. This morning, I had a better look. It sits on a knoll about a hundred yards from camp along a well-worn trail. A small payotte about three and a half feet in diameter has been built around a deep clandestine pit. Half of a sawed-off gasoil drum is fitted with a plastic toilet seat and positioned over the hole. There is, of course, an open doorway. Newspaper lies nearby, to tear off pieces for wiping.

Not far from the well, a pathway weaves a short distance through a dense grove of trees leading to the shower. The other half of the gasoil barrel is perched on a small wooden platform built between two stout limbs. A rickety, hand-built wooden ladder leads up to the barrel, where water is poured into the half barrel. A shower head hangs from a hose that has been fitted into the tank's opening. A clip fastened near the shower head keeps the water from flowing out until needed. A woven stick and five-foot tall grass screen encircle the shower space, leaving a three-foot gap for entering. The floor of the shower has thick layers of gravel that was brought up as core samples. This, of course, is after it had been washed in search of diamonds. I couldn't help but move some of the gravel around with my sandals. A diamond may have been missed.

Any camp member desiring a shower at the end of the day was expected to haul at least two buckets of water from the well in the morning, climb the rickety ladder and pour it into the barrel where it would heat to lukewarm throughout the day…if all went well and it didn't rain.

Most of my morning was spent washing clothes. Using the gallon pails, I lowered them into the well, drawing up water to be heated over a small camp cook fire. The water is light brown and contains various floating particulates, including tiny red swimming bugs barely noticeable to the naked eye.

Three flattish rocks were spaced in the fire ring for balancing the wash tubs, as well as the cooking pots. Once heated, the wash tub was set aside and the second filled with water and placed over the fire. Part of a bar of Palmolive soap was shaved into the hot water in the first tub. Several pieces of clothing were added, then fiercely beaten with a stick! The beaten clothing was hung on the line to cool and drip, while a second load of dirty laundry was added to the soapy water. This was repeated until all the clothing was washed, hot water from the second tub added, as needed.

Finally, all the washed laundry hung dripping on the line, waiting to be rinsed and wrung. Then I twisted and squeezed the excess water out before rinsing the pieces in the second tub, then cooling, and ringing them again, before hanging them on the line. As the clothes were drying, I added small pieces of wood to the fire to make coals for the iron.

After the waistbands, collars and cuffs had been ironed and rehung on the line in the fresh air, I surveyed my morning's work, amazed at how clothing could come out so clean after being washed in murky water.

While I was doing the laundry, Dennis, the kitchen helper, was preparing the camp's drinking water. He drew water from the well and brought four buckets to the propane stove. Seven gallons are poured into a large eight-gallon, soot-blackened enamel pan. The water is boiled for thirty minutes over the open campfire, then six gallons are poured into one of the six-gallon Berkey water filters. The water hauling and boiling is repeated to fill the second filter.

The remaining hot water from the enamel pan is poured into a large wash tub holding the morning's breakfast dishes. Dennis had prepared oatmeal early this morning for Fred and David McDonald. He is responsible for fixing breakfast, while I will be taking over preparing the lunch and dinner meals. Dennis had waited for me to finish with one of the wash pans so that he could finish the morning dishes.

I tackled our payotte next, moving the crudely constructed stand this way and that, before settling on a spot near the foot of our bed. Then I neatly stacked our clean and folded clothes on the shelves. I hung minnow traps from cup hooks and found niches in the woven grass construction to store small items.

Then it was off to the small garden plot. There was a parking area in front of the kitchen, beyond which existed a small, unfenced garden. Cucumber and tomato seedlings had previously been planted. Wayde and I planted several varieties of lettuce, radishes, pole beans, beets, and garlic cloves. The soil was loamy and moist from last night's rain.

Approximately twenty yards from the kitchen stands a flimsy aluminum Sears & Robuck's shed used for food storage. There are rows of empty shelves. However, boxes of supplies are labeled and stacked against the metal walls, most unopened.

I went to my payotte and came back with a small pad of paper and pencil and began taking inventory:

Seven 50 lb. bags of rice
Twenty cases (each 48 – 12 oz). tomato paste
Eight cases (each 16 – 12 oz.) canned corned beef
Twenty-five lbs. yellow onions
Six 8 oz. boxes of baking powder

One case, 35 count each boxed macaroni and cheese
Twenty-four 24 oz. bottled applesauce
Twelve 15 oz. canned asparagus
Twenty-four 4.5 oz. canned mackerel
Twelve 5 oz. canned tuna
Four 12 oz. canned ham
Twenty 3.5 oz. canned green beans
Twenty 3.5 oz. canned baked beans in sauce
Eighteen 3.5 oz. canned potatoes
Twenty-four 3.5 oz. canned spinach
Twelve 2.5 lb. cartons of oatmeal
Twelve 2.5 oz. cartons of weevil infested cornmeal
Two 26 oz. cartons iodized salt
Three gallons of vinegar
Two 3 oz. tins of black pepper
Six small tins ground cinnamon,
Six small tins ground nutmeg
Five small tins curry powder
One case of twenty-four 12 oz. dried prunes
Two cases of twenty-four 12 oz. dried mixed fruit
Twelve 14 oz. pkg. dried white beans
Two 25 lb. bags weevil infested flour
Twelve 3.8 oz. pkgs. chocolate pudding
Twelve 8.8 oz. pkg. noodles
Six 12 oz. canned franks
Twelve 3.8 oz. pkgs. vanilla pudding
Nine 12 oz. pkgs. raisins
Two cans 32 oz. powdered eggs
Two 50 lb. bags sugar
Six 6 oz. boxed tapioca
Forty-two 12 oz. Treet, (Amour Star compressed canned meat)
Four gallons of cooking oil
Fourteen 4 oz. instant hot chocolate
Twenty 8 oz. jars instant coffee crystals

Twelve 14 oz. powdered milk

To the list I added:
3 oz. alfalfa seeds
2 oz. radish seeds

I am not a "Betty Crocker" cook. Formulating and preparing recipes for *How to Prepare Common Wild Foods*, had eased me into innovative cooking. But was I up for the challenge of turning the supplies in the storage shed into flavorful and interesting meals for the men in camp?

I started sprouts in Fred's and my payotte. I had soaked a spoonful of radish seeds in an empty can, filled with drinking water last night. This morning, I rinsed them well and lined the can with a soaking wet white cotton handkerchief, then added the rinsed seeds to the center. I folded the handkerchief over the swollen seeds and sprinkled more drinking water over the top. Hopefully, within four or five days we will have fresh sprouts – enough to add a touch of green and nutrients to our diets. I will just need to remember to give them a daily fresh rinse.

I had return to stocking the shelves, but the inside of the aluminum shed was sweltering so I took a walk along the path that passed the outhouse to see if I could find the mango trees that Fred had told me about. I had asked Wayde if he would like to join me, but he was preoccupied playing with the monkey and the two black kittens.

I found the mango grove about a half mile along the path. They were so tall! My only chance of gathering any would be if they fell to the ground. I will return later, after a storm or strong wind, when there might be windfalls.

By the time I returned, it was time to cook a meal for the five of us – David, Jean Charlot, Fred, Wayde and myself. I prepared our meal over the campfire.

First, I gathered handfuls of savannah grass and layered it on the ground beside the firepit's rocks. Next, I mixed a can of the franks with cans of baked beans, in one of the 2-quart aluminum pans, adding a half teaspoon of dried mustard. The pan sat at the edge of the fire; I turned it occasionally to heat the ingredients evenly.

I poured cooking oil, two inches deep, into the cast iron skillet, balanced on the firepits rocks. As the oil heated, I mixed cornmeal, powdered egg, powdered milk, salt, and a dash of curry powder with drinking water to form a soft dough. The dough was shaped into pones and fried in the oil until golden brown. I drained the cornpone on the mat of grass that I had gathered earlier, then arranged them on a metal plate. In the other small pan, I heated two cans of spinach. Wayde helped me carry the food to the table.

David said that the meal was a welcome change from canned corned beef and boiled rice.

Jean Charlot was ill with malaria and couldn't eat dinner. He retired to his tent at the onset of his symptoms.

Speaking of corned beef and rice, that is the diet of the forty Guinean workers divided among the three camps. They are paid the sum of 50 sylis, the equivalent of $2.50 in U.S. dollars, one cup of rice, a tin of corned beef and a can of tomato paste per workday. David calls the workers "Lampietti's rice machines".

After dinner Fred, David, Wayde and I relaxed around the table, lit by a kerosene lantern. Suddenly our peaceful evening was invaded by a large hatch of termites. They flew into our faces, hair, nostrils, mouths and down our backs. David quickly extinguished the light, diminishing the onslaught. We retired to our quarters.

April 9th Wednesday – We slept so well last night! The buzzing of the cicadas is already becoming a soothing song of home. In the distance we hear the drums of Kaya. I love so much about being here!

A small group of workers came into camp this morning with a bucket of fish! I selected some to use in a chowder for tonight's dinner.

This has been another productive day. Fred wired the payottes for electricity. When the gasoline arrives from Kissidougou we can run the generator for a brief period each evening. Fred also wired the electric stove. What luxury that will be when the fuel arrives.

Wayde and I did laundry, scrubbed the kitchen shelves and table, boiled water to wash all of plates, silverware, and cooking utensils. Then worked in the garden planting scallion seeds and transplanting tomato starts.

Then we tackled the supply shed and stocked the shelves, stacking the spare cases of food along one wall. Afterwards, Wayde and I followed a bush road to nearby Faraco Creek to cool off in the water after the oppressive heat of the supply shed. There were some women from one of the nearby villages doing their laundry, but they grabbed the clothing and quickly disappeared through the tall savannah grass as we approached.

The creek is very shallow, so we built a dam above the road to form a small pond about three feet deep.

Camp laundry takes so much time, hauling bucket after bucket of murky water from the well, heating the water and washing a few items at a time in the limited-sized wash tub. Why not bring the laundry to the creek and scrub in on the stones as the native women do? It would save me hours!

Back in camp I fileted the fish we'd received this morning and prepared a chowder. I also made a marinated bean salad, hush puppies and a chocolate tapioca pudding for dessert.

Fred was displeased because I had the meal finished before he was ready to eat. I attempted to explain that it was difficult enough to prepare a meal over a campfire, without having to do it in the dark. All members had arrived from work an hour earlier and were ready to have dinner. David and Jean Charlot said that their mealtimes were normally around 5:00 P.M. I served dinner at six-thirty. They both had hearty appetites, ate plenty and were full of compliments about the meal. Fred, on the other hand, continued to sulk and ate very little. He retired to the payotte early.

The animals had provided much amusement today. The lame chicken took a liking to me after I had taken David's splint off her broken leg. The puppy, Frank, spent the day pouncing on the kittens, which protested by arching their backs, hissing, spitting, and dancing sideways. Sange found a pair of David's pants hanging on a chair in the kitchen and picked through his pockets, examining every scrap of paper before tossing it to the ground. Then the monkey stole hush puppies from the table and fed them to the kittens.

At David's and Jean Charlot's urging, I played the guitar and sang folk songs at the kitchen table before retiring. Fred had his back turned when I got into bed, so I don't know whether he was asleep. I quickly nodded off.

I was awakened by the distant sound of a vehicle approaching. I woke Fred and we went to the kitchen and lit a lamp. David and Jean Charlot soon joined us. The wait was agonizing, listening to the vehicle slowly make its way to camp. We now knew by the sound that it must be a Land Rover, rather than the Mercedes truck.

Finally, the Land Rover arrived, driven by Momodu. There were no others with him. The vehicle carried gasoil and the remaining food and supplies from the Russian truck.

The workers in their camp had also awakened to the sound of the approaching vehicle and crowded into our camp to enthusiastically greet Momodu, who had brought gifts for them.

In a mixture of English and French, Momodu gave our camp updates. Missing were the five workers left at Kissidougou; they had been commandeered by Camp B! Tony has found a used Poclain in Conakry and has been working on getting it ready to be freighted to Kankan via rail.

Poor David Salsby had gone on to Camp B when we parted in Kissidougou, as planned, only to find that it had been moved and no one had bothered to leave David a note as the where. He was upset that he had to drive all the way back to Kissidougou and wait for news. Fortunately, a Camp B Land Rover came through and David was able to leave the borrowed Land Rover with Jean Paul and get a ride to the new camp.

Furthermore, Jean Paul at the PDG office is still without a radio to communicate with Conakry. The radio had been repaired, but the local government confiscated it because Jean Paul could not produce the permit papers needed for radio transmissions. Those papers are in the PDG office in Conakry.

Momodu is the camp's main Guinean driver. Even though he is a general DDX driver, he works mainly with Tony Robinson, the camp's mechanic. Momodu is extremely devoted to Tony; however, he addresses all the Caucasian men in camp as "Boss Man".

The Guinean driver is also the hunter, trusted with the camp's only rifle and shotgun. Thin and wiry, Momodu stands approximately five feet, nine inches tall, and I believe him to be in his mid-to-late thirties. He almost always wears a toothy grin and is a bit of a ham.

Although Momodu's main language is Mandinka, he can make himself understood by using a combination of French and English. He is most often seen wearing a used pair of women's pink, bell-bottomed, pull-on pants, which hang almost to the ground, covering callused bare feet. He wears the pants with a blue, or sometimes yellow, short-sleeved T-shirt. Momodu always wears the billed canvas hat that Tony gave him last season.

Since Momodu has aligned himself as Tony's sidekick, he has the strongest and most frequent Guinean presence around camp, and we have all grown fond of him.

As I was leaving the kitchen for the night, Momodu handed me six lemons and two limes!

April 10th Thursday – Fred got the generator started today and the small two burner stove hooked up. I stocked the storage shed with supplies that the Land Rover transported last night. Then, I baked some banana bread from bananas that had been over-ripening in the stalled Russian truck. Under close watch, to prevent scorching, it was baked over the campfire in the cast iron skillet, and it worked!

I have taken over the morning and evening dish washing chores after a couple of the camp members observed Dennis washing dishes with cold brown water drawn directly from the well and using a grimy rag with no soap. Amoebic dysentery is known to be prevalent in this region.

Beginning the daily process of water filtering, I had Dennis haul four buckets from the well to one of the large wash tubs, which had been set on the open campfire and allowed to boil for thirty minutes. After cooling for half an hour, six gallons are poured into one of the Berkey filters. Meanwhile, Dennis hauled water to fill the other wash tub and began the boiling process.

I shave a small amount of Palmolive soap into leftover hot water from the first batch of water, thoroughly wash the dishes, then rinse them with the leftover hot water from the second Berkey filter filling.

It takes several hours for the boiled water to filter through the Berkey's black ceramic filters. I clean the filters late in the afternoon before preparing dinner.

Dennis will have hauled another four buckets from the well so that I can repeat the morning's water routine this evening. This water processing routine assures that we have enough drinking water for everyone in the camp, as well as clean dishes. I suppose when guests from other camps wander through, we will sometimes have to ration.

Dennis is a native Guinean, and unlike the majority of the Malinke people, he does not align himself with the Muslem beliefs, preferring the ideology of his tribal heritage. The stern-faced man stands approximately five feet seven inches tall. He has a prideful bearing, seldom smiles, and doesn't take instruction well – especially from a woman. He speaks a little English, so he and I can communicate. However, he prefers not to talk to me unless necessary.

Officially, Dennis is the camp cook. However, he is satisfied with me doing lunch and dinner, while he cooks breakfast. His breakfasts consist of either oatmeal or cornmeal mush. He brings a pot of water to a boil and stirs in the oatmeal or cornmeal, until it is thick enough to glop on the spoon. I demonstrated that by adding some raisins, and perhaps a little cinnamon or salt, to the oatmeal, it would make the breakfast more palatable for the camp members. A little salt added to the cornmeal mush wouldn't hurt, either. Dennis frowned at my oatmeal demonstration, then immediately dumped the mass into the fire, and proceeded to make a fresh batch of oatmeal by his accustomed method.

Dennis is never in the kitchen without his apron – a dingy yellow, stained article of clothing worn thin from washing and speckled with burn holes from firepit coals. This piece of treasured attire is usually worn against his shirtless chest. His khaki pants rise above his ankles and, like the apron, are thread bare and tattered.

Later this afternoon I walked to Faraco Creek with Fred and watched him wash gravel from the core samples brought up by the jumper drill, using a set of three siroccos. The siroccos are large bowl-shaped screens, each with a different size of mesh ranging from large to small. The gravel is roughly separated into three piles. The largest gravel is washed first in the largest screen, the rotating action of the washing pulls the heaviest gravel toward the center. The diamonds would be found in the center where the heavier gravel concentrates. The two other piles are similarly washed in the smaller screens.

Fred didn't find any diamonds in the samples but did find minerals that indicate the likelihood of discovering them. Perhaps the hole that the jumper drill is currently working on will eventually yield some.

For dinner, I served a marinated bean salad, macaroni and cheese, and a banana tort in an oatmeal crust.

After the meals' dishes had been washed and put away, I sat at the table sipping a cup of water. The lukewarm, purified water serves its hydrating purposes, but it has the bland, flat, taste of nothingness. How I miss the cold, clear water from my mountain home in Idaho.

This evening, the sky began clouding over and darkening, promising rain. I developed a plan of action. After dinner, Fred went back to the creek to wash gravel. Out of the lower corner of the mosquito netting I cut a circle, just big enough to fit over a large mug. Securing the netting in place with some string, I set the mug in a level, open area near the food storage shed, out of sight.

Tonight, the rain came. Snuggled in bed, beneath the mosquito netting, I listened to it pattering on the thatched roof. Once I knew that Fred was sound asleep, I quietly climbed out of bed, slipped on my sandals, and crept through the dark to claim my waterfilled mug.

Sitting alone in the kitchen in my dampened nightgown, I removed the mosquito net filter and took a sip of cool water. It wasn't the water of my Idaho home; it didn't carry its snowmelt iciness. Rather, in the rainwater I tasted the scent of the savannah grasses, and the effervescence of a heavily clouded Guinean sky. This was the true taste of my African home…not boiled and purified, but straight from the heavens. As I slowly swallowed the last cherished sip, I heard Fred call my name loudly enough to awaken the entire camp. The mug was quickly placed on the table, the circle of netting tucked into the small pocket of my nightgown.

"I just needed to get a drink of water", I whisper to Fred as I slip back under the mosquito netting.

April 11th Friday – Dawn had just begun when Momodu the driver, turned hunter, entered camp.

"Boss man! Boss man! I got meat! I got meat!" Momodu shouted, standing in the open doorway of our payotte.

We hurriedly dressed. David and Jean Charlot were now up, as was Wayde. The small doe was hanging from a pole secured between two trees, and a mere twenty yards from our storage shed. Within an hour the camp workers had arrived, skinned, gutted the deer, and cut it down. Then quartered the deer as I wiped down the kitchen table to use as a surface to cut up the meat. The camp workers took the entrails, including the liver, heart, and kidneys.

I cleaned the small kerosine refrigerator and started it. It would not hold the entire deer, but it would keep some of the meat fresh for a couple of days. Then I took the short walk to the mango grove to collect some mango leaves. I wandered a little further and found a boggy area in a dense part of the forest. There were ferns growing along the edge of a seep. At the base of the maturing fronds, tightly curled fiddleheads were still forming. I snapped one off and nibbled it. It had brown scales, like the edible ostrich ferns growing in Idaho, and the crisp, yet slightly mucilaginous texture! I gathered about twenty of them, nibbling two as I wandered back to camp with an armload of mango leaves.

The deer was lying quartered on the kitchen table when I returned. I stood the ferns upright in a large water-filled can, then set about processing the deer meat. I had Wayde stand on one of the stools waving a branch back and forth to keep flies from landing. I cut a section of the backstrap and cut it into thick, boneless steaks, two for each camp member's dinner tonight. I cut a good portion of the haunch into ample cubes for brochettes for tomorrow's dinner and stew the following day.

I spent a couple of hours cutting the remainder of the meat into very thin strips along the grain. Sange kept trying to steal strips of meat to feed the puppy and Wayde's kittens. After putting the leash on the monkey's harness and tying him to one of the table legs, I proceeded to marinate the venison strips in a mixture of oil, salt, pepper, warm beer, sugar and finely minced red African peppers. I set up empty boxes in the center of the storage shed, then placed layers of mango leaves on top. After four hours of marinating, I laid the strips of venison on the leaves and left the meat to dry to jerky in the hot enclosure, keeping my fingers crossed that the meat wouldn't cook in the heat.

Momodu, driver, turned hunter.

Then Momodu showed up with a second deer! A big buck. He wanted a photo taken, so I borrowed Fred's camera. Momodu hammed it up as I snapped the picture.

The second deer will go to the workers' camp to supplement their diet. Part of the deer will be taken into the village of Kaya and sold to purchase soap and salt for the workers' camp, any funds remaining will go to Momodu.

When Fred returned from the field late this afternoon, he moved the generator to a location further from the camp so that the noise it generated wouldn't be so bothersome.

I made potato salad to go with the venison steaks. The salad was made of canned potatoes, well rinsed, then cubed. Quarter inch-pieces of crisp fiddlehead fern, and a chopped onion were added. The salad was marinated in a mixture of olive oil, fresh lime juice, salt, pepper, and a touch of dry mustard. I was able to fit the salad in the kerosene refrigerator to chill before dinner.

My son and I walked to the creek where Fred was washing gravel. I washed the laundry, then Wayde help me carry the wet load back to camp to hang and dry. After hanging laundry, the two of us walked up to the wild mango grove hoping to find one on the ground. We danced with joy when we saw that there were dozens of windfalls! I tied a knot in the side of my shift; Wayde took off his shirt. We filled our clothing with nearly three dozen ripe, juicy mangoes!

Back at camp, I peeled and diced enough mangos for everyone to have a large helping for dessert. Then I started the cook fire and fried Puri Indian flat bread in the cast iron skillet.

Tonight, we had electric lights to eat our meal by!

Everyone enjoyed the tender, mild flavored venison as well as the salad, fried bread, and mango.

Tomorrow, I expect to have bread from Kérouané. Momodu had to make an emergency trip to Kérouané with the Land Rover. One of the wives of the chief of Kaya began hemorrhaging badly. There is a hospital, of sorts, in Kérouané. Momodu doesn't believe that the woman is going to live. He told David that he would find some bread in the village and bring it back with him when he returns late tonight or tomorrow morning, depending on road conditions.

Lightning had been striking in the distance all evening. A brush fire flared up across the savannah. If we listened carefully, we could hear the dry grasses crackling as they burned. The flames receded over the horizon. I was relieved that it hadn't come in the direction of the terrace. I drifted off to sleep listening to the pounding of gasoil drums, the faint sounds of the goat skin-covered bara, and chanting from the Guinean workers' camp, celebrating the gift of venison meat.

April 12th Saturday – The day began working in the garden planting peas and watering the rows of sprouting plants. The well has dried up. I hope that it rains soon so that water won't have to be hauled up from Faraco Creek to be boiled and filtered for drinking water.

This morning, I baked an upside-down apple cake, using bottled applesauce and cinnamon, in the cast iron skillet on the kerosine stove.

It was a hot day, so I cooled down this afternoon by taking a shower with the lukewarm water from the barrel. However, before doing so, I waited for a spitting cobra to leave the grass-screened shower area. It was stretched out across the pebbled floor, most likely enjoying the coolness of that shaded area. All I needed to do to frighten the snake back into the bush was clap two sticks together. There are a lot of snakes in the savannah and surrounding forested area, but this was the first that I had personally seen.

Later, I wrote a long letter to Mom and Dad, with the puppy at my feet and the monkey in my lap. Maybe the Mercedes truck will roll in one day soon and take the mail out. I still have the letters that I wrote in Conakry that I hadn't mailed.

Wayde spent the day at the hydraulic pit with David so that he could swim in the Baoule Stream. The pit is located next to the tributary. A heavy gasoil pump sits partially submerged at water's edge, to which a stout hose, fitted with a large nozzle, is attached. The hose forces high-pressure jets of water to remove the layers of sand and rock along the riverbank, exposing the kimberlite. The slurry of sand, gravel, and small river rocks is scooped up with buckets and poured into a crudely fashioned, homemade trommel screen attached to a small gasoil engine. Buckets of river water are poured over the mixture as the engine shakes the slurry through the screens to be sorted.

For dinner I made venison brochettes, mashed potatoes, canned asparagus, and of course, the cake I had made earlier. The upside-down cake certainly surprised everyone around the dinner table tonight.

David had put in a hard day and retired for the night. Jean Charlot followed shortly afterwards. Fred stayed and helped me with the dishes and put on the *Waylon and Willie* cassette tape. When the song, *Don't Cuss the Fiddle* played, Fred grabbed ahold of me and swung me around in a polka-like jig, leaving me breathlessly giggling like a schoolgirl. It was so thrilling when Fred let his playful side show.

Again, today has been wonderful, leaving me happy and fulfilled even though the well is out of water and the Mercedes is long overdue.

April 13th Sunday – Jean Charlot left for Kissidougou this morning to try to obtain gasoil. Production in the hydraulic pit, where he works with David, has slowed to a snail's pace as fuel is rationed to keep things operating at some level. He is expected to return by late tomorrow evening.

After watering the garden this morning, I walked one of the forest trails along the terrace and discovered a wild banana tree; however, the bananas were not ripe. The trail led me to a spot above the savannah overlooking the jumper drill rig where Fred works. I watched him for a while from my hillside perch.

Unlike David's hydraulic and trommel screen setup, Fred takes core samples from the packed earth of the savannah using an old jumper drill. The drill was fueled with diesel, which in Guinea, was more difficult to obtain than gasoil.

The jumper drill's engine is mounted on a skid frame. A collapsible mast, supporting the wire winch rope, is mounted to the frame. The cylindrical drill rod, a hollow tube with a cutting edge at the bottom, is rotated and hammered into the ground to collect the core sample.

Soon, I ventured on. I traveled the path along the terrace for approximately another mile. The village of Kaya could be seen in the distance, and off to the left was a small lake. I later learned it was called "Floating Grass Lake". I walked down the hill and across the savannah toward the water. The ground became very spongy as I neared the water's edge. The matted grass sagged beneath my feet. Once I gingerly made my way to the edge of the lake, I saw movement in the water and soon realized that it was inhabited by walking catfish, some struggling in the shallows. I knelt along the grassy edge and attempted to grab the fish, but only succeeded in getting very muddy.

Once back at camp I changed out of my muddy shift and prepared a chocolate tapioca pudding for tonight's dessert. Afterward, Fred, and I went to the creek where he washed samples, and I washed clothes. We stood up from our chores, hearing a Land Rover approach. The vehicle stopped, straddling the creek. It was Simon, the young man from New Zealand that I had met in Conakry!

Simon had come to our camp to see if he could trade for some parts needed in Camp B and was headed to David's pit beside the Baoule. He will overnight in camp, then proceed to Conakry, a journey of over five hundred miles, to get supplies...his workers are out of rice.

Clouds were beginning to form and thicken across the sky. As I finished the laundry, I left Fred to complete washing his samples and returned to camp to hang the wash. No sooner had the wash been hung, the wind began to blow. Then the rain came, falling in a solid sheet! I chased the flying clothes through the muddy camp.

Wayde came running to me, toting a terrified monkey, and shouted above the howling wind that the storage shed had blown away! I ran to where the shed had previously stood and spotted it fifty feet beyond, smashed against a tree, resembling a giant, crushed empty beer can. When the shed embarked on its airborne journey, it took half of David McDonald's tent with it.

Above the deafening thunder, I yelled at Wayde to help get the flour, oatmeal, and other packaged goods out of the wet and under the thatched roof of the kitchen. He promptly elicited the aid of half a dozen Guinean workers standing, bewildered, beneath the shelter of the kitchen.

The rain continued to sheet; wind almost bent the trees to the ground; lightning struck nearby, following the deafening thunder. The ground was obscured by an inch of water! After twenty minutes the storm calmed.

David and Simon showed up from the hydraulic pit about ten minutes after Fred arrived. Everyone was soaking wet.

After changing into my last set of dry clothing, I began preparing venison stew while the remaining members of the camp did what they could to dry out the wet interiors of their tents and payottes. David will take refuge in Tony's tent tonight. Simon has resolved to sleep in the cab of the Land Rover.

That evening, Simon was particularly complimentary about dinner. At Camp B, meals have been corned beef and rice for days…until the rice ran out. David told Simon that this was no longer a "camp", but a country club with electric lights and good food.

After the dishes were done, Simon and I played four games of backgammon, I won all four, plus a game of cribbage. Fred puttered around doing various chores that he'd been wanting to finish.

The air smells rain-fresh and the cicadas have resumed their singing. It has been another wonderful day. I never want to leave Guinea!

April 14th Monday – The black kittens seemed to have trouble crawling off Wayde's bed, their bellies still bloated from eating the strips of drying venison jerky ruined by yesterday's storm. The puppy was stretched out beneath the kitchen table passing gas, while Sange was stretched out on the ruins of David's tent holding his stomach. The chicken hadn't partaken of the spoils and sat in the warmth of the early morning sun, preening.

The well now has water.

The camp workers busied themselves with emptying the kitchen of the food supplies and stacking it in Bill's payotte until a storage payotte can be built where the Sears and Robuck's shed had previously stood. However, a payotte for David McDonald will be built first to replace his destroyed tent. That was started this morning under command of the former Chief of Kaya, payotte building master, and should be completed late tomorrow.

I checked the garden and found zucchini and beet seedings up. The tomato and cucumber vines lay prone to the ground, a tangled mass. The remainder of the morning was spent making banana custard from overripe fruit, and yeast onion rolls, which I deep fried. The rolls were ready to sample by the time everyone had returned to camp for lunch.

During the afternoon I walked up to the wild mango trees expecting windfalls. Not only had the wind knocked down hundreds of mangoes in various stages of ripening, but it had broken large fruit-ladened limbs off the trees! What a mess.

I wrote letters this afternoon to send off with Simon. He had decided to stay another night and help David with Pit #3. The pit was dug close to the river, which is rapidly rising due to last night's deluge. It may cave in before gravel is reached.

David McDonald is a twenty-two-year-old from Nashville, Tennessee. He is an attractive young man with a well-developed medium built physique, blue eyes, blond hair, and a rugged complexion. His dream had been to be a motorcycle racer, but his parents put him through college, instead. Fresh out of college last year, he found himself in the heart of Guinea earning nine hundred dollars a month at his first job as a geologist. Now, he's wondering what the hell he's doing here another year.

David spends his days at the hydraulic pit working harder than five local workers put together. When he returns to camp, first he asks me what's for dinner, then ambles off to the shower before retreating to his tent, where he continues to wade through the novel, "*War and Peace*".

At mealtimes David is either animated or moody…seldom in between. I have noticed that his moods seem regulated by the current stock of beer, which has recently been in short supply due to the missing Mercedes. His seating position is at the head of the table, in one of the collapsible camp chairs. David tends to become bored when there is no stimulating conversation happening around the table. He amuses himself by burning insects that he sees crawling along the table, using the tip of his cigarette. If he isn't smoking at the time, the unfortunate bug will get encased in a drop of candle wax. These sadistic pastimes are accentuated with sound effects consisting of high pitched "eeks" as the poor six- or eight-legged victims writhe in agony.

David can also be extremely entertaining with his uncanny ability to mimic the voices and mannerisms of camp members. When he imitates Tys, I laugh so hard my sides ache. He also does a great Jean Paul.

I admire David's intelligence. He has a broad English vocabulary and I often have difficulty understanding what he is saying when he lapses into one of his philosophizing moods, which usually happens around beer number three. David also speaks French as well as any of the other camp members, including Jean Charlot.

David and Wayde get along great together. David addresses Wayde as "Private Ephram" when he issues orders. Wayde responds with a salute and a "Yes, Sir!"

Recently, David read me a letter he had written to one of his girlfriends back in Tennessee. The letter showed a great deal of creative writing ability, with a charming touch of bullshit.

The camp gossip is that David has a Malinke girl that he met last year. She doesn't come into camp; he goes to visit her some nights at a nearby village. He takes her gifts of tinned food.

I enjoy being around David, but he tends to draw into himself, at times. That said, we have also spent hours sitting in the kitchen with a late cup of instant coffee, visiting. He treats me with respect and kind regard, whereas I tend to "mother" him a bit.

April 15th Tuesday – We had expected Jean Charlot to be back last night, but he hasn't shown up. So, we expected him to arrive today, or this evening at the very latest. There is no more gasoil for running the hydraulic. The mystery continues to build here at Camp Baoule. Where is Jean Charlot? Where is Tony – he was expected days ago? Where is that elusive Mercedes? Does such a vehicle exist?

I took the wash to the creek. Due to the lower flow, our double sheets were a trick to clean and rinse without getting silt in them during the "rinse cycle." Fred is out of fuel for the jumper drill, so he took the day off to go to the hydraulic pit with his siroccos and help David handwash the gravel. Wayde and I went along to enjoy the river. Even though the river's water is murky, the overall appearance of the place is enchanting. Tall, leafy trees snug up to the water's edge. The river is wide at the hydraulic pit, and shallow. My son and I waded across the waist deep water to a trail on the opposite side.

Fred had told me that about a quarter of a mile up the trail, entering a rain forest, is the third diamond exploration site. Core samples must be collected by hand since the ground is saturated with moisture and would bog down any motorized vehicle. A Sierra Leone Banka drilling team is producing the core samples.

The team's rhythmic chanting could be heard long before we reached the site. There are eight workers in the team. Four men shoulder a large, circular, wood platform on which four other men stand. The workers on the ground are spaced around the platform, which rests on their shoulders. The platform is rotated as the men trot around in a circle, chanting. The four men atop the platform ram a large, hollow casing into the ground. Ram. Rotate. Ram. Rotate. Ram…the casing is driven deeper with each rotation. The men wear khaki shorts, nothing more. Sweat glistens and muscles bulge as they work and chant. The men did not seem to mind that I sat and watched, spellbound.

Wayde soon grew restless, so I rose and followed him back down the trail to the river. Simon had left with the Land Rover to head to Conakry. Fred left his Land Rover for David to drive back to camp when he had finished the gravel washing. As Fred, Wayde and I walked the two miles back to camp we encountered a local man and his son. They had been plowing a casava field using a team of oxen pulling a hand plow. They were having a lunch of boiled potatoes and offered one to share. The three of us sat beside the two, sharing smiles, and potatoes.

Malinke father & son
Plowing cassava field.

Further on down the road we paused at the workers' camp. There are six sleeping payottes and one community camp kitchen. The workers sleep six to a payotte. Their beds are head-to-the-wall, making a spoke-like formation. Beds are raised platforms padded with savannah grass. In the center of the payottes hang small reed baskets in which fish and strips of meat are dried. The camp surroundings are littered with discarded tomato paste cans and corned beef tins. Large empty rice bags lean against payottes, crammed with personal belongings.

Upon returning to camp, we had lunch from leftover last night's dinner, then Fred returned to Faraco Creek to wash core samples. Meanwhile, I made an apple crisp with applesauce topped with a sweetened oatmeal-cinnamon topping for dessert. I prepared canned mackerel for fish patties, using some stale leftover breadcrumbs and an egg that David's chicken had laid. I covered the bowl and let the ingredients meld until the mixture was ready to form into patties and fry. To spruce up the mackerel patties I made a green mango salsa with fresh lime juice, a generous dash of salt, and finely minced African pepper. I also heated up canned spinach and cooked a pot of rice.

David returned from the pit distressed. The Banka drilling team were bitterly complaining about their food rations. After David, Fred, Wayde and I had finished dinner, the eight Sierra Leone men came to camp and had a meeting with David at the kitchen table. David went with me to Bill's payotte, where the food was temporarily stored. We had plenty of Treet, which David said the Sierra Leones wouldn't eat. Most of the rice, tomato paste, and corned beef had already been used to pay the Guinean workers. The men wouldn't eat any of the dried fruit, since they weren't accustomed to food that was sweet. They would eat canned potatoes, canned mackerel, and canned baked beans in sauce, so David gave them the rest of our supply of those items.

When David gets to Kérouané he will purchase extra supplies such as sugar, tea, bananas, and rice out of his own pay, to help supplement the Banka team's diet. Tomorrow is Wednesday, Kérouané's weekly market day. But we can't go to Kérouané without the Land Rover that Jean Charlot took, since the one remaining in camp doesn't have enough fuel to get there and back.

Fred, David and Wayde retired early. After the kitchen was cleaned up and dishes washed, I sat and listened to the night sounds of the savannah…the cicadas, distant drumming from the village of Kaya, occasional cries from night birds. I love this place, my place in Guinea. I enjoy washing the clothes in the creek; working in the garden; hauling water up the rickety ladder anticipating a cool shower later; planning meals from our odd assortment of supplies.

April 16th Wednesday – Another day with no sign of Jean Charlot, the Mercedes truck, or Tony. Raynor is now expected back from his vacation. Will there be no Raynor? There is mention now of the "Dark Hole" which swallows up everyone leaving Baoule Flats. With all the fuel gone and food supplies running low, we may end up walking out of here.

Yesterday, David brought Wayde a baby bird, so the better part of my day was spent fashioning a crude bird cage from reeds and vines. I even added a little thatched roof.

I pared the meat of a coconut and dried it in the sun for the curry I made for dinner. There is no meat, so the curry was made with mixed dried fruit and served over a bed of rice with the dried coconut sprinkled on top. I also made pan biscuits cooked over the campfire in the cast iron skillet. The meal was popular, which is a good thing. With the dwindling supplies there will be a lot more curry appearing at the dinner table.

Grasshoppers have decimated much of the garden. I replanted the lettuce today. I do keep alfalfa and radish sprouts growing so there are always some to add to the dinner plates.

Wayde had been spending much of his time with David at the hydraulic pit, but he and David are in camp today. There are also several of David's Guinean workers idling around camp. Fred is tinkering under the hood of his Land Rover.

Once darkness falls, I make my nightly visit to the Bog, the camp's name for the outhouse. I imagine the men who use the

Bog during the daytime can relax on the seat and finish their business with no problem, as they gaze out the wide opening at the peaceful wooded landscape beyond and greet passersby. I, however, sit at the edge of the toilet seat, ready to spring up at the first sound of anyone meandering past, since the Bog sits alongside the trail leading to one of the local villages where some of the workers live. Morning visits for me are too social. Guinean workers pass by on their way to work. There is no way to avoid their notice, so as I sit there on the toilet seat, they greet me.

"*Ca va.*"
"*Oui, ca va.*" I answer.

Venturing to the Bog at night is an adventure. Walking up the trail from the camp, the way illuminated by a flashlight with a wavering, weak battery, is like hiking through a mine field. Columns of fierce Guinea ants march across the path at various points along the way. These points vary from day to day. The columns are easy to step over in daylight, but are seldom seen at night, even when the moon is full. When stepping in their pathway angry Guinea ants race over the meager protection of rubber sandals, gripping between toes with their painful bites. They then race up legs, back, stomach, and head, biting along the way. I have often danced to the Bog in agony and danced my way back to the payotte covered in red welts.

I am never alone in the Bog. Thousands of termites can be heard chomping away while sifting sawdust in my hair.

After my nightly Bog visit, I retire to the payotte.

April 17th Thursday – Last night the sounds of an approaching Land Rover could be heard whining on its way to camp. Its approach woke everyone out of a sound sleep. The camp came alive!

John Charlot and driver, Momodu, had returned with two homologues, five Guinean workers, one goat, two drums of fuel, four cases of beer, potatoes, onions, cheese, pineapple, and a case of motor oil. It was amazing to watch all of this come out of one Land Rover.

Jean Charlot had met Tony in Kissidougou. Tony had been heading to our camp with workers and supplies. However, Jean Paul, at the Kissidougou house, and the other Camps (B and C), raided our supplies, since they were in greater need than they perceived Camp A, in Baoule' Valley, to be. So, Tony transferred his workers and a few choice items to Jean Charlot's Land Rover and returned to Conakry to load up with more supplies for our camp.

The mysteriously missing Mercedes truck is in Conakry with worn out tires and no replacements available in the capitol city, so we won't see it for a while. Tony plans on going to Sierra Leone after delivering our supplies, to search there for tires.

The Russian truck with the drill parts for our camp had the parts unloaded in Kissidougou, then returned to Conakry. It is unlikely that we will see the second jumper drill this season. Perhaps not even next summer since Lampietti refuses to authorize further transportation of the drill parts, now stuck in Kissidougou, while the drill itself is sitting disassembled in Conakry.

Simon found no rice at the PDG warehouse in Kissidougou, so he had to go on to Conakry which would take him an extra four days to return to Camp B. Meanwhile, his workers are completely out of food.

Furthermore, the Guinean government issued an order to send the Sierra Leone Banka Drilling team back to their country and hire Guinean laborers to replace them. David said that the Guineans have neither the training nor the muscle to do the job, so that part of the diamond exploration would need to be shut down.

It is good to see Momodu back. He immediately requested to go hunting. He returned from the hunt with no meat but did bring a turtle that he had found for Wayde.

It has been raining during the late afternoons. There is concern among camp members that the rainy season may be coming early this year, and the exploration may not be able to continue beyond June 1st.

The grasshoppers have now leveled most of the garden, except for a few scraggly tomato plants, a cucumber vine and one zucchini plant which has just begun putting on blossoms.

I did not have my usual energy this afternoon. I managed to do the wash in the creek and making an evening meal of raisin biscuits to go with ham and white bean soup and a marinated potato and alfalfa sprout salad. There were sweet, succulent pineapple chunks for dessert!

Both Fred and I decided to retire early.

April 18th Friday – As we were getting ready to go to bed last night, I heard a vehicle approaching. It was Tony! He had made a rapid journey but was only able to obtain two drums of gasoil. The Mercedes truck is operational again and is waiting in Kérouané for two Land Rovers to go to bring its cargo to camp.

It had unloaded crates of furniture at Jean Paul's household in Kissidougou.

We were informed that fuel remains in short supply, so there will be none for operating our unnecessary equipment, such as the kerosene refrigerator or the generator throughout the remainder of the season.

Tony also brought mail! I received a letter from Mom and Dad, and one from a friend, Dorian. Mom and Dad had returned from their vacation in Mexico the first of April and found my first letter from Dakar waiting. My brother, sister-in-law and their children spent Easter with my parents.

Until the Land Rovers go to Kérouané to bring back supplies, we remain low on any sort of meat, except for the Treet, which neither the workers, monkey, kittens, dog, or chicken will touch. Perhaps the walking catfish living in Floating Grass Lake will. Wayde and I took a hike to the lake with a tin of Treet, hooks, and fishing line. The grass beneath my feet was soggier than before, and felt at times, that it was going to give way. We moved across it tentatively.

As we left the grass at the lake's edge and stepped into the water, we sank almost up to our waists in mud. With line tied to our wrists, we baited the hooks with the Treet. No bites. Finally, Wayde was able to grab a minnow. I cut it in half and baited our hooks. Within minutes we each caught large walking catfish! We caught eight more within the next half hour, breaking their necks and tossing them onto the grass. Having caught the ten fish, we worked our way out of the mud and the bank's edge and onto the grass. I threaded the fish onto a twig to carry them back to the camp.

As we were hiking along the path with the string of fish, our camps payotte builder, formally chief of Kaya, stopped us and was jabbering rapidly in a mixture of Mandinka and French. I could not understand what the man was saying, but Wayde, who had picked up some French and Mandinka from afternoons spent playing with village children, was able to know that it was related to the fish. At first, I was concerned that the man was upset with us catching the fish, but Wayde said that was not the case. He wanted to know if his people could go fishing at the lake. Well, of course! It was their lake, wasn't it?

Once back at camp, Wayde and I took clean clothes to the creek to bathe and change. I prepared dinner of filleted fish, cornmeal battered and fried, along with steamed cornbread, mixed dried fruit cobbler, boiled potatoes, and spinach.

The evening was spent drinking beer (lots of beer) and enjoying Tony and his wild and crazy tales of the past couple of weeks. Then David put on the *Waylon and Willie* tape. I retrieved my guitar from the payotte, and we all sang along, *Mammas Don't Let Your Babies Grow Up to Be Cowboys*, then the mournful song, *It's Not Supposed to Be That Way*.

David paused the tape, Tony would give a dissertation about the missing Mercedes truck, and we'd all sing, *It's Not Supposed to Be That Way*. Then David told his tale of woe about running out of fuel for his hydraulic pit…*It's Not Supposed to Be That Way*. I lamented about the workers running low on food…*It's Not Supposed to Be That Way*. By the time we all retired for the night, our sides ached from laughter.

During our celebration, several of the local villages were having a celebration of their own, their drumming reverberating across the savannah.

Fred had gone to bed early, not wanting to take part in our noisy celebration. He was sound asleep, pillow folded over his head to filter out some of the racket.

April 19th Saturday – Yes, I had a slight headache this morning, but that wasn't the focus of Fred and my argument. Our doorless payotte faces the main entrance of camp and sits close to the camp kitchen. Workers are always walking by the open doorway in the early morning hours, often while we are still in bed. Anyone can look right into our bed. I must dress and undress each day under the bed covers – the only privacy the payotte affords.

I have lived with this lack of privacy with no problem until this morning when Fred wanted to make love. I refused unless he covers the doorway with a sheet or something to give us privacy in the stark light of day! Fred became very angry, our argument reverberating throughout the camp. Fred got up, dressed, and stormed off, leaving me in tears. He refused to speak to me or to eat the morning meal I prepared for camp, since Dennis was on vacation.

However, while I was watering and working in the tattered garden after breakfast, before leaving to fuel the jumper drill, Fred came and told me that he was having a door made for our payotte.

Tony was off to Conakry this morning. He was to have taken the Sierra Leonians with him, but successfully argued his point to keep the Banka drilling team. The homologue, a Guinean government official overseeing our camp, who had the authority to make decisions concerning the camp's operations and wellbeing, finally agreed.

Wayde went to Conakry with Tony. They will return within three to four days, barring complications. Shortly after Wayde and Tony departed, Fred was back to camp with the tractor and told me to climb in. He said that there was a lot of excitement at Floating Grass Lake. I got into the tractor and Fred drove over to a terrace where we could look down onto the lake.

There were nearly a hundred Malinke women up to the waists in the lake tossing walking catfish onto the grassy shore, where children were dashing about with sticks to clobber the flopping fish. Hundreds of fish were being picked up and loaded into grass baskets. On our way back to camp, Fred and I spotted five antelopes.

After the fishing hole slaughter, several of the mud-splattered women converged on the mango grove and gathered up all the fallen fruit. This they brought to my payotte and made a large pile of mangos beside the doorway. The group and I stared at each other and smiled. I was honored that they had finally decided to be friendly to me. A couple of them reached out and touched me, then pulled back laughing. Some of the women were nearly naked; others wore tattered men's shirts or shorts. One of the younger women wore a pair of shorts that I recognized. Several times I had washed them in Faraco Creek. They had a pocket coming apart from the seam that I had planned to stitch up but hadn't gotten around to it. They belonged to David. Was this his rumored young native girlfriend? She was very thin and did not look well.

Jean Charlot had left early this morning with the Land Rover to pick up the fuel that had been left in Kérouané. He returned in time for dinner.

I fixed corned beef and noodles, canned asparagus, fresh pineapple and mango salad, and coffee flavored custard. This evening, we sat around the table after dinner and talked about our day. Fred and I talked about the antelopes we had seen.

Ebrahim, one of the homologues has taken off on foot to Banancora, approximately twenty miles away. A runner had come from the village to tell him that his wife was seriously ill.

This evening Fred brought me some wildflowers and said that he was sorry that he had made me cry. I forgave him and feel very close to him tonight.

April 20th Sunday – This morning we slept in until eight. We closed the newly constructed grass door and tried it out for privacy, then it was off to the drill site for Fred, and off to the garden for me.

The rest of the day was spent puttering around in the kitchen and going to the creek with Fred while he washed gravel. The small tropical freshwater fish that live in the creek provided me with amusement until a blue dragonfly stole the show by whizzing around my head catching gnats. Once one had been captured, the dragonfly would fly to a nearby long blade of grass and devour the gnat. This scenario was repeated several more times, the dragonfly nearly landing on my nose at one point.

Ebrahem returned just in time for dinner. He had good news about his wife. She is going to be fine. But he brought other news…I am considered a white witch woman. While walking through the villages on his way back to camp he was repeatedly told this story about a white witch woman who chased away the evil spirits from Floating Grass Lake. It was then safe for the village women to fish there. According to local beliefs, and

Ebrahem was one of the believers, the lake held the spirits of the evil ones. At times, when a villager went toward the water's edge, they would disappear, never to be seen again. The evil spirits had reached up through the grass and pulled them under. Sometimes at night the ghosts would float above the water, their haunting eeriness gloating over the lives they had stolen.

Having walked to the lake across the undulating grass, I could understand how easily one could fall through, especially during the rainy season. The small lake was so filled with rotting vegetation that will-o'-the-wisp would likely be seen; frightening villagers who had no understanding of bioluminescence caused by oxidation produced by organic decay.

I attempted to explain, with the aid of Jean Charlot, that I was no white witch woman, but that did nothing to convince Ebrahim. The final word on the topic was that witches are not self-proclaimed.

This evening's meal consisted of beans and canned franks, fried wheat bread, onion rings, and applesauce with raisins and cinnamon for dessert.

Jean Charlot, the Frenchman, is one of the geologists who works in the hydraulic pits with David, the only married, as well as non-English speaking member of Camp A. He stands approximately five feet, five inches tall, has short brown hair, brown eyes, and always wears a cheerful smile when around camp members. He and I have tried to engage in some polite conversation, but since Jean Charlot speaks no English and I, no French, the only thing that we can do is the standard French greeting when our paths cross. Then we bob our heads and grin.

There have been occasions where we need to communicate concerning medical supplies, which I have been assigned to dispense, and worker problems, when no one else is in camp to translate. Then Jean Paul and I enter a complicated game of charades and whomever was attempting to communicate with us most often walks off more confused than had nothing been said, at all.

Jean Charlot often seems depressed and hides in his payotte. At first, I would coax him out of hiding so that he would join us at the dinner table. However, I realized he was doing that for me, rather than himself. So, now I take his meals to him when he chooses to be alone. He likes his desserts, so I always take in a little extra when I think that he is feeling blue.

Jean Charlot does not like to have his meals without wine, which is in short supply here since only beer is part of the camp's provisions. Anytime someone goes to Conakry, they always bring him a large jug of wine. He is always more cheerful when he has his wine and tends to linger around the table after meals with the rest of us. Otherwise, Jean Charlot goes back to his payotte to write long letters to his wife.

It must be difficult for Jean Charlot to sit among the rest of us as we visit. Only David speaks French well enough to communicate with him. I understand that Bill is fluent in French, as well. But David often retires to his quarters to read *War and Peace*, rather than linger in the kitchen. And Bill has yet to return from his two-week break.

One day Jean Charlot came to me with a group of photos of his wife and young children. I spent time examining each and nodding approval at his attractive family. I was pleased and honored that he shared the photos with me.

I admire Jean Charlot's calm demeanor. I have never witnessed him display anger or frustration. He accepts things with grace, which is an asset here in WAWA (West Africa Wins Again) land.

April 21st Monday – I watered the garden this morning, then headed to the creek to do the laundry. I wish it would rain again as it was extremely hot and humid today.

As I was enjoying doing the wash in the creek and cooling off, Fred showed up in the tractor. We visited while he filled a water drum for the drill. If it weren't for our frequent meetings at the creek, Fred and I wouldn't visit much. During the evenings after meals, Fred logs samples, reads reports, or writes in his journal. Either he goes to bed after I am asleep, or I find him sleeping when I wind up my day late.

During the afternoon, I mended one of Fred's three shirts, peeled onions, diced mangos, and cooked white beans for our evening meal of beans with ham, curried pearl onions, and mango-banana salad.

Another homologue arrived, making three at the table, now – Ebrahim, the youngest; "The Count" (because David says he acts like one); and now Sly (because David says he looks like a rock star.). Sly walked twenty miles from Banancora.

The monkey and the puppy were fun to watch romping around the kitchen this morning.

The lame chicken is no longer with us. This afternoon during lunch the hen hobbled up to a large sore on David's foot and pecked it, causing David to leap out of his seat and hop around in agony. David then sent the chicken off to the workers' camp to turn into soup.

I retrieved salve and a bandage to dress the wound on David's foot. It was more of a bumpy, weepy rash and had become infected from being scratched. I applied the salve and bandage. David said that it was feeling better all ready.

I was exhausted from the hot day, as was everyone in camp. After meeting Fred at Faraco Creek this morning, I hauled an extra bucket of water to the shower. Fred was reading reports in the payotte, so I enticed him to come and have a shower with me.

The water was clearer than what had been hauled from the well, and not as silty, so the shower nozzle sprayed, rather than dribbled. The woven grass enclosure made the area feel cozy in the soft light provided by the candle that I had lit and set above us on the barrel platform. We bathed each other and rinsed off, lingering in the small intimate enclosure after drying off. Then we returned to the payotte, hand in hand.

Fred fell quickly asleep, while I curled up with a flashlight and book, *Bury My Heart at Wounded Knee*.

April 22nd Tuesday – "Kitty, Kitty, Kitty!" Everyone in camp is looking for Wayde's kittens. They didn't come into the kitchen this morning for their reconstituted powdered milk. I checked Wayde's payotte where the kittens curl up on his bed. But they weren't there! Sange is acting strangely. She clings to my neck with furrowed monkey brows.

I walked around the payottes and searched through the nearby forests, looking for fur and blood. But nothing. They couldn't have just vanished into thin air. Fred was comforting, saying they are probably out in the savannah grass somewhere hunting. That could have been possible, but by day's end, they hadn't reappeared. I don't want to have to break bad news to Wayde if they don't return.

Fred took the new homologue, which will be working with Fred's crew, Momodu, and me in the Land Rover. Our first stop was Pit #1, which David and his crew had managed to save from the rising river. However, when we approached the pit, we saw that a group of clandestine miners were working the area. Those who saw the Land Rover approaching took off running through the tall savannah grass. Others were in the pit, engrossed in shoveling gravel, and didn't notice the approaching vehicle until the last minute. Momodu had brought the rifle in case we saw any game. Now, on the homologue's orders, Momodu held the miners at gunpoint.

Clandestine miners operate outside of the law, resulting in most of their production to be smuggled and marketed illegally. The methods of their mining have been proven to be inefficient and wasteful. The secretive nature of their activities, their geographical distribution, and their ability to sneak across borders, makes their capture difficult.

The clandestine pits had been deeply dug using worn out picks and shovels. Water had been bailed out of the rapidly filled holes using buckets. The homologue was terribly upset by the renegade miner's which he determined to be Lebanese. Taking the men as prisoners was problematic. They would have to be transported, fed, and housed. Instead, it was decided that their tools would be confiscated, as well as the gravel. Momodu lowered the weapon and the clandestine miners fled into the savannah. Fred told the homologue that this pit had yet to produce any diamonds and to haul all the gravel the illicit miners had dug would not be worth the effort. So, the mishmash of broken tools was taken, plus I gained three hole-free buckets for my kitchen.

From Pit #1, Fred drove the Land Rover to the Sonamba River and parked it at the crossing. There is a place to ford the river a short distance upstream, however, recent rains have made fording currently impossible. When the river drops to fording level again, and all the Land Rovers are back in camp, one will be parked on the Madina side of the river for access during times of high water.

We were ferried across the river to Madina in a large dugout canoe piloted by a young boy using a broken shovel as a paddle. The canoe, crudely carved from a large tree, could ferry eight or nine people at a time. Once we were across the Sonamba River, we walked along a narrow path through tall grasses, past mango and banana trees, and intriguing living fences. The fences had been fashioned out of thorny sticks stuck in the ground, where they had taken root and grown into lush, green, impenetrable, thorny hedges. I also noticed, hanging from several mango tree branches, grass-woven bee skeps.

The town on Madina consists of thatch roofed huts made of clay mud applied over handmade bricks. Momodu is a friend of Madina's chief's son. We were invited into the son's hut. It was about the size of Fred's and my payotte. We sat on prayer mats spread across the floor. The chief's son has three wives and fifteen children. Many of the children entered the hut and sat in a squatting position, smiling at us.

Our host asked Momodu if anyone would like some honey. I thought that he meant would anyone like to purchase honey, since he had just sold Momodu and the homologue cigarettes.

I nodded, “Yes.”

The chief's son opened a large crock, took a ladle fashioned from a gourd, glopped it into a good-sized gourd bowl and handed it to me with a small spade-shaped wooden spoon. Smashed in with the dark, amber honey were all stages of developing brood, dismantled bees, tiny floating rafts of wax, golden blobs of beebread. I stared into the bowl; wooden spoon clasped tightly in my hand. Momodu was sitting next to me.

He leaned over and whispered, “Eat, or you will dishonor our host.”

I took a bite. The honey was sweet and soured. Momodu bumped me slightly. I took another bite and smiled at our host. He was grinning broadly, seeing that I was appreciating the treat. Momodu was also grinning broadly because he knew my discomfort and was curious to see how much I could eat without bolting for the doorway to empty my stomach.

After the third bite I asked Momodu to tell his friend that I was enjoying the honey so much that I wanted to take it back to the camp to share it with the others. Momodu could return the gourd bowl on his next visit. Momodu gave me a look. I'd like to think that the look meant that he realized I was smart for a white woman. But I knew it only meant that I had escaped this situation, but there would be plenty more coming up.

We had a tour of the village's two wells – deep open holes lined with ironwood. Over the years deep grooves had been worn in the wood by the rope hauling up buckets of water. On our way back to the dugout, we shook hands with women and children lined along the path to bid us farewell.

At the Madina crossing, children crowded into the dugout to ride back across the river with us. The canoe rocked and swayed as our young oarsman struggled with the heavy load of passengers.

For dinner I served curried canned chicken over rice, topped with freshly grated coconut, diced mango, and finely minced African pepper; a marinated salad; and apple tapioca pudding.

After dinner and until dusk, Fred, Jean Charlot, David, and I searched for Wayde's kittens.

April 23rd Wednesday – Momodu, "The Count", one of Fred's Guinean drillers and I took off in a Land Rover for Kérouané around 10:00 this morning. I had been reluctant to go, but Fred encouraged me, saying that I needed a break from camp chores. It was market day in the village, so I took a couple of things to trade for fresh bread, and hopefully, meat.

We stopped in the small village of Kaya where Momodu purchased a goat to sell at the market in Kérouané, he also picked up four passengers. Women, several who had brought mangos to my payotte a couple of days earlier, crowded at the window to look at me and pat my head. We were tightly crammed into the Land Rover, me, holding the doomed goat on my lap.

There was a large barge on the far side of the river, ferrying vehicles, and livestock across the Milo. However, the water was low enough to ford. The Land Rover made a running start and water came up over the hood. I held my breath until the vehicle was out of the river!

The wide Milo River rises in the southern outcroppings of the Fouta Djallon plateau of Guinea, northeast of Macenta. It flows 200 miles north, past Kérouané and Kankan to the Niger River.

The market was a lot of fun. It was much smaller and cleaner than the one in Conakry. I wore a shawl over my shift to afford myself privacy when I needed to use the public toilet. Fred's driller, who speaks Mandinka and English, assigned himself to me, acting as my guardian and interpreter. I was surprised to see some American products, all demanding more sylis that I thought they were worth! Where would the Malinkes source canned ham? And tuna?

There was a big, skinned N'Damas bull hanging at the edge of the market and women lined up with their pans. Beside the carcass stood a wooden table with a scale. As each woman approached, chunks of meat would be cut from the hanging beast and weighed. It wasn't just meat, there was also gristle, fat, and pieces of intestine added to the scale. Bartering would begin. The buyer of the meat would reject some of the gristle, the butcher would reluctantly add a bit more meat. A little less fat…replaced with a bit more meat. Finally, the butcher would toss up his hands and make a shooing motion toward the buyer, who would then quickly scoop the meat into her container and hand the butcher the required sylis. The only other meat that I saw in the market was monkey. There were a couple of dead ones lying on a piece of cloth and at another vender, a live one tied to a post. The live one was large and had a blue hind end.

Dirt pathways passed between rows of women sitting on the ground beside their wares, piled on sections of cloth or pieces of cardboard. There were globs of ground peanuts resting on pieces of torn paper bags, pyramids of lemons, limes, and mangos, woven reed baskets holding chicken eggs, long loaves of weevil infested bread, tomatoes, casava, and pineapple. And I had items to trade!

The trading didn't go as well as I would have liked. The meat had all been sold before the line of women had ended, so many walked away disappointed. I was able to trade a tin of nutmeg for a nice, ripe pineapple. The nutmeg was discarded, and the tin, greatly admired by the vender. I will bring more tins of nutmeg next time. Mixed, dried fruit was viewed suspiciously. I had brought a dozen bags of it to the market, thinking that it would be a great item to trade. I even opened a bag and handed out samples, most of which, once tasted, were spat on the ground. The women did not care for the fruit one bit! However, one bread vender took pity on me and traded a weevil infested loaf of bread for a bag of dried fruit.

Momodu changed some American dollars on the black market, seventy-five sylis to the dollar, so that I would have money to make purchases. I had managed to acquire most of the items on Fred's list.

The Land Rover had been parked in front of a tailor's shop. One of the tailors, a nice-looking young man, probably in his twenty's, handed me a note written in French. Of course, I couldn't read it, so I took it back to camp and David read it to me. It turned out to be a love letter!

> Chere Madame,
>
> Le volupte de vaus addresser mes salutations les plu respectueuses vraiment ye

vous ames pas par impolitesse mais des que ye biens ai vu, je ruis tombe de amoureux vour y e vour tres bien,

Par Daouda Camara
Translated by David,

Dear Madam,

The voluptuousness from you, send my greeting most respectful. Really, I am not sure if my soul is out of rudeness, but as soon as I saw, I liked you. I have fallen in love. You can see for yourself very well.

By Daouda Camara

In the future, I will make certain that any Land Rover I arrive in at Kérouané, is parked far, far away from the tailors' shop.

I was tired from marketing and the long, rugged journey to Kérouané and back. I relaxed for an hour, then prepared dinner of creamed canned chicken, the sauce made with the cheese packets from the boxed macaroni and cheese, and powdered milk. The boxed noodles were cooked, and the chicken sauce served over the top. The sliced bread I brought from the market had very few weevils. I hope that vender is up for another trade next time I go to Kérouané on market day. The pineapple was served for dessert.

As we were finishing our meal, a Land Rover arrived with Wayde, Tony and Raynor Shaw! I cooked up another pot of food as everyone visited around the table. Simon and his homologue were half an hour behind Tony and showed up as the second meal was being served. Simon may stay in our camp for a couple of days.

Dennis, the cook, also returned with Simon. He had been away for about a week on vacation. Dennis presented me with a woven handbag that he had bought in Sierra Leone. I thanked him for his thoughtful gift. Now there will be help in the kitchen. Good thing, too, with twelve to feed. We haven't even enough plates or eating utensils for twelve. Plus, our food supply remains low.

Tony brought fuel with him, and lots of beer, plus twenty-four cans of 7-Up for making shandies. He also brought corned beef and rice for the workers, plus a large bag of potatoes for our camp. Raynor retired early. He was not happy – someone had taken all the bedding from his tent.

Wayde had a good cry over his missing kittens, but soon zonked out, having had only a few hours of sleep during the past few days.

Tony, David, and Simon stayed up way into the night drinking shandies, a beverage made by mixing 7-Up with Heineken beer. I asked Tony where some of the Kérouané venders would get American canned hams and tuna. Tony said that the only way would be to steal from our supply trucks. That's why any stranded vehicle headed for camp is put under guard.

This evening, I discovered a far more romantic and appreciated note than the one I had received in Kérouané. It was pinned to the mosquito netting above our bed:

You are away
For only a day
And all I do
Is think of you.

I love you,

F.

April 24th Thursday – It was barely daylight. Fred had already left for work. I saw movement out of the corner of my eye. It was a green mamba. It had slithered under the ventilation space and was swiftly moving across the floor toward the bed. My heart raced; what if it came into the bedding? It was moving so swiftly that I had barely had that thought as it slithered onto the bed, across my chest and disappeared out the other side of the payotte.

The first thing that I did this morning was, using a hand saw, cut down three trees, about six inches in diameter. Then cut each into two four foot lengths and hauled them home to the payotte. Camp members heard the small trees fall.

By the time Fred came from the field for lunch, I had dismantled the bed, dug the first twenty-inch-deep hole, and sank in the post, adding and tamping sand to set it firmly into place. I had heard some heckling around the kitchen table before Fred showed up, took the shovel from me, and began digging a second hole. I was glad for the help, as my hands were blistered from sawing down the trees. He finished setting the other five poles. Together we hoisted the newly arrived plywood onto the six supporting poles.

When we were in Conakry, Fred had acquired a heavier piece of plywood, which had just recently worked its way to camp. First the plywood had been stranded on the crippled Russian truck, then transferred back to Conakry before being loaded onto the Mercedes and left in Kissidougou at Jean Paul's, then hitching a ride with one of the Land Rovers to Camp A, strapped to the roof.

While Fred went to get some lunch, I repositioned the foam pad and made up the bed, which was now forty inches off the floor. Now we had a more comfortable and safer bed!

I spend late morning washing the clothes in the creek while Fred washed samples and Wayde searched for the kittens.

Dennis and I worked together to prepare dinner for twelve people this evening. It was great to have someone help peel onions, dice potatoes, and fetch supplies from the storage payotte. I had earlier learned that Dennis is a cook by name only. He can open cans and heat the contents, and cook oatmeal, but that is the majority of his culinary skills. However, he makes a handy sou chef.

Camp members were fed in two shifts, ending around eight this evening. After dinner everyone sat around the table and visited with the homologues, being entertained by their stories. Whatever their formal religious affiliation, many Guineans still adhere to locally based beliefs, regarding themselves as living in intimate association with the supernatural world. Obviously, the camp homologues are deeply rooted in this ancestral ideology.

Aside from proclaiming me a white witch, they had many other supernatural beliefs. The first interesting one they spoke of is of a "magic shirt" that is woven in Kaya by a nyamakalaw, a special artisan. A nyamakalaw spends their entire life perfecting special secret skills that are passed down from generation to generation. The creator of the shirt weaves some of the customer's hair into cotton fabric. The "Magic Shirts" are very thin and lightweight, but they are bullet-proof. It takes about five paychecks to purchase one.

But the next belief made my hair stand on end. The homologues claim that the Lebanese steal most of Guinea's diamonds by turning invisible and walking across the border to sell the illicit bootie in Sierra Leone. The clandestine miners can't afford the bone required to turn invisible themselves, only the notorious dealers have those sorts of funds. Recently some bones were obtained for the homologues, so they could more effectively pursue the perpetrators by becoming invisible.

"What kind of bone?" I asked.

"The forearm bone of a black cat," I was told.

April 25th Friday – This morning Tony, Raynor and I set off in a Land Rover for Simon's camp near Bounoudou. Simon and his homologue were following behind us with hydraulic pipes strapped to the roof of the vehicle. Fred had spent the better part of last night urging me to take this journey. I was reluctant to leave Wayde behind searching for his kittens, which I now was certain would not be found. Fred assured me that he would take Wayde to the jumper drill project on the savannah with his crew of four Guinean laborers.

Once on our way, I was glad for the break. Our mission is to locate some trained hydraulic workers to help David with his pit. The river has been rising and it is feared that the current pit will cave in. We stopped in Kérouané to wait for Simon.

While waiting, we feasted on brochettes and mangos. We waited for over an hour and a half, but there was no sign of Simon. Tony decided that Simon had had mechanical trouble, so we headed back, not looking forward to the long, bumpy return. Just as we crossed the Milo River outside of Kérouané, here came Simon. The load of heavy pipes had broken free, and Simon and the homologue had to stop to reload and re-tie them. We didn't leave Kérouané until three in the afternoon.

The route to Bounoudou was beautiful and the road could validly be claimed to be one! There were wide valleys surrounded by mountains, draped in capes of tropical green; villages built on terraces, surrounded by banana orchards and pineapple fields. The difference I noticed about the villages along the route to Bounoudou, compared to the villages of Madina and Kaya, was the cleanliness. These villages were not littered with refuse, even though goats, chickens and oxen freely roamed the streets. The people here are also more productive, creating a farmed area with a variety of crops, rather than relying on wild harvesting.

We turned off the main road onto a bush route leading toward the camp. It began to rain a little, which made the red clay road extremely slick. As the Land Rovers, slid and slithered along I began to appreciate the ruts leading to Baoule' Valley, Camp A, which at least partially held the tires in place. As we traveled closer to Bounoudou, there were many streams to ford, and bridges in need of repair.

One place along the way was extremely rough. We were following Simon's Land Rover when it nearly flipped over on its side while climbing a steep, slick slope. It could not complete the climb with its heavy load of pipe, so some were loaded to the roof of our camp's Land Rover and strapped down. Then picks and shovels had to be put to work, breaking up the ground to provide the needed traction. Simon said that the road would soon be impassable if the rain keeps falling.

We arrived at dusk. The camp quarters and sleeping accommodations were in abandoned white stucco buildings. The small stucco structures were built by DDX and the French, providing housing for Russians doing the company's geological work here in 1977-1979. Much of their equipment, including the old Russian truck used by DDX, was left behind.

It is nice to have a day off from cooking and to be served a meal prepared by someone other than myself. We were served sauce over spaghetti noodles.

As we were sitting around the table sipping beer, the driver of the Mercedes showed up on foot. He had been instructed not to attempt to bring the heavy truck to Camp B. However, against those instructions, the Mercedes was bogged down about half a mile from camp. Tony rounded up a crew of the camp's Guinean workers and went to work extracting the truck from the mire. Once freed, the Mercedes was driven two kilometers before it slid off the road and became mired up to its fenders. Eight men were left with the truck to guard the food and supplies – and one drum of gasoil, enough to last just two days.

Simon had his "houseboy" heat water so that I could clean up. Simon also insisted that I use his bed and mosquito net for the night. He slung a hammock outside and was most likely eaten alive. I went to bed feeling very pampered.

We had hoped to be back at Camp A late this evening but knowing about the WAWA (because it seems as though West Africa Wins Again about eighty percent of the time), I'd left a note on Fred's pillow stating that I was thinking about him and loving him.

April 26th Saturday – The Mercedes was pulled from the muck this morning and I finally got a look at the illusive truck. Simon thought that the truck may be a diesel-powered Mercedes-Benz Langhauber, dating from 1959. Much of the body of the large khaki-colored truck was encased in mud, and its tarp-covered long bed heavily spattered. Mud was packed around the wheel wells. As its cargo was unloaded, I was happy to note that it carried supplies for our camp as well as David's pit. Our camp will be its next stop, but two Land Rovers will need to be sent to Kérouané, since it would be difficult for the Mercedes to make the journey into camp. Tony sent it on its way, telling the driver that he must return by the route he entered. The driver did not come the shorter way to Bounoudou as we had but had come from Kissidougou via an easier route. The Mercedes truck should reach Kérouané within two days.

The main Bounoudou pit is very large and deep. Two pumps on rafts float in the pit to extract the water which seeps into the hole overnight. Tony and Simon were correct, Simon's project is superior to Davids. Simon's workers have better training, work harder and longer hours. I hope that the workers that we are returning with will be able to help David's operation.

I went with Simon, Pip, and the homologue to the main pit where I watched the emptying of the jig and the washing of the gravel. Diamond recovery is based on a series of mechanical concentration techniques to reduce the quantity of non-diamond gravel. Here, this was done by a small mechanical jig, left behind when the Russians were evacuated from the camp. Once the gravel was sorted, Simon, Pip and the homologue separated the rough diamonds. Over twenty diamonds were found, including a 2-carat! The 2-carat resembled oily, pale-yellow glass.

While Simon finished washing gravel, Pip drove me to camp where I prepared a lunch of salmon, and macaroni, plus a salad of marinated onions and tomatoes.

We left Bounoudou at five in the afternoon. About halfway to camp a tire on the Land Rover went flat. As I watched Tony and Raynor replace one threadbare flat with a threadbare spare, it was difficult to imagine how we had made such a long trip over rutty, rocky roads without all the tires having gone flat!

The trip had been a fantastic adventure, but a tiring journey back to Camp A. We arrived around midnight. I was too exhausted to eat, but fixed Tony and Raynor some dinner.

Fred said that he was glad to have me back, but his actions were rather distant. Perhaps being awakened from a deep sleep had something to do with it.

April 27th Sunday – I rearranged our dwindling food supplies in the new storage payotte, preparing for that which was being brought. Bill will be returning soon to reclaim his tent. A padlock had to be installed to discourage theft, which has become a big problem. David had moved into his new payotte while I was visiting Camp Bounoudou.

It was overcast during the morning. After waiting an hour, I decided that the threat of rain wasn't going to blow over and went to do the laundry in the creek, anyway. Before leaving, I took a minnow trap from one of our payotte walls. After the wash had been done, rung out, and piled on a mat of grass, I baited the minnow trap with a piece of stale bread, hoping to examine more closely some of the tiny fish that inhabited Faraco Creek. I caught three of the two-inch tropical freshwater fish. Each had three spots on their sides, a line of little blue dots, green ear plates and fringed red tails and fins. After examining them, they were released.

Fred was very distant today. He had been since my arrival last night. I don't understand why but think perhaps it is because of the trip to Bounoudou with Tony and Raynor. This theory doesn't make sense; it was Fred who asked them to take me, then worked at persuading me to go.

Both Tony and Raynor noticed Fred's attitude. When they asked me about it, I could no longer hold back my tears. Both men were very kind and reassured me that Fred was a difficult person to understand and communicate with. Knowing that I had neither a Guinea visa nor a required identity card, they told me that if I ever needed help leaving the country, that they were my friends and would assist me with any problems which may arise. I now realized how heavily my situation had been weighing on not only me, but others, as well.

But I do not want to think about leaving Guinea. I love so much about being here. It is different from my Idaho home with its towering, snowcapped-mountains, crystal clear rivers, and mixed conifer forests so familiar to me. But Guinea has become familiar, too – how the morning fog pillows above the tall savannah grass; how the scent of morning resembles freshly mown hay; how songs of the night insects lull me to sleep, and the lilting chorus of birds awaken me.

Later in the afternoon Tony announced that he needed two Land Rovers to go to Kérouané to meet the Mercedes. I volunteered to drive one of the Land Rovers. Tony declined my offer, saying that I do more than my share, as it is. Tony felt that Fred should step up and do it. Fred did not want to volunteer. Tony told him that everyone should draw straws to see who would go, since everyone benefited from eating the food and using the fuel. Fred refused. He said that the Mercedes may not have reached Kérouané, yet, and going might be a waste of his time.

Then Fred added, “Besides, I don’t need to volunteer for anything. I brought Darcy. That has been my contribution.”

What? I was his contribution? My eyes stung with tears, as I turned away and walked up past the Bog to the mango trees beyond, tears streaming down my cheeks. Leaning into one of the bigger trees, I wrapped my arms around her in a tight hug.

I heard someone approaching. “Mom? Are you okay? Tony told me what Fred said and that you are upset. And that you came this way.”

“I’ll be alright. It is just adjusting to a new understanding.” I said, as I sat and leaned against the tree. Wayde sat beside me.

Wayde said, “Tony and David left. Fred said that they couldn’t use his Land Rover because he was saving gas. So, Tony asked to borrow one of his spare tires, because Tony got a flat when you guys were coming back to camp. Fred has two, but he wouldn’t give Tony one.”

When Wayde and I returned to camp, Fred had left to wash gravel in the creek. Raynor took me aside to fill me in, not knowing that Wayde had already done so. Raynor stated that Tony and Fred had had a heated conversation over Fred’s spare tires, which were in good shape. Fred said that he wasn’t here to accommodate anyone. He was here to work in diamond exploration. That was what he was paid to do. Finally, Tony took David’s spare, which was worn to the point of being next to useless.

It was getting late, so I prepared a dinner of canned hotdogs, dipped in cornmeal batter and fried, canned beans in sauce, mashed potatoes, and a green mango salad. While preparing the meal, the hurt turned to anger. I don't understand Fred's attitude, but it is helpful to realize that I am not alone. I wish Fred's behavior could be discounted as having a bad day. Unfortunately, too many similar situations have been witnessed.

Tony and David returned around 11:00 this evening in the loaded Land Rover. They had encountered the Mercedes loaded down with passengers and their assorted belongings. Still fuming over his encounter with Fred, Tony flew into a rage and he and David threw all the baggage off the vehicle. Suitcases flew open, chickens squawked as they scattered, the workers fled in fear, and the driver of the Mercedes was fired. He had been carrying nearly twenty passengers in the truck with no liability insurance and no brakes!

I reheated the dinner I had set aside for Tony and David, and retired to bed, relieved that we had more food supplies.

Fred had retired ahead of me. He had not eaten any dinner. His stomach growled. It served him right.

April 28th Monday – The shipment of food was extremely disappointing. No vegetables, we are down to two cans of spinach. There was also no meat, all we have left in stock is one half case of tuna and three cases of Treet, which no one would eat. The last time we tried to feed Treet to the puppy, he rolled in it. There was no salt, which had been requested a couple of weeks ago. What had arrived were two cases of cornmeal, four cases of stale cookies, two cases of limp saltine crackers, two cases of cooking oil, and two more cases of Pringles potato chips to add to our two cases already on hand from the last supply arriving from the Kissidougou warehouse. The shipment was mostly junk with little food value! No peanut butter, no tins of ham or chicken. We did receive a case of mayonnaise – to use with what?

Tony is returning to the driverless Mercedes for the fuel and rice. Raynor and I are going in another vehicle, Fred's, to help haul the fuel. Fred needs the fuel to continue work tomorrow. I took two cases of tomato paste, we are always being sent cases and cases of it, but very little corned beef. Also, a case of saltines was added, along with a case of cornmeal and a case of the mixed dried fruit. There was little hope of selling or trading the mixed dried fruit, since the last attempt received no enthusiasm for it.

It is not market day in Kérouané, but when we arrived, locals came to the Land Rover to see what we had, and we sold the wares out of the back of the vehicle.

We were able to trade one case of tomato paste for fresh vegetables, fruit, and bread. The second case traded for 750 sylis worth of tire repair and tube patch work. The saltines brought 80 sylis per box; the cornmeal, 100 sylis. The tubes of Pringles were enthusiastically grabbed up for 50 sylis each, the content promptly dumped out. The Guinea women love containers for stashing their stuff!

Women were still hanging around the Land Rover. Everything had been bartered or sold but the case of mixed dried fruit – twelve bags. I pulled a bag out of the box and women rushed forth. I was offered 200 sylis! And the women were clamoring for more. Another 200 sylis, then another! I was thinking to myself that these women certainly developed a sweet tooth quickly. Handing out another bag, I glanced up.

What did that woman have hanging from her ear lobes? Was that a pair of prunes? And there, a woman wearing a necklace made of strung mixed fruit; and another, dried apricot earrings. The clamor was all about fashion statements! That case of dried fruit sold for 2,400 sylis!

We returned to camp just ahead of the visitors – Tys, Jean Paul and Mr. Gueye. I quickly tossed together chowder from fresh fish some worker had brought me early this morning. I fried corn meal hush puppies and a peeled, diced marinated cucumber and onion salad.

There were twelve to feed tonight. After dinner, the arguments began. I escaped to the payotte to get some chores done. Raynor came in, feeling depressed that little will be done concerning our fuel and worker situation. Our camp was the least productive of the three camps, so we were told that we were at the tail end of the supply chain.

After things calmed down in the kitchen, the gang, having shouted themselves hoarse and not having any beer to temper their moods, retired. I joined Raynor in the kitchen to listen to the first part of Raynor's favorite play on the cassette player, *The Importance of Being Earnest*.

April 29th Tuesday – I awoke extremely fatigued, partly from yesterday's shopping and selling expedition, and staying up late listening to *The Importance of Being Earnest*, but mostly from fighting off three columns of Guinea ants that had had marched through Fred and my payotte during the middle of the night. One of the columns had climbed up one of the support posts and came right across our bed, biting as they went! Fred and I fought them for an hour or more before succeeding in diverting their direction toward the tent Tys was occupying. We had returned to bed riddled with bites and holding back giggles, imagining a colony of ants trailing into Tys bed.

It hasn't rained in six days; the garden is suffering, and the well is dry. Water must be hauled from the creek. The creek is getting skinny, and I find that washing our clothes is becoming difficult in the shallow water. The sand and grit that accumulates doesn't easily rinse out.

Part of the afternoon was spent soothing ruffled feathers between Dennis and Ebrahem, one of the homologues. There are many ruffled feathers flying among individuals in camp. Tys was angry with Fred for helping himself to sheets, bedding and plywood from the Sultan House while in Conakry. Which recalls a camp joke.

If there was a river of beer flowing through camp, Lampietti would try to walk on it, Tony would try to drink it, and Fred would try to steal it.

There were twelve to feed again, with tuna and a couple of cans of corned beef to work with. I made corned beef and herbed tomato sauce over steamed rice; boiled casava leaves and a fresh fruit salad.

While we were having dinner, Momodu came running through camp foaming at the mouth. In his hand he clutched a half empty bottle of Wesson oil that had been filled with hydrogen peroxide.

"Boss man! Boss man! What in here! What I swallow!"

"Battery acid," Tony told him.

Momodu collapsed at Tony's feet and started retching and gagging. Everyone was laughing at the poor, traumatized man. I took Momodu to Fred and my payotte and gave him some antiacid tablets and told him to go home and rest.

After dinner, Mr. Gueye called a meeting and gave a speech which had to be translated from French to English. Then problems were discussed with everything being translated from one language to the other. Tys did the translating. Little was accomplished, but no tempers flared. The meeting ended at 11:30.

Fred had gone to bed. I thought that he was at the Bog, so accepted a shandy, made with warm Heineken and warm 7-Up while I waited for Fred's return. When he didn't show up, I got worried and went in search of him, finding him safely tucked into bed, sound asleep.

In camp at the end of the day it is customary for everyone to say good night when retiring. Fred has been the exception. I don't like to see him alienate himself from the rest of the camp. His distance makes things difficult for me. I am the one everyone comes to with gripes, complaints and accounts of disputes involving Fred. Do they think that I have influence at all over him?

April 30th Wednesday – Tys and his party left this morning and camp members felt relieved. Tony left, too. Fred's used Poclain is to arrive in Kankan, where Tony plans to pick it up. It is a far cry from the new one that had been shipped from France, then stolen from the dock in Conakry. The used Poclain excavator is a 1965 PPM model, having a 360-degree rotating excavator on a three wheeled tricycle under carriage. Tony also plans to swing through Kissidougou to obtain three drums of fuel. David's pit will close until Tony returns, due to the lack of gasoil.

Before Tony left, Momodu came to Tony and exclaimed, "Boss man! Boss! That stuff I drink make me well! A big worm this long (indicating about three feet) came out of me dead!'

No wonder Momodu was so skinny.

It poured down rain this afternoon. There was a parade of cuts, abrasions, infected insect bites and swellings marching to the door of Fred's and my payotte throughout the day, so I busied myself playing nurse. I did have time to write my brother and sister-in-law a letter.

Fred has been down all day and extremely distant, I found out later that he was upset over a couple of comments about him which came up during last night's meeting. The comments were aimed at him by Tony and Raynor. Fred didn't tell me what the comments were.

David assisted me with dinner, which I greatly appreciated. He seemed to sense that I was a little distressed over Fred's evident disregard of me, today. We had curried tuna over mashed potatoes, cassava fritters and rice pudding with raisins and cinnamon.

Fred and I talked about our personal problems, but I don't believe that anything has been resolved.

SECTION TWO
May

May 1st Thursday – I did the laundry this morning, filtered drinking water and straightened up the payotte and the kitchen.

Tony returned with three drums of fuel, but Fred's expected Poclain had not arrived in Kankan. There was no word as to where it might be. The trip along the back road from Kissidougou to camp was extremely rough and Tony predicts that the route will not be a plausible way back to camp in the future.

It was a restless day for me today. Things seemed to move slowly. I think that I have become accustomed to the challenges and drama that has been prevalent around camp. Today, there were no challenges to sort out or personal drama to untangle. The day was flatlined.

Tony brought some meat from Kissidougou and fixed brochettes for dinner. I made sides of chili and corn bread.

After dinner Fred took me aside and suggested that we bring the bottle of whiskey to the table that had been set aside for a special occasion. We had planned on doing this tomorrow night, being Fred's birthday. However, Tony will be leaving again for more fuel and wouldn't be able to join us.

Sharing a special occasion a day early so that Tony could participate, revealed Fred's thoughtful side…a trait not often displayed. But it softened my heart when he did.

It didn't take Jean Charlot, David, Raynor, Tony and I long to finish the bottle. Fred had retired early, soon followed by Jean

Charlot and Raynor. I stayed up with David and Tony until there was not a drop left.

Tony Robinson is British with a Yorkshire accent. I enjoy hearing him talk, especially when he gets "hot under the collar", which occurs frequently. His ability to speak his mind, with temper and insults blazing from his voice, while laughter dances in his eyes, never fails to amuse me. Tony, a Gemini, reminds me of my cousin Brook, also a Gemini. They have a stinging honesty, letting people know exactly what they think about them and why. And yet, people crowd around them, eager to be in their company. Is it the laughter in their eyes?

Tony has a vitality which enables him to go full bore. After a two-day drive, with only a couple of hours of sleep, he will still have the energy to sit late into the night and carry on a lively conversation. When I witness Tony beginning a marathon evening of storytelling, I go to Fred's and my payotte for a small tube of superglue and put it in my pocket. Tony has a repaired denture that can come unglued mid-story. Tony hands me the unglued pieces, which I dry off and apply the superglue. Then I attempt to keep the repaired denture out of Tony's reach while the glue dries. Often, Tony gets the teeth out of my hand before drying is completed and the denture ends up sticking to his tongue. Everyone at the table is howling in laughter by this time. Once things get straightened out, Tony picks up mid-sentence and carries on with his tale.

When I first met Tony, he warned me about the WAWAs (West Africa Wins Again). It didn't take me long to understand Africa's challenges. Tony meets each one of them enthusiastically and fearlessly head-on. Any time there is a WAWA, it's Tony who's the first to volunteer to go tackle it. And Tony usually wins.

I would have guessed Tony to be in his thirties, but he is in his forties. His features are rugged and masculine. His hair is blondish, his eyes are blue. To me, he resembles the actor Tom Jones, but is far more attractive.

The happiest times in camp are when Tony is around. His sense of humor keeps smiles on our faces and laughter in our hearts. He can find humor in most situations. But most admirable of all, Tony finds humor in himself.

May 2nd Friday – Today was Fred's birthday. I wanted to celebrate it with him and bake a spice cake. However, he said that he wanted to spend it with his five workers, to not have to deal with people in camp, and to wash gravel at the creek. Tony and David were taking two Land Rovers to Kissidougou for fuel. Fred urged me to go along with them, saying we needed a break. Raynor offered to keep Wayde with him doing survey work.

I reluctantly packed some things in my rucksack for the overnight trek, wondering if the hurt Fred inflicted was intentional or that he just didn't want to be bothered having me fuss over his birthday.

David and Momodu rode in one Land Rover while Tony and I rode in the other. We stopped at a place in Kankan that Momodu knew of and had a couple of beers. David really enjoyed the German beer, a definite improvement over Heineken. The "bar" consisted of a table and a few chairs at the back of an Asian woman's home – a round hut with packed mud siding and thatched roof. She was from Viet Nam and married a Guinean man, whom in turn, ran out on her.

The woman makes a quiet and secretive living off her "bar", as this being a Muslem community, alcohol is frowned upon. The

Muslim faith has grown at the expense of other faiths, particularly Christianity, which in Guinea is associated with white people. This attitude was strengthened by memories of the country's former French colonial rule between 1891 and 1958, when Sékou Touré, a devout Muslim, became the country's first president. Hers is not the only surreptitious bar in the area, however. We traded some tomato paste for the beer, which was selling for 160 sylis each.

At 10:30 this evening, we arrived in Kissidougou hot, tired, dusty, and hungry. Bill Davis, the camp boss that I had yet to meet, was returning from his vacation in Wales, and was at Jean Paul's. So was Tys, and his wife who had flown to Africa recently from the United States to be with her husband. The reception we had received was quite hostile. Tys and Jean Paul seem insensitive to the fact that the mining at Camp A has lost days of work due to the lack of gasoil, the fuel that they are responsible for supplying and transporting to camp. Tony stated that we will be loading six drums of gasoil tomorrow, like it or not.

I wasn't certain how Bill Davis would react toward me since he hadn't wanted Wayde or me at camp. He pretty much ignored my presence. David had confided that Bill was concerned about how he could refrain from being himself in Wayde's and my presence. Unlike the gentlemanly conversation engaged in by other members of camp, Bill's language was filled with profanity. Raynor said that Bill could make "sailor talk" seem like the insipid dialog from *The Water Babies* movie when compared to Bill's own brand of profound verbiage. Bill was afraid that I would be offended.

We were all hungry, but there was no place to eat except street venders that normally made brochettes, but the venders were out of meat. Tony, David, Bill, and I went to the guest house and fumbled in the dark attempting to light lanterns and set up camp beds. I had brought some saltines and canned tuna in my rucksack, so that was what the five of us had for dinner, along with a couple of warm beers.

We retired to our cots, but the mosquitoes and the heat, from keeping all the windows shuttered, made sleeping difficult. In the middle of the night, I had to go to the bathroom. It was totally black in the guest house and none of us had flashlights, due to the batteries having died long ago. I started feeling my way along the walls and bumped into someone's camp cot. Through the blackness of the night came an onslaught of profanity and I instantly knew it was Bill Davis. He had startled me.

"I'm sorry. I was trying to find my way to the bathroom." I apologized.

Bill replied, "...sorry I scared you, but would you mind getting your fuckin' foot off my mosquito net – shit!"

"I'd offer you some shit, but I just have to pee," I replied, then made my way to the bathroom.

Dead silence. Then a loud guffaw erupted from the cot. David and Tony joined in. And I hurried off to the closet-sized bathroom, which consisted of a half barrel partially filled with sawdust and fitted with a toilet seat. I felt around in the dark and finally located a large nail pounded into the wall, skewering torn pieces of newspaper.

As I felt my way back to my cot, the men again erupted into laughter. I smiled to myself; I had scored some points with Bill!

May 3rd Saturday – It was around 7:30 when I awoke. We all went to get the gasoil loaded, then had brochettes for breakfast prepared by one of the street venders. They certainly tasted good!

We headed out of Kissidougou toward Kankan around 11:00, Bill riding with David and Momodu. Our first flat tire happened about eight kilometers out of Kankan. Two kilometers later, we had the second flat tire, so after using our last spare, we returned to Kankan and went back to the Vietnamese woman's beer bar while the tires were being patched. It wasn't until four-thirty that we were able to leave the city. Tony had hoped to be back to camp before it got dark because the one remaining headlight on his Land Rover had burned out as we had entered Kissidougou last night.

Momodu was left at Kankan to wait for the Mercedes and for the train arriving from Conakry on the fifth. Fred's Poclain was to be on the train. Tony didn't have any funds to leave Momodu, so he gave him some expired fuel coupons to try to sell on the black market.

Black marketing fuel coupons, expired or not, was a risky business. Activities such as this, have been condemned by President Sékou Touré, regarding it a threat to government economic planning. The PDG passed resolutions requesting members to be vigilant. Throughout the country, the militia was given authority to prosecute illicit traders in black market dealings.

Tony drove his Land Rover ahead of David's so that we could make more time while it was still light, pulling miles and miles ahead of David…who was well-known to be a cautious driver. Tony, not so much so. I held onto the edge of my seat or braced myself against the dash, as the Land Rover bounced over exposed rocks and plowed its way through ruts. The gasoil barrels sloshed and skidded back and forth in the rear of the vehicle. Fortunately, there wasn't enough room in the back for them to tip over, but I wasn't too certain that one wouldn't end up in the front, securely pinning me to my seat.

As dusk approached, Tony pulled over to wait for David, but after a thirty-minute wait, his Land Rover still hadn't arrived. So, Tony turned his vehicle around and headed back, now dusk, and with no headlights, to search for David's Land Rover. Two Guinean Army Land Rovers came up behind us, passed Tony's Land Rover, then flagged us down! They had just forded a river and both vehicles had each lost one of their headlights, so they were going to commandeer Tony's! Only Tony didn't have any.

Tony was worried that the officers in the Guinean Army vehicle would come across David's Land Rover and commandeer his lights. However, his were still in place when we finally backtracked to where he had stalled with a flat tire, and no jack handle. Tony and David got the tire changed. Bill joined Tony and me for a change of conversation. Now, in total darkness – not even a sliver of moonlight had yet to rise – we rode close behind David's vehicle, following the illumination of his taillights.

It hadn't been more than twenty kilometers later that one of Tony's four-wheel drive gears jammed up. Tony had to make some temporary adjustments which allowed his Land Rover to continue, but without four-wheel drive.

I don't know how Tony managed it, but he forded the Milo River, went through bog holes, and up steep, and deeply rutted hillsides, with no four-wheel drive and the dim guidance of David's Land Rover's mud-caked taillights.

We arrived at camp at 1:30 A.M., exhausted. I fixed some fried potatoes and corned beef for dinner and left the weary drivers and Bill to eat. I went to take a shower. However, there was no water in the barrel, so I walked to Faraco Creek. The quarter moon was now up, its light giving the savannah the illusion of a vintage sepia-toned photo. I bathed in the soft light, the cicadas singing their nonstop chorus, welcoming me home.

When I returned to the payotte Fred was awake. He said that he had missed me and was glad that I was back. I felt very happy at that.

May 4th Sunday – The day passed slowly. I spent a couple of hours washing clothes. Raynor had noticed that the clothes that I washed and hung for Wayde, Fred, myself and sometimes, David, turned out cleaner than when the Guinean washman washes his. So, I have added Raynor's washing.

Aside from hauling water to boil and filter, I also carried buckets of water from the creek to the garden and to the shower barrel. Faraco Creek is about a quarter of a mile away, but I enjoy the task.

By late morning it had begun to rain – a continuous drizzle, not enough to sate the garden or fill the well. Just enough to be annoying and make everything wet. I fixed a dinner of crispy fried tuna croquets, served with boiled potatoes and a curry sauce, canned spinach, and mango pudding.

There are still food supplies missing from the storage payotte. I, alone, have permission to remove food from there. Bill Davis has learned of the missing supplies, so he put the key for the lock on a leather shoelace for me to wear around my neck.

Fred and I retired early tonight. He had his nose buried in his journal, re-reading his reports. I leaned in for a kiss goodnight and he pulled away.

"Are you angry that I went to Kissidougou with David and Tony?" I asked.

He turned to me angrily. "Why would I be angry? Sometimes you seem too needy, and I just want you to go away for a while."

He blew out the candle and turned his back to me. When he was sound asleep, I left the bed and went to the kitchen. It was empty and quiet. Needy? Was I? I lit a candle and sat thinking. How does he see me?

Through the fog he finds her
Shivering in her river of fear.
In her need he senses her lure
And dares not venture near.

A woman drowning is a fearful sight,
Even the bravest of men take heed.
For a floundering woman in her fright
Will drown another with her need.

Wary Sir do not let your pity rule.
Let your head and heart be sound.
The currents of apathy are cruel.
But clutched to her breast, you drown.

The riverbanks are crumbling inward,

As the icy fog grows thicker still.
When echoes of her pleas are heard
He retreats to diamonds and the drill.

Is this how Fred sees me? If so, he does not know who I am. But I am beginning to learn more about living with him. He is an unreliable teeter-totter. I can't trust that he won't jump off when I am on the high end.

May 5th Sunday – I woke up this morning with mild malaria symptoms – fever, chills, and muscle pain. It didn't stop me from wanting to make love to Fred during one of his rare approaches, though. He said he loved me and was sorry for being so distant last night.

We decided to walk to Fred's drill site together, and then beyond toward the Baoule Stream. Fred carried the shotgun in case we spotted Guinea Fowl. However, halfway there I found myself too weak and was fortunate to get a ride back to camp with Raynor, Tony, Bill, and a homologue. Tony was feeling down with malaria symptoms, too. I gave Tony some aspirin, then went to my payotte and slept.

Later, I got up and made an Italian pasta with corned beef sauce, potato salad and fried bread.

Everyone sat around the table in a foul mood because the beer had been gone for four days. Fred returned from his long walk, having seen no Guinea Fowl. He ate the dinner that I had set aside for him before retiring to the payotte.

David told a joke after Fred had gone to bed.

"Fred enters a bar with Darcy. 'A beer please…on second thought make that two.'" Everyone laughed.

I didn't think that it was very funny. I guess when things hit that close to home, it's difficult to feel the humor.

I was the last one to go to bed since I had slept during the day.

May 6th Monday – I was still feeling ill, today. Last night had been a restless one with fever and chills. The sky was overcast, so I didn't do the laundry for fear that it wouldn't dry before the rain came. I was correct.

Most of the afternoon was spent making tamales. I had found some large wild banana leaves and boiled them until they were pliable. Then I coated the leaves with a cornmeal mush seasoned with lime juice and finely minced African red pepper. The filling was made of mashed, cooked beans mixed with corned beef and some tomato paste. The tamales were tied with strips of banana leaf and steamed in one of the dish pans on stones set over an open fire. While the tamales steamed, I made Spanish rice, then peeled and diced ripe mangos for dessert. The process was time consuming, but doing something took my attention away from my malaria discomforts. Plus, I basked in the appreciative comments of eleven hearty eaters.

Today, at the hydraulic pits, David shot a six-foot spitting cobra, trapped in the bottom of one of the holes. Tony brought the hooded head back to camp, and even in death the cobra looked vicious.

Tomorrow, I plan to go to Kérouané with Tony and one of the drillers. The plan is to purchase fresh produce and bread at the market as we wait for the Mercedes. If it doesn't show up, someone will have to return the following day. Our supplies now consist of a half case of corned beef, three cases of tomato paste, eight cans of tuna, rice, tea, a case of dried fruit, instant coffee, soda crackers, cornmeal, dried minced onion, a bag of raisins, and seven cans of spinach. There had been two cans of chicken, but they disappeared in the night. Our supplies won't feed the eleven members in the camp for long. I will take one case of tomato paste for trading.

May 7th Tuesday – We didn't leave until 2:00 P.M. for Kérouané. Tony, Raynor, Dennis, and Latiff, one of Fred's drillers, also went. I still felt shaky this morning, with chills, fever, and a sore throat. I swabbed some of the pus sacks from my tonsils, gargled with hydrogen peroxide and took an antibiotic tablet.

Bill had entrusted me with the camp's meager funds plus the surplus soda crackers, tomato paste, and a case of mixed dried fruit to sell at the market.

Fording the river was a bit touchy, but the Land Rover made it across. It had been our hope to see the Mercedes upon our arrival, but it never showed up. I was more disappointed by its nonarrival than usual. Perhaps it was that I wasn't feeling well. Or perhaps it was that the Poclain hadn't arrived via train, as expected.

Momodu was nowhere to be found. We learned from a friend of his that after the train had arrived without the Poclain, Momodu had left Kankan. Apparently, he had done very well selling the expired, black-marketed coupons and had split before the swindle was discovered. Tony was confident that he would show up at camp within a day or two.

The supply-ladened Land Rover was greeted with enthusiasm, as there is a country-wide food shortage. Aside from what could be sourced locally, food in Guinea is scarce. This is partly due to the poor condition of the rural roads and the lack of reliable vehicles for maintaining roads and transporting food.

We did well bartering the spare supplies that we had brought. However, we had arrived too late to purchase N'Damas meat. I managed to obtain bread, limes, pineapple, and coconuts, plus 8,500 sylis. Sadly, I couldn't score any dried mixed fruit sales. Perhaps the women discovered their dried fruit jewelry would disinigrate in wet weather or provide tasty treats for pesty bugs.

It began to rain, and the venders packed their merchandise before we could complete making purchases needed for camp.

With Tony in charge, the bar was certain to be our next stop. This one, the only one in Kérouané, consisted of two tables and six chairs. There was an adjoining payotte with a table and two chairs, plus a bed where the owner's daughter slept, and entertained, for a price. At the bar, a small bottle of 80 proof Gin sold for 200 sylis. The Gin was very poorly distilled and had a harsh taste. Raynor, foreseeing the pause at the bar, had purchased four bottles of mango juice, which, when mixed with the Gin, made the liquor go down more smoothly. Raynor shared the mango juice, and I lost track of how many mixed drinks Tony, Raynor and I consumed.

It began to rain in earnest. Tony finally decided to check the level of the river to make certain that we could still drive the Land Rover across. The verdict? Impassible. We were stranded on the Kérouané side of the Milo.

Tony went to Momodu's friend's payotte and explained our situation and we were invited to stay the night. The three Guinean occupants, a husband and wife, plus a grown son, slept in one bed. Raynor slept in the son's single bed. Tony and I slept on a straw mat on the floor. Tony's feet were in my face all night and in the morning, I accused him of giving me athlete's foot of the ear.

May 8th Wednesday – This morning we went to a small neighborhood market Momodu's friends had told us about and purchased beef, onions, carrots, and bananas. I was particularly excited about having purchased carrots, a rarity in markets. But there were also several cans of chicken as well as canned corn – all American products. If I had had enough sylis, I would have been tempted to make a purchase as a treat for camp. But the prices were way too high. Were these black-marketed items that had been stollen from one of our supply trucks?

The level of the river had receded and was passable. We made good time getting back to camp. Bill met us at Kaya. He and Momodu, who had arrived on foot early this morning, were heading toward Kérouané to see if we had run into trouble returning to camp.

Bill was pleased that we had done so well selling at the market and purchasing most of the things that the camp had needed. I thanked Bill for looking after Wayde in my absence. He replied that he enjoyed "hanging out" with my son. I was also told that he found my work in camp invaluable and plans to speak with Lampietti about paying me something for my work this year. Bill will also give a recommendation for my return next year. He knows how keen I am about returning to Guinea.

I had a lot of laundry to do this afternoon, so spent three hours in the creek scrubbing out dirt.

I fixed stew for our evening meal, plus onion rolls, and a salad made of green mango, sliced tomato and avocado. Tomorrow it will have to be tuna or corned beef, again. But I plan to freshen up the meal with a fresh, grated carrot and raisin salad.

One of Fred's Guinean workers brought word that the Mercedes truck had arrived in Kérouané, so Tony and Bill made the trip back this evening. False information. Tony and Bill returned around 2:00 A.M. No sign of the Mercedes.

May 9th Thursday – I did laundry again today. The Guinean camp had the day off. There is no gasoil to continue work in David's hydraulic pits or fuel for Fred's savannah jumper drill. In desperation, Tony and David went into Kérouané again in search of the Mercedes, determined to track it down.

Moving hydraulic pump downriver.

Since mining operations were shut down today, it was decided to make use of the time moving the big heavy hydraulic pump a mile down river to a new location. A raft was constructed from debris found along the banks of the Baoule Stream and empty gasoil drums. It took the four of us – Bill, Raynor, Fred and me – to wrestle the pump onto the wobbly, crudely built raft. Each of us positioned ourselves at a corner of the raft. Most of the mile was between knee deep and waist high, allowing us firm footing to keep the raft stable. However, there were several sandbars where we needed to push and shove our way through. That was by far the most strenuous and exhausting part. There were a few areas deep enough to swim. This, too, was difficult because the raft teetered this way and that, free from our footholds. Had the raft tipped enough to dump the pump into the river, I doubt that it could have ever been retrieved.

We saw a medium-sized alligator sunning on the bank. It flipped into the water and quickly swam upriver, away from our strange floating entourage. It made me feel safe, knowing that the large aquatic reptile regarded us as a frightful sight, rather than an afternoon meal.

Finally, we reached the gravel bar where the hydraulic pump would be set up. We were all exhausted by the time we got it unloaded and securely in place. Here, a Land Rover could easily cross the savannah to supply the new site with gasoil and workers.

Tony and David returned this evening in time for dinner. No Mercedes. However, they had been able to purchase five small bottles of Gin.

Tomorrow the Land Rover heads for Kérouané again, hoping for the arrival of the Mercedes. Aside from being out of fuel, I had used up the canned tuna for this evening's meal. Now, we have only corned beef for meat.

The Gin was mixed with warm 7-Up and consumed around the table this evening. Fred wasn't in a celebratory mood and had gone to bed early, as had Wayde, but the rest of us got sloshed and had a lot of laughs – which was exactly what we needed. We witnessed Bill attempt to light a fart, only it backfired, and he singed the hairs on his butt, which sent the rest of us into fits of hysterics. Even long after the mishap, one of us would start laughing, setting the rest of us off, again. Bill laughed the hardest!

I felt very close to camp members this evening – Fred, David, Tony, Raynor and Bill.

Bill Davis is a 5-foot, 5-inch tall, chain smoking Welchman with brown hair, green eyes, and a stocky build. I believe that he is around thirty-five years old. Bill currently lives with his mother. A couple of weeks ago, while on vacation, Bill proposed to his girlfriend, Margaret, of three years.

When Bill first returned from his vacation, the workers chanted and carried him around on their shoulders. Even though Bill speaks fluent French, he yells at them in his vulgar English. He will even physically shove them around. But they laugh and obey him. Should any other member of camp attempt such antics, the workers would revolt. Perhaps, to them, Bill is a Nyamakalaw, a person born with the inherent ability to negotiate the forces of nature.

Bill is a terrific camp boss, too. To the outward eye, Bill appears to be a person of outrageous grossness. He belches, lights his farts, and spews out a steady stream of the most vulgar words I have ever heard. The Guinean and Sierra Leone workers laugh and say that he has been touched by a spirit. The fact that Bill can get the workers to work when no one else can, is a source of amazement to everyone in camp. When Bill gives the order, workers will labor in the mines even when there have been no rations to feed them. Intuitively, they know that to Bill, they are not, as David has said, “Lampietti’s rice machines”. They are valued as human beings, and he loves them.

Bill is wonderful with Wayde. He has made it known that both he and I are welcome in camp. Wayde calls him "Uncle Bill". I am keeping my fingers crossed that Wayde learns some of Bill's humanity and not how to light a fart. Bill has taken Wayde to work with him and on short one-day jaunts to Kérouané.

When the Guinean and Sierra Leonian workers greeted Bill with such enthusiasm when he returned from his vacation, I didn't understand. Now I do. Bill is a lover of humanity. Beneath his crass exterior is the most tender heart that I believe I will ever know. Bill is a man that one can trust to be honest, fair, and kind.

May 10th Friday – I went to Kérouané with Bill and Raynor this afternoon. No Mercedes truck, although Bill did find a driver who has claimed to have seen the vehicle in Kissidougou at 8:00 this morning.

We had brochettes at the market and purchased bread, coconut, bananas, tomatoes, and avocados.

As we were waiting for the Mercedes, we stopped at the bar for a drink. I drank too much, but really enjoyed myself as I walked arm in arm between Bill and Raynor in search of the Mercedes. The two men were really a riot and they had me cracking up at their antics. We had a great time.

After waiting until dark for the missing Mercedes, the three of us stopped to visit a friend of Bill's, who ferried us across the river in a small, motorized scow. The river had been too deep when we had arrived this afternoon, so the Land Rover had been left on the opposite side of the Milo. We had crossed on the large commercial barge, which normally wasn't operational due to lack of fuel.

I fell asleep in the Land Rover on the way back to camp. Once there, I couldn't keep awake and went to bed and fell asleep fully clothed.

May 11th Saturday – I spent all morning and part of the afternoon catching up on the laundry. Later, Raynor took me to the Banka drilling site and one of the hydraulic pits. It was an enjoyable excursion.

We had visitors come today, via Land Rover, a man named Brian Loyd and another man, Howard Bills. With them was Alan Kingston, a new member of our camp sent here to survey a new road and airstrip to be built next year. They brought disappointing news. The Mercedes has broken down about thirty kilometers outside of Kissidougou.

Momodu shot a small deer and Dennis cooked it African style.

The animal was gutted and skinned. Then a cut was made lengthwise, down the center of the ribcage, and the carcass splayed. The splayed carcass was cut across the center, forming four pieces, two with front legs and two with back.

A new fire ring had been built and large chunks of wood burned, forming good-sized coals. The venison was laid directly on the hot coals and turned about every ten minutes. It took about thirty minutes of roasting this way. Part of the meat was well done; other parts, such as the thicker flesh of the haunches were medium to rare, but well heated all the way through.

Dennis had spread a thick mat of green savannah grass over the center of the kitchen table. Ash was lightly whisked from the meat using a bundle of short grass. The hot pieces of meat were lightly rubbed with a mixture of cooking oil, lime juice and

African pepper…camp is still without salt. Then the meat was placed on the center of the table. We cut delicious chunks of it from the bones or tore apart well-cooked ribs and ate the venison with our hands, juice dribbling down our forearms.

While the meat was cooking, I had made a large pot of rice, and tore the bread we had obtained in Kérouané into chunks.

There was little else to feed everyone as our food supply is nearly gone. So is the workers' supply. We haven't any corned beef, or meat of any kind, except for Treet – which everyone agrees – is a non-food, and boiled empty cornmeal cartons would be preferable. We are down to rice and tomato paste. And mango.

Brian Loyd brought two cases of beer, which were quickly consumed.

Fred went to bed early. He is losing weight, and I am worried about him.

Raynor and I met on the trail to the outhouse and visited for a while. I think that his fiancé, Janis, is a lucky lady.

Dr. Raynor Shaw is a thirty-one-year-old geologist. He is very, very British, with an articulate pattern of speech. His appearance is always neat and tidy. If I had but one word to describe Raynor, it would be gentleman.

I already consider Raynor a close and sincere friend. He has a good sense of humor and a very sensitive nature. In many ways, Raynor reminds me of my brother, Gregg. They are both Aquarius, so perhaps that explains their strong and regal appearance, plus their natural, social grace.

Raynor is over six feet tall, has brown hair, blue eyes, and a generous nature. I am attracted to his love of small creatures and appreciation of his environment. He, as I, truly loves it here in Guinea. However, I suspect with Raynor's awareness of the natural world, he would love most places outside of city dwellings.

I plan to keep in touch with Raynor after leaving Africa.

May 12th Sunday – Tony, Bill, Wayde and I left for Kissidougou this morning in the Sierra Leone's Land Rover, rather than Fred's, which is currently without a clutch. We went the "back way" fording the Baoule stream near Madina. It was quite a feat and there were moments when I doubted that we would make it across without getting stuck.

When we arrived at Jean Paul's I was certain that sparks were going to fly because Bill had really been working himself up over having run out of food to feed the workers. However, when Bill saw how distressed Jean Paul was over the situation, he cooled down. Our food for camp is here in Kissidougou, but there isn't much. However, there are two cans of chicken! Gasoil is scarce, also. Jean Paul shared a rumor about why the entire country is thirsty for oil. Apparently, President Sékou Touré made a public statement criticizing Russia. The statement angered General Secretary Leonid Brezhnev, so he ordered the tanker of fuel enroute to Guinea to return to Russia. Tony, Wayde and I will be returning to camp in the morning with three drums of gasoil and enough food to last four or five days. Once the supplies are delivered to camp, Tony will return to Macenta where the stranded Mercedes sits with a seized-up engine. He may have to go to Sierra Leone for parts, so we will be without Tony in camp for a while.

Bill will be flying from Kissidougou to Conakry tomorrow morning to, hopefully, get enough food from the Sultan House storage to last the remainder of the season. He will have to hire a truck to transport it.

What a mess!

Jean Paul, his wife, and two children joined us for dinner at the brochette place, chunks of skewered meat roasted over a grill and served with rice and mango.

I went to bed early on a cot set up for me in the guest house, but Tony woke me later and we visited until 2:30 this morning. I don't know how Tony gets by on so little sleep. He had written a poem that he had wanted to share with me. It gave me a window into his emotions and thoughts:

Reality, by Tony Robinson

Swim before the mist of dreams,
Your soul awakens by the means,
If indeed the chance to dream
Has whetted senses no longer keen.

Salvation, yes indeed, is yours,
As you approach Utopia's shores.
I know Utopia is in the sky,
But to reach it, one must fly.

It is said it's the perfect place.
Is there room there for my face?
I see others, their numbers many,
But one like mine, there isn't any.

I am realistic, give me grace.
Please, kind person, find my face.

Tony wistfully spoke of Anna, the girl who had recently left him to marry another. I wish that he wasn't still hurting so much over it. My hurt over Fred's and my situation probably won't get better for a while, either. I feel that we are far apart, emotionally.

May 13th Monday – Bill bought a plane ticket for Conakry, to fly in a rickety, old Russian military plane. It is hard to believe that an airplane of any sort flies out of this place! He is on a mission! Determined to get the supplies that our camp needs in Conakry, rent a truck and drive it back to camp. Supplies were supposed to be delivered to Kissidougou on a bi-weekly basis, but that hasn't been the case. Bonnie chance, Bill!

Latiff, a Sierra Leonian and Fred's main driller, had returned from his vacation and was headed back to Camp A, this morning with Tony, Wayde and me. We took the rugged, but much shorter way back.

About thirty miles out of Kissidougou the steering shaft broke when Tony hit a large rock submerged between two mud-filled ruts. Our combined efforts managed to move the Land Rover off the road. Traveling along this road was minimal, so when Tony saw a Land Rover crammed with passengers approaching, he made a hasty decision and jumped aboard.

He called over his shoulder, "I'll get a Land Rover at camp and be back sometime tonight with welding equipment."

A churn of mud, a hasty wave – and Tony, the WAWA man, was gone. In the glove box he had left his wallet and I.D. card. He took no water, no money, and no food. He also had been using a list of villages that we were to pass through on our way back to camp with the kilometers between each noted, so the four of us wouldn't get lost. Thankfully, that too, was left behind.

Latiff knew English, but we seemed to have little to say to one another. We sat in the sweltering cab, windows rolled up, avoiding the swarm of mosquitoes. Finally, the oppressive, enclosed cab became more of a problem for me than the mosquitoes lurking outside. So, Wayde and I exited the vehicle, and I opened a can of glutenous corned beef, sliced open a loaf of bread and sandwiched the congealed, canned meat between the loaf. I cut it into three portions, and Latiff, Wayde and I had lunch, sharing sips of water from Tony's canteen. After lunch Wayde chased butterflies while I did what I could to assist Latiff, because it was obvious that he had a plan.

Latiff started digging around in the back of the Land Rover, surfacing with Tony's toolbox. He squiggled under the vehicle on his back, then squiggled back out. There were still some threads on the unbroken part of the shaft, he said, then wiggled back under the vehicle with a small metal saw. After about thirty minutes, he scooched out and disappeared into the bush. I stood leaning against the Land Rover, awaiting his return. We had been stranded for several hours by now.

Finally, Latiff returned with some stout sticks and long, thin vines. Back under the chassis he went, dragging the sticks and vines with him. After about thirty minutes he resurfaced and announced that if we go along very slowly, the repair may hold well enough to get us some distance closer to camp. I would need to use the list of villages we were to encounter to follow the route Tony had been taking. We would attempt to reach the nearest village before dark. It was now 6:00 P.M.

When we reached the first primitive village it was obvious that there would be no place to get food or to sleep, other than the Land Rover. The water from the village well looked clear enough to drink, so I refilled Tony's canteen. Latiff asked if we should sit and wait or continue.

I impulsively said, "Onward!" I often wondered, throughout the night, just how foolish that decision might have been.

The road was extremely rough and hazardous, especially after the heavy rains of the previous day. Latiffe had already skillfully maneuvered the crippled Land Rover around two large trucks stuck fast in the mud – neither was the one Tony had boarded. There were native men trying to dig out of the situation. Neither Latif nor I spoke Mandekan nor French, so there was no way to ask about Tony. I needed confirmation that Tony had come this way. That I was guiding us in the right direction. Roads, if you can refer to them as that, went every which way. What if Tony took a different route on his return?

Another ten kilometers along, the Land Rover's wheels fell through a bridge. The bridge spanning a fast-flowing stream, had been constructed of two long logs positioned side by side, with a three-foot gap in the middle. The right tires slipped into the gap, leaving the left wheels spinning in the air. The vehicle was suspended there for about an hour before a truck approached the bridge in front of us. Since the truck couldn't cross the bridge with us stuck there, he and Latiff secured ropes between the two vehicles. The truck slowly backed up, pulling the Land Rover's tires free from the gap. Then the driver jabbered in Mandekan, angrily wagging his finger at us. But Latiff and I just smiled…the steering shaft had held together!

We proceeded onward with me checking the kilometers between the villages and Latiff avoiding ruts and obstacles. But ten kilometers later, we were stuck fast in mud that came halfway up the door! Latiff had to crawl out of the window. It was dark, now, and there would be few, if any, vehicles passing through. We had only seen six during the entire day, one of them taking Tony.

Latiff headed off toward a village that was, according to the map, five kilometers away. Within three hours he returned with six men. They pushed and shoved until the Land Rover broke free from the mud. Each man was given a tin of corned beef, which pleased them a great deal. I opened a can for Latiff, Wayde and myself to share. We ate our rations with slices of raw onion. There are now four tins of corn beef to take to camp. As we were eating, I imagined Tony safely back at camp eating rice and tomato paste.

Again, Latiff's repairs had held fast. We slowly made our way along until around 3:00 A.M., when we reached the town which was supposed to be the one before Madina. But I had been to that town before, and this wasn't it. This was a large village called Banankoro, so we had to backtrack to the previous village, which was 13 kilometers away, reaching it around 4:30 A.M., Latiff pulled over at the fork in the road and we slept in our seats, Wayde stretched out across our laps.

May 14th Wednesday – Around 6:30 A.M. we were on our way again. We arrived at Madina about three hours later. Now I was in familiar territory. I directed Latiff down the narrow foot path to the river where the water was shallow enough to ford the Land Rover. I also knew there were deep holes that had to be circumvented and I was uncertain as to where they were. So, I waded into the water and walked through the broad stream in front of the Land Rover to show Latiff the way.

We were close to camp! Since there were no fresh Land Rover tracks at the fording point, I knew that Tony hadn't left camp, yet. I was greatly relieved, having feared that we may have missed him when I had directed us to Banancora yesterday, and had to backtrack. We arrived at camp around 10:00 in the morning. Tony was going to be so surprised to see us!

Fred gave me a casual welcome home. He was engrossed in changing a tire. Raynor surprised me with his enthusiastic and warm welcome. Then Raynor asked, "Where's Tony?"

"What do you mean, 'Where's Tony? We had trouble, a broken steering shaft and Tony got a ride to camp to get a Land Rover and welding equipment to repair it. Latiff managed to get it fixed well enough to work our way back."

Tony had not returned to camp. No one had seen nor heard from him. I suddenly felt sick with worry. Where was he? He had left his wallet and I.D. behind. Who were the people who had picked him up? Where had they taken him?

The morning went very badly. I had a knot in the pit of my stomach as I busied myself doing laundry and stocking the storeroom with what little food had been brought in the Land Rover. Raynor came to the storeroom and said that he had worried about Wayde and me when we hadn't returned last night, as expected. He was very relieved to have us back. He said that he had missed me. It was nice to know that someone had.

As I was preparing a dessert for our evening meal, Tony showed up! He was in the company of a Swiss couple, Gene and Ola, from the mine, Aredor, located over the mountain near the village of Gbenko. They had walked with Tony up and over the mountain and across the Sonamba River, to show him the way to camp.

Tony had picked up his ride with a group of illicit Lebanese diamond buyers who had taken a road away from where Tony was heading and got stopped at one of the barricades. The group was arrested and taken to jail at Banancora. Having no Guinea I.D. card, Tony attempted to profess his innocence, which didn't set well with the guards. Tony is sporting a sore-looking bruise on his side where the muzzle of an AK14 was shoved into his ribs.

Somehow, Tony managed to get a message to Banancora, where someone came to the jail to verify that Tony was who he had said he was, and to pay his bail. Tony was on his way to the Aredor mine shortly before we arrived in Banancora during our hapless detour.

The Aredor mine is located a little over twenty-four miles from Dabola. This area of Guinea is positioned in a diverse range of rock formations, including volcanic and sedimentary rocks very different from the areas being searched in Baoule Flats.

At Aredor this morning, Tony had heard that we had been through Banancora in the Land Rover, so Tony knew that Latiff and I were attempting to find our way back to camp. Communication via jungle vine?

I liked the couple who had shown Tony the way home. They will be passing through this area again on Sunday and hopefully stay to have dinner with us. Here in the middle of West Africa, there may be dinner guests from another camp! I rode with Tony in the

Land Rover as he took them back to the river and their trail up over the mountains.

I prepared dinner with some of the beef that I had bought in Kissidougou. Having had no refrigeration, it smelled a bit off, so I cooked it well done. I also prepared an apple crisp and a salad from the now wilted produce purchased in Kissidougou.

This evening Raynor asked me to take a stroll with him. I accepted. We had a good visit on our walk and when we returned to camp, I had hoped that Fred might show a slight bit of jealousy. He had been treating me with cool disregard since I had returned from Kissidougou. Surprisingly, Tony was the one who exhibited a jealous reaction.

I suppose that I shouldn't have been surprised at Tony's reaction. Except for Fred, the camp members have formed a close alliance. Since I am the only woman here, the men in camp have become protective. They let me know that I play a big part in this camp's function…that I am appreciated. I have become someone that they can confide in; speak to of the women awaiting their return; share the photos of their loved ones; express themselves on a deeper level than "man talk." Platonic love has developed among us. I love everyone here in camp, even Fred, from a place deep in my heart.

May 15th Thursday – I slept in late this morning. I suppose the lack of sleep over the last two nights had finally caught up with me.

Tony and Alan left for Kissidougou this morning. So did Brian Loyd, Howard Bills, and the homologue. Tonight, there will be only ten people to feed instead of fourteen.

Since Jean Paul has claimed that no more gasoil is available, we have had to put aside a barrel to use in emergencies, such as getting out of here when the food runs out. Work stopped at the pits today due to lack of fuel. Fred will be the only one working since he has enough fuel for five more days.

When I went to do the laundry, Fred was at the stream washing samples. He wanted to know what was happening with us. I tried to explain – but I couldn't put into words all the emotions that I had been feeling and was currently feeling. His distance and lack of interest in me – us – had confused me. It felt as though there was little between us to build on. I struggled to live with a man that I couldn't understand. My love had dwindled, in part, due to the lack of fuel needed to keep it burning. Fred just nodded his head in agreement. He expressed the desire to remain friends and relinquished me, calmly and with lack of emotion. I was no longer his lover and fiancée. I sat beside the stream feeling that losing the love we had started didn't matter to Fred one way or the other.

I felt depressed after our conversation. Fred finished the washing of the gravel and left. I remained at the stream. About an hour later Raynor showed up. He had been wondering where I had been and carried the laundry back to camp for me. He helped me rinse the laundry in hot water that Dennis had heated for me and helped hang it up. Later, he had taken it from the line. Fred's, Wayde's and my things were neatly folded and placed on the bed in the payotte.

Fred and I had decided to continue sharing the payotte. I don't know how long I will be comfortable doing that.

After dinner everyone sat around the table and visited. Fred seemed happier this evening than he had in a long while. I am glad that he isn't hurt, and I am surprised at my own lack of pain. I believe that most of the hurt is behind me. We haven't shared our decision with the other members of camp, but Tony and Raynor seem to sense the change.

Tony shared Howard Bill's description of PDG: Working for PDG is like living on a mushroom farm. They keep you in the dark and feed you a bunch of shit.

Raynor and I stayed up late this evening, listening to Poems by A. E. Houseman and Sir John Betjeman on the cassette player.

My favorite Sir John Betjeman poem was *Slough*, written a couple of years prior to WWII. I hadn't known A. E. Houseman's poetry, but quickly became a fan.

May 16th Friday – Everyone slept in this morning since there is no gasoil and there has been declared a day off. We planned a picnic at Kamaradou Falls on the Milo River. There would be about a mile hike along a steep trail to the falls. I wish that Tony, Alan, and Bill were here to join us. Wayde had chosen to stay in camp and help Dennis with the boiling and filtering of the water.

I had made soft flat bread to fold over a curried tuna filling. Crackers, applesauce, cookies, and tea were also packed in the picnic basket Fred had purchased in Dakar.

This morning David and Ebrahem got into a row about workers' rations. Ebrahem went to his tent and sat sulking in his chair after getting the worst end of the shouting match. When everyone went to leave, Ebrahem refused to go. I went and asked him to please come and join us. Still, he refused, preferring to sit there and continue to pout.

Then Raynor walked up to him with a shotgun and basically told him that if he didn't get his butt into the Land Rover it was going to get filled with buckshot. "So, get your shoes on, we are leaving in two minutes."

Ebrahem glared at Raynor, then burst out laughing. Ebrahem laughed and smiled all the way to the falls and back.

Two Land Rovers were driven across the savannah to the Milo River, where a crude path on the opposite side led up to the falls, about a mile beyond. Leaving the Land Rovers, we forded the river and headed up the jungle path with homologues, Faloni and Katsura, clearing the way with machetes. The way was a steep, winding, path filled with creepers and stones, and bordered by all sorts of intriguing vines, fruiting, and flowering trees.

The wind came, then rain sheeted down. There was little choice but to continue onward. The steep and sometimes treacherous trail became slick with mud. Fred had fallen behind during the steep climb. At the top of the mountain, we found an old abandoned Russian magazine, ore carts rusting outside the entrances. The group took shelter there, while Raynor and I set out in search of Fred.

About a quarter of a mile back we found him safe, huddled beneath the shelter of a stone outcropping, reading his French dictionary. He joined us on the hike back to the abandoned magazine. Everyone had stripped and wrung rainwater from their clothes and dumped it from their boots. A fire had been built in one of the bunker rooms, but the area became too smoky, and the building had to temporarily be abandoned. When most of the smoke had cleared, we re-entered the shelter and spread out our picnic lunch.

The rain was relentless. Around 3:00 A.M., we left the shelter and proceeded the last quarter of a mile to Kamaradou Falls. The falls were stunning! The Milo River lazily meanders along, spread wide from bank to bank, before it suddenly leaps through a narrow gorge of dolerite columns, becoming a loud, angry, frothing, body of water, before gathering itself into a large pool. These falls are the most beautiful that I have ever seen. From a vista slightly above the falls, we looked beyond the gorge where the river now calmly meanders through the lush green of the jungle forest. Mists rise, as if reaching for rain clouds resting above the mountain tops.

Cold but grinning, we returned to the magazine, gathered our things, and made our way down the steep, muddy path to the Land Rovers. As we jounced along on our way back to camp, we saw several Guinea fowl. But, alas, the shotgun was at camp.

It felt great to get into dry clothes and warm up. I made sloppy joes out of corned beef and homemade barbeque sauce. It was served over flat bread left over from our picnic. We also had a tomato salad and boiled potatoes.

After dinner Raynor, David, Fred and I hung out in the kitchen listening to the music on the cassette player that Bill had brought. Aside from an Irish music tape, Bill had a tape recording of Famoudou Konaté playing the djembe drum. According to Bill, Famoudou is a Malinke musician from Sangbaralla, a village in the Hamana region. He began drumming in community festivals when he was eight years old. Since then, he had become the lead djembe soloist for Les Ballets Africains de la République de Guinée. Bill acquired the recorded tape while in Conakry when returning from his vacation in Wales.

I enjoyed the Irish music but must admit that it is going to take some time to gain an appreciation for djembe drumming.

Fred was in great spirits today. So was I. Fred had been very affectionate and attentive.

May 17th Saturday – I slept in late this morning, getting up around eight. The first thing accomplished was typing David's hydraulic pit report to Lampietti. David hasn't looked well lately and doesn't seem to have his normal energy. The sore on his leg hasn't cleared up, even with the antibiotic salve that I have applied. And when he was shirtless yesterday on our hike, I notice two smaller sores on his torso.

Fred carried the laundry to the creek for me and I spent a couple of hours washing.

The afternoon went slowly. I made chicken and noodles with one of the canned chickens, plus for dessert, rice pudding with lots of raisins and cinnamon. I am still fretting over what to feed the company tomorrow. Our supplies are rapidly dwindling, again.

I had expected to see Bill arrive today, but he hasn't returned. Hopefully he will be loaded down with food and supplies when he does.

This evening, we sat around the table looking at one another wishing we had some beer and the raucous company of Bill, or the humorous ramblings of Tony. What a dry, witless bunch we are tonight.

May 18th Sunday – I acted as field assistant to Raynor. We started at the Baoule Stream and surveyed a line to the terrace – a total of 1.24 kilometers. Some of the going was rough working through the eight-foot-tall savannah grass. Raynor took the time to lecture on the meandering streams and rivers that flow through this area, as well as various mapping procedures. Even though the Baoule would be considered a large river in the United States, here it is classified as a stream, since it is a tributary of a larger source. The information that we gathered today will be used for mapping the area.

Later this afternoon Raynor surprised me by asking me to go to England for a couple of weeks after leaving Guinea and before returning to the U.S. I told him that I would consider it, but I doubt that I will be able to afford to.

We returned later than planned. Our guests, Gene and Ola, the Swiss couple from Aredor had arrived from over the mountain. They had camped along the Baoule during the night. They apologized for not being able to stay for dinner since they had to swim across the river and climb the mountain before dark. However, they did have a large lunch before they went on their way.

I really enjoyed seeing Ola again. She is a terrific person, twenty-eight years of age, who has an adventurous spirit. In Saudi Arabia, where she spent two years, she had her own camel and would trek alone across the desert to visit various oasis's. Ola invited me to come spend a week with her in Aredor, which I plan to do toward the end of this season, or next year. She has promised to teach me some African cooking and Mandekan. Ola speaks six languages.

Gene and Ola had brought another Aredor member, a red bearded British gentleman named Ted Smith.

I made corned beef hash with potatoes and gravy, corn bread and pickled beets for dinner. As we were finishing the meal, one of the men from the Sierra Leone Banka driller's camp came and invited our camp members to a celebration. I tried to get Fred to go to the camp with me, but he became testy and snapped that he had better things to do. So, David, Raynor, Wayde and I went. There were a few women from one of the neighboring villages attending, also. There was a mixture of traditional drums, including a djembe and several bara drums, that were accompanied by singing.

This performance was followed by a meal cooked in a large iron pot set on an open fire. It held a bush meat stew, which included Guinea fowl and monkey. A smaller pot, containing cooked, mashed casava root, sat cooling by the fire. As guests, our camp members were instructed to eat first. Even though we had just eaten, it would have been considered rude if we did not partake. First each of us scooped some mashed casava root from the communal pot into the palm of one hand and flattened it into a bowl shape. Then we scooped some of the mixed meat stew onto the casava and ate the food from our cupped hand. It was very spicy – those little red African peppers! I believe that the meat in my serving was a small piece of some sort of bird and the knuckle bone of a monkey. The small amount of meat gnawed from the bone was stringy and chewy.

Things became more boisterous and joyful after the group finished the meal. The drumming now sounded from pounding on an empty gasoil drum, accompanied by the beating of pots, pans, and buckets, creating a freeform blend of noise accompanying the wild and uninhibited dancing.

Raynor recorded some of their songs with his tape recorder and promised to send a copy to me when I return to Idaho.

No sign of Bill, Tony, or Alan. We had been straining our ears all day for the sound of an approaching Land Rover.

May 19th Monday – We have been out of kerosine for nearly a month, so the refrigerator hasn't been functioning. The beer and soft drinks have been gone for five days. Tepid filtered water or tea (there is no sugar for sweetness) is all there is to drink. When it rains, I do still capture a cup of rainwater, which I guiltily drink in secret.

The morning was occupied in the field with Raynor, finishing surveying the jumper drill line. I spent the afternoon doing the laundry and fixing the evening meal.

Around dinner time we heard an approaching Land Rover, so I threw the last tin of tuna into the curry and listened intently to the vehicle whine and lurch its way into camp. It was Bill! I could have rushed to him to give him a huge hug. Instead, I followed the lead of other camp members and shook his hand, grinning broadly.

Bill brought fourteen cases of beer and a Land Rover packed with food supplies! The truck that Bill had rented is parked in Kérouané, under guard, protecting seven drums of fuel. It will be picked up tomorrow.

We received mail! I had a letter from Mom, as well as one from Fred's mother, Valerie. Valerie has no inkling of her son's and my current relationship situation. She addresses me as "Daughter." There was also a small package. My mother had sent my tarot card deck.

After a late dinner and a few beers, the camp retired for the night.

May 20th Tuesday – I took off to Kérouané in the Land Rover with Raynor and Alan. Fred still refuses to make any trips for food or fuel. I feel that he should, if only for the change of scenery. David drove another Land Rover, as it will take two to haul the fuel, and Latiff drove the tractor. The river is high, and the tractor will be needed to ford the river and bring the fuel drums back and forth across the Milo.

It took all afternoon to load the Land Rovers with the gasoil. The river was too high to make fording possible, but the tractor was able to manage. The heavy drums of oil had to be brought across the river via the tractor, one by one. What added time to the crossing and loading was that the tractor had to go approximately two kilometers downstream to access a place shallow enough to cross. Raynor and David had ridden across on the tractor to help Latiff load each drum of fuel. Alan and I, with the help of Latiff, loaded the drums into the Land Rovers. While in Kérouané, Raynor purchased a chunk of beef for tonight's, or tomorrow evening's meal. Tony is expected to bring Lampietti to camp when he returns in a day or two.

It was a terrific day, at least for me. There were a couple of minor WAWAs. Raynor got the Land Rover stuck in a mud hole and we barely managed to get it pulled out with the tractor. In Kérouané, David had his camera confiscated by the PDG police. He had been spotted taking photos of the children crowded around him. Guinean law forbids photos being taken of Guinean people at work, play, or worship. Nor is taking photos of villages, artifacts, or other similar scenes allowed. In other words, only photos of the natural scenery are permitted. David will now have to go through a complicated maze of forms and visits the PDG offices in Kissidougou and Conakry, in hopes of retrieving the camera.

Tony was at camp when we returned, having come to camp via the Madina route from Kissidougou. With him was Lampietti and four of Lampietti's crew. While crossing the river, one of Lampietti's vehicles got stuck in one of the deep holes. It was still there.

Tonight, I had a dozen people to feed. I prepared brochettes, mashed potatoes, canned spinach, and a mango crisp, for dessert.

It was 11:00 P.M. when we went to rescue the stranded Land Rover. I attempted to persuade Fred to join us, but he was in one of his noncommunicable moods. The rest of the camp went, accompanied by a half of a case of beer. Two Land Rovers were taken, plus the tractor. Lampietti's vehicle was seriously bogged down, and it took quite a few tugs with the tractor to dislodge it.

Upon our return, Raynor, David, Tony and I visited. After Raynor and David retired for the night, Tony and I continued to visit until 4:00 A.M., after which I helped him get a bed set up in a Land Rover by loaning him my pillow and bedspread. His payotte is housing guests and there is no place for Tony to sleep.

May 21st Wednesday – Tony took off this morning for Kissidougou with two Land Rovers, the other driven by Latiff, to pick up six drums of gasoil.

I spent the morning washing clothes, returning from the creek in time to make a tuna and macaroni salad with an avocado dressing for lunch. For dinner, I fixed an Italian pasta dish using corned beef, finely diced green mango and onion, dressed with a tomato sauce thinned with beer and a dab of sugar. It worked. A pickled beet salad was made using a finely diced cucumber (one of the two in the garden, to add freshness). For dessert I prepared an applesauce crisp. Lampietti kindly complimented me on the meal.

According to Raynor, I was the only camp member to receive a kind word from Lampietti. Meetings had been held all afternoon and our distinguished guest had been harshly critical of everyone.

After the kitchen was cleaned up, I retired to the payotte to write letters home. Raynor came to wish me good night and seemed very disheartened. I invited him to stay awhile, and we sat on the grass mat to visit. Fred was in the kitchen having a private meeting with Lampietti. When he came to the payotte, he and Raynor went over the details of the day's meeting.

I took the opportunity to return to the kitchen, where Lampietti was returning paperwork to a briefcase. I asked him to consider hiring me for the following year. He said that he would give my request consideration.

May 22nd Thursday – I was back in the stream with a bucket of dirty clothes this morning.

For lunch I made various spreads that could be served on crackers, since we have no bread. Then I worked on dinner all afternoon to have food prepared for everyone in camp. Brian Loyd, Bob (a Welchman), and another homologue had arrived early this afternoon. There will be nineteen for dinner.

I made a large pot of white beans, intending to use one of the three canned hams that Bill had brought from Socamer, the European grocery store, while in Conakry. He had purchased the hams with his own funds, as a treat for our camp. However,

Lampietti confiscated them for his group to enjoy on their journey back to Bounoudou, Camp B. This distressed Bill.

So, I used four cans of corned beef, chopped, and added to the beans. Then whipped up a barbeque sauce to make it all palatable. I baked corn bread and made a lime dressing to drizzle over a platter of sliced fresh tomatoes. Dried fruit was soaked until soft, then chopped and mixed into white flour and baking powder to form a batter, then simmered in a pot of sugar water flavored with pineapple juice, resulting in dessert dumplings. I fed the group in two shifts.

After the meals had been served, the kitchen was used for a meeting with Lampietti. Candlelight lit the table, as there were no more batteries for the flashlights nor kerosine for the lamps. The meeting lasted until 8:00 P.M.

Bill left the meeting in a pissed-off mood. He had handed in his resignation and said that he is leaving in the morning. The major disagreement with Lampietti revolved around wage increases for the Sierra Leones. The Sierra Leone Banka drilling team also resigned.

I am greatly saddened over Bill's impending departure. The two of us have become good friends. Bill is vital to this camp. Everyone goes to him with problems of all sorts – personal and business. Jean Charlot will be leaving, also. Lampietti has another job for him elsewhere, most likely replacing Tys at the Sultan House in Conakry.

Raynor was in a great mood after the meeting. Lampietti had much praise for Raynor's work here. He has instated Raynor as our new camp boss. Raynor will make an excellent camp boss for us, but I don't believe that the Guinean workers will embrace his leadership as they had Bill's.

After the meeting, Lampietti, his V.I.P.s, Fred, Tony, Raynor, and I sat around the table and visited. As we were doing so, Bill stormed out of his Payotte and snatched up the cassette player – the only thing in camp still with viable batteries – and a cassette tape, the recording of Famoudou Konaté playing the djembe drum, then returned to his payotte. He turned the volume of the player up full blast and the entire camp seemed to vibrate with djembe drums.

Bill returned and lit into Lampietti, djembe drums beating in the background. Lampietti would pull away from the table and confer with Raynor, then Tony, then Bill. Bill would take Raynor aside and they would have a mini conference; then Alan, who had retired earlier, but rejoined the group when all the shouting and general commotion had begun, would be drawn to the side by Tony. Fred sat and watched the unrehearsed drama.

Finally, Bill stormed back to his payotte, yelling to the group, "He's a cunt!" Referring to Lampietti.

Lampietti looked around the table and asked if there was anyone there that could calm Bill and get the racket (music) turned down? Everyone looked at me.

I asked to enter Bill's payotte and he welcomed me in. He was shaking with anger, so I put my arms around him and held him tight. I could feel him calming. I asked him if he would please turn down the music and he turned the cassette player off. We sat on the edge of his bed, holding hands. I could feel that he was beginning to calm down.

Bill then got up and yelled out the payotte opening, "He's a cunt!" then returned to the edge of the bed and sat down again and lit a cigarette. So, maybe he wasn't that calm.

I took Bill's hand in mine and turned him to me. I had tears in my eyes, thinking about his leaving. I told him that the entire camp would suffer if he left. It was he who had gone to Conakry and found gasoil and loaded up supplies at the PDG warehouse to feed the workers, as well as members of our camp. It was he who had rented a truck to haul everything back. And he did these things with his own money, with no guarantee that DDX would reimburse him. There was not one other member in camp who would have done that. Bill had what it took. The exploration was dead without the workers, all of whom stood with Bill. I asked him to please speak with Lampietti in the morning before he left; after everyone had rested and thought things over.

"Please, Bill. Please, don't quit." I pleaded, giving him one more hug and left.

As I was returning to the kitchen a message came from the workers' camp that Latiff was very ill. I grabbed the first aid kit, and Tony and I went to the camp. Latiff was writhing with stomach pain. I applied gentle pressure to the appendix area. Assured that it wasn't an appendicitis attack, I asked when he had his last bowel movement. The answer shocked me! The man needed a laxative. I gave him some tablets with instructions to take them with lots of water. Raynor showed up and walked Tony and me back to camp.

Fred, Tony, Raynor and I sat around the table discussing the outcome of the meeting until 2:00 A.M. We were all very distressed by Bill's resignation.

May 23rd Friday – When I got up around 7:30 and went to the kitchen, there sat Bill and Lampietti drinking instant coffee. During the early morning hours, the two had reached an agreement. Bill was staying on as camp boss. I felt like crying with joy! But I contained myself.

Lampietti thanked me for the hospitality that I had extended to him and his group. He said that he would be in touch concerning my request for employment next year. However, he cautioned that I was not to bring my son. I would have to make other arrangements for him. Guinea diamond camps were too dangerous for children.

Latiff, feeling himself again, took the tractor to assist Lampietti's party across the river, jokingly asking me if I would like to wade across to guide the fleet.

Tony and Bill went into Kérouané to see the local governor about obtaining extra fuel. They were to return by this evening. I suspected that camp wouldn't see them until tomorrow sometime. Those two would likely be spending the night sleeping on the floor of the bar. I was correct.

I helped Raynor survey – or I had intended to. It was a long walk to the site. We sat down on the hillside overlooking the savannah and floating grass lake. It was so beautiful and peaceful that we ended up sitting there and visiting. There was little accomplished today.

For dinner, I prepared hash, curried rice, beets, and the first zucchini from the garden. This evening was spent listening to Oscar Wilde's play, *The Importance of Being Earnest*. Sitting there with Raynor, having spent most of the afternoon, and now evening, my feelings are going a little deeper than is appropriate.

Particularly considering the growing distance between Fred and me. Raynor has indicated that his feelings are growing deeper, too. We both are aware that this is not the time nor the placc to allow our feelings to grow beyond friendship.

May 24th Saturday – This afternoon, I moved out of the payotte and into a recently vacated tent. It had been Ebrahem's, who had taken over Jean Charlot's payotte. Fred had finally driven me out of our payotte by yelling at me for giving some malaria medication to an ailing homologue, claiming that the supplies belonged to him and weren't to be doled out – especially to the Guineans. They were to receive quinine tablets, only. Quinine tablets were a preventative but did not adequately address the symptoms of malaria. The homologue had come to me in a very ill state.

There were ample supplies of malaria medication. We had gone through less than half of what had been brought. As far as I was concerned, since I had procured and paid for a lot of it before coming to Africa, it was part of our first aid supplies. However, Fred saw things differently. I had accessed his personal supplies.

The entire camp had heard Fred raging at me. After I had moved my satchel of clothing, pillow, and the candlewick bedspread to the tent, Raynor came and said that I needed a walk to calm myself down. We didn't talk, just walked. When Raynor returned me to my new quarters, he told me that Fred was a selfish man and wasn't worth getting upset over. Was he selfish or just driven to do the work he had undertaken, and I had become more of a distraction? For me, love is a hard thing to separate from the heart once it has been given.

Communication between Fred and me had progressively grown more distant and tense. I think that we both knew that something was going to blow up. For me, the tenseness caused me to consistently go to bed with knots in my stomach. Would Fred hold me? Would he speak to me or ignore me when I spoke to him? Would he recoil from my touch? Well, I will feel less lonely sleeping by myself in the tent. Fred seemed in total agreement that it was time for me to leave.

However, later this afternoon, he called me to the payotte. He fastened the door behind me. I thought that it was so that we could have a private conversation. Instead, he practically tore my clothes off, and without my consent, took me sexually. I was very angry, but dared not cry out for fear that half the men in camp would barge in. Should that happen, I don't think that Fred would have fared well. With those thoughts in mind, I was able to calm myself, realizing that Fred lacked the ability to cope with people, including me. My leaving had caused a surge of possessiveness.

He didn't apologize. I didn't expect him to. What he said was that he was ready to be my husband. I couldn't be honest with him at that moment. I couldn't bring myself to tell him that it could never be. I just said that I needed time alone. Still, it was difficult for me to take my heart out that door, knowing that we were never to be lovers, again.

Tony cornered me later, saying that Raynor was becoming emotionally involved with me and Tony worried that someone would be getting hurt. I later spoke with Raynor, echoing Tony's concern. Our friendship had begun to extend beyond just friendship. He had a girlfriend back home and he was not available for romantic involvement. I was feeling damaged from a dysfunctional relationship and romance for me had to be somewhere far down another road. Otherwise, Tony would be right…someone was likely to get hurt.

We mutually agreed to "cool it".

After dinner, which I had managed to prepare under the influence of five or six beers, I read Tarot cards. Back in Idaho, I read cards professionally, as a sideline. I had over forty regular clients. I would frequently "hire out" at parties, where I would dress up as a gypsy, set up my little tent and read for tips. I always read while sober, which I wasn't tonight!

Alan, Tony and Raynor asked me to read their cards. Usually, the cards are read in private, but the guys wanted to see what each other's predicted. Using a Rider-Waite deck, I do a variety of layouts, but tonight it was just the basic Grand Cross using only the major arcana.

With each reading, the death card appeared. The three men enjoyed their readings and a lot of discussion followed. However, at first, I was troubled by the death cards, before realizing the card was probably referring to the death of a camp's relationship – Fred's and mine. That made sense to me, at the time.

Raynor and I were the last to retire. Our goodnight was tense, and I was sorry for the uneasiness in a friendship that had previously been so natural.

The musty tent and uncomfortable folding cot made me realize how sheltered the payotte had been in comparison. The tent flap didn't close all the way, mosquitoes entered, and I now had no net to drape above my bed. But I welcomed the fresh air coming through the unzipped section. Most of the men in camp slept in tents such as this. I laid awake in my unfamiliar surroundings, beneath the bedspread folded in half to give me extra warmth.

A shadow crossed the front of the tent, then stopped. Then crouched. My heart pounded and suddenly I felt alone and unprotected – which I was soon to discover, was far from the truth.

As quietly as I could, I crept from the cot to look through the gap in the tent doorway. Some ghostlike form crouched there.

"Who's there." I said in the firmest voice I could muster under the circumstances.

"Latiff." The answer came. "Go back to sleep. I am protecting you."

He was dressed in a thobe, rather than his regular work clothes.

May 25th Sunday – This morning one of the Guinean camp hunters brought me two large cane rats. At first, I didn't know what I was to do with the big rodents. They were dead, so obviously they weren't brought as pets for Wayde. The worker signed that they were to eat. I thanked him for the gifts, wishing that I had a tin of corned beef to give to him. Instead, I unlocked the storage payotte and indicated that he could choose something from there. He selected one of the three remaining bags of green split peas. Then he indicated that he would skin and clean the rodents for an additional bag. I gladly accepted.

Raynor and I met on the way to the Bog. It seems that the path is becoming a social trail, rather than one traveled due to necessity. We talked a long while and concluded that we should allow our friendship to travel a natural course, rather than try to manipulate it. It had been difficult for us since our discussion yesterday.

David has been quite ill, lately. It tends to come and go, but it doesn't act like malaria. He is pale and lacks an appetite. With what is available to eat in camp, lack of appetite isn't surprising.

Raynor came to my tent this afternoon and showed me some of his pictures of Janis and read me some passages from her letters. They have known each other for three years. By the partial content of her letter that Raynor shared, she seems deeply devoted to him. I can easily understand why. Raynor and I discussed the possibility of Janis and him coming to Idaho someday to visit.

Tony took me aside later and wanted to know what was going on between Raynor and me. I told Tony that Raynor and I intend to remain friends and allow our friendship to grow naturally. Tony still cautioned me that there was more to Raynor's attention than mere friendship.

Sometimes it is hard for Tony to communicate his feelings concerning serious or personal matters, so he writes them down on paper. Tonight was the second time that he has communicated with me in this manner and both times it has been easier for me to understand his true nature. I write my answers to his and we pass the note pad back and forth.

My mood had not at been its best today. The events of the past few days have depressed me. Even Bill sensed my mood and slipped me a note of encouragement.

It read, "I, too, have suffered outrageous misfortune. But I have remained me and intend always to do so."

The camp was out of milk, flour, and cooking oil, so I didn't even have a way to fry the cane rats. I remembered how Dennis had prepared the small deer, African style, by laying the meat directly on the coals and turning it as it roasted.

I built a hot fire and laid the skinned and gutted carcasses directly on the coals. Once I was certain that the animals were thoroughly cooked, I brushed ash from the meat, cut it into pieces and rubbed the pieces with a mixture of finely minced garlic from the garden, African pepper, and lime juice. I domesticated the meal with a side of split pea soup, adding a can of tomato paste to the cooking water to give it some flavor.

At the dinner table, only Raynor asked what the meat was. He seemed satisfied with my answer, "Bush meat."

When I went to my tent this evening, I found a bouquet of wild lilies. Instinctively, I knew that they were from Fred. I went to his payotte to thank him. He said that he was sorry that he hadn't done similar things for me before it was too late.

Again, this evening, Latiff came in his white thobe and crouched in front of my tent.

May 26th Monday – Before daybreak, I awoke to rain on the canvas of the tent. I peeked out of the flap opening and saw Latiff still crouched there. I quickly dressed, then exited the tent.

"Latiff, come to the kitchen and I will fix us some coffee."

He followed me the short distance to the kitchen, and I lit the small campfire set under the shelter of the thatched roof overhang and put the pot of water on the edge of the flames to heat. I added some instant coffee crystals to two mugs. Once the mugs were filled with the steaming water, I carried them to the table and sat across from Latiff.

"Latiff, thank you for guarding me my first night in the tent. I felt safe with you there. Now the tent is my home and I feel safe there alone. Do you understand?"

Latiff nodded as we sipped the hot coffee in silence. Then he stood, nodded, and walked back to the workers' village.

It had continued to rain this morning, but when it cleared a little before noon, Fred, Wayde and Ebrahem took off for a couple of days to visit Banancora. It disappoints me that Fred will readily take off to sight see when he flatly refuses to budge when fuel or food needs to be brought into camp. However, since he would be traveling through villages larger than Kérouané, Fred promised to bring some needed supplies upon his return. He had taken three cases of tomato paste for trade. Raynor had also given Fred fifty sylis of his own money to purchase candles, matches, flashlight batteries and juice for the camp.

Speaking of which, supplies still leak out of the storage payotte, an item here, an item there. I wear the key around my neck. Do we have a food thieving ghost?

Tony, Alan, and Bill took off for Kissidougou to get fuel. Only Raynor, David, a homologue, and I are left in camp. Raynor and I spent the day walking the survey line and returned to camp past 6:00, totally exhausted. We had walked about four kilometers surveying today, much of it through rough terrain. At one point we startled a group of wild pigs. Raynor jumped about three feet in the air when they unexpectedly flushed out of the tall grass. The pigs were equally startled and charged off, squealing. My sides still ache from laughing so hard! We also saw some Guinea fowl and a small crocodile sunning itself along the banks of the Baoule.

Both David and Raynor were feeling out-of-sorts today. I think that Raynor is over-tired. But I feel David's illness may be serious. He is out of it. Raynor slept for a few hours, then I woke him and gave him the mashed potatoes he had requested.

I fixed dinner by moonlight since there is no kerosine or candles for light. There are two small candles and a flashlight that are being held back for emergencies. Things are bound to improve.

May 27th Tuesday – No one returned today. Tony's party was expected.

David has been extremely ill. He has lost weight, and he says this throat hurts. Since he complains of night sweats, I make certain that he has extra filtered water to drink. Normally he gets up and goes to the hydraulic pits, regardless of his lack of energy. But this morning, he felt too weak to do that. Raynor expressed concern, also. If there were a place in this part of Guinea, with a medical service, Raynor said that he would take him there. Perhaps in Conakry. David doesn't seem interested in getting things checked out, since the severity of his illness comes and goes. After a couple days of having no energy, he rallies and returns to work for a couple of days.

With David's absence today, there were labor disputes. The Banka drillers refused to cross the river because it was running too high and swift, plus they said that there were crocodiles in the area, and they were afraid to enter the water. The Sierra Leones and the Guinean workers at Bill's hydraulic Pit #5 had an argument among themselves and quit working. The tractor broke down, so Fred's team of workers could not move the drill to the new drilling site.

Poor Raynor. He was beside himself. With all the workers idle and complaining, they trouped into our camp with various desires. They wanted a little salt, which the camp finally had after Bill's trip to Conakry. Their shoulders hurt and needed muscle rub liniment; a little sugar for their tea; a minor cut tended to; an extra cup of rice; aspirin – you name it, they wanted it. These were not unreasonable requests, but they put stress on Raynor.

Additionally, Dennis, the camp helper, was ill and said he couldn't work. I took over his chores of cooking breakfast, hauling water to be boiled and filtered, building, and tending the cook fire. Fortunately, there were just Raynor, David and me, so the few extra chores were not a burden. However, the table holding the water filters collapsed, denting the canisters, and leaving us temporarily short of water.

As I said, poor Raynor. He looked at me with a haggard expression and said, "What if Bill had resigned in earnest? I don't think that I would make a good camp boss!"

I picked some fiddlehead ferns to cook up as fresh greens for David. Later in the afternoon Raynor and I went out with the range finder to measure a broad channel by the Baoule Stream. I drove the Land Rover again today. I am amazed at the places one of those things can go. It is the only functioning vehicle left in camp and I was apprehensive that I would get it bogged down in a mud hole. But that didn't happen.

David had slept all day. I woke him up this evening to eat the food I had prepared for him. The steamed fiddleheads were tasty with the salt. David ate them, plus the last cucumber from the garden. He also ate quite a bit of the chicken and dumplings that I had prepared. However, we are all weary of a diet of canned meat and are hoping that Tony brings some fresh beef when he returns.

Just as I was finishing cleaning up the kitchen, the darkening sky clouded over, and it began pouring down rain. We have no light except for the emergency flashlight. Raynor and I sat in the dark kitchen and listened to the remainder of Raynor's tape, *The Importance of Being Earnest*, while rain pelted the thatched roof.

With Fred away, I slept in his payotte under the protection of the mosquito net and luxuriated in clean sheets and a warm blanket. It was a treat compared to sleeping in the cramped tent on the small cot, with its sagging, lumpy mattress. Plus, having a warm blanket instead of the skimpy, candlewick bedspread that provided little warmth against the night's chill.

I listened to the rain and wind as it raged through the trees outside the payotte. I wondered where I will be in a month…or a year from now.

May 28th Wednesday – Raynor woke me from my peaceful sleep. It was time to prepare breakfast, since Dennis was still feeling ill. David, however, was feeling much better and was eager for breakfast.

After breakfast I spent the remainder of the morning doing the laundry. The morning was overcast, the creek was swollen, and the air chilly after last night's rainstorm. During the afternoon I studied some French and composed my formal letter of employment application to Mr. Lampietti.

Wayde, Fred and Ebrahem returned from visiting the Aredor mine just as I was getting ready to prepare dinner. I was excited to have Wayde home and to hear about his adventure. I was also eager for the goods that they had brought with them for the camp.

Fred unloaded a big box of produce from the Land Rover, consisting of bananas, onions, oranges, potatoes, and juice. Wayde followed, carrying candles, batteries, and matches. Instead of heading to the storage payotte, Fred marched past the kitchen to his own payotte, Wayde following behind, and deposited the items there. Then he returned to the kitchen and informed us that he would dole out the supplies as he saw fit.

I thought that Raynor was going to fly right out of his chair and assault Fred! I wanted to, myself! But Raynor controlled his anger. I was able to talk Fred out of a banana, one small candle and a bottle of juice for Wayde, Raynor, David, and me.

During his trip, Fred had witnessed ten clandestine miners under arrest, being marched between two armed guards. The prisoners were tied together with bush ropes.

I had prepared extra food for this evening's meal, expecting Tony, Bill, and Alan to arrive from Kissidougou, but they had not. Assuming that they couldn't obtain what was needed in Kissidougou, I surmised that they had to go on to Conakry.

Just as I was finishing the dishes, Bill puffed into the camp. He was on foot and out of breath. The Land Rover is at the Madena crossing, opposite the Sonamba River, unable to ford. Alan is waiting there. Tony had heard that a truck with gasoil was enroute to Kissidougou and stayed to meet it. When it didn't show up, Tony caught a ride to Conakry with Jean Charlot, who had been in Kissidougou at PDG guest house. Bill said that while they were in at Jean Paul's, there were several messages that came through on the now functional radio.

Tys has resigned from his post at the Sultan House and Jean Charlot will be filling the vacated position.

When recalling the second radio relayed message, Bill's face was red with rage. In the future, no member of DDX will be allowed to visit the Aredor mine. Fred had spent one night at Aredor, then told to leave. He had done too much snooping around, entering forbidden and secure areas. Against the security guard's orders, he also took photographs of the mine's Poclain in action. Aredor mine had previously provided a back-up supply for machinery and vehicle parts when something was urgently needed in one of DDX's mines. No more. Lampietti had been scheduled for a visit on June 8th. That has now been canceled. And my growing friendship with Ola? Once ousted from Aredor, Fred and Wayde's second night had been spent at Ebrahem's house in Bounoudou.

Bill angrily chastised Fred for his "arrogant and inconsiderate" actions at the Aredor mine. Fred turned and walked away before Bill could finish his tirade.

Tony will stay in Conakry until he can acquire several barrels of gasoil to bring back to camp in a rented truck.

I rode with Raynor and David to pick up Alan. He had gotten a ride across the river on the dugout canoe. Once back in camp I reheated some dinner for Bill and Alan. Bill still appears pale and exhausted. I am certain that his confrontation with Fred didn't help. I hoped the food would perk him up, but he hardly ate.

Alan Kingston is taller than Raynor by a couple of inches. He has curly brown hair and brown eyes. Alan is basically quiet and soft-spoken. I thought that Raynor was immaculate, but Alan?

He always looks as though he just stepped out of the pages of a men's clothing catalog. He wears matching briefs, T-shirts, and socks…I know this because I do his laundry. He also wears pajamas. I met him by the light of a quarter moon when returning down the path from the Bog. He was endearing – looking like a over-stretched little boy.

Alan doesn't care for camping or isolated places. Why Guinea then?

"It was all just a big mistake." He claimed.

His main ambition is to find the right woman, marry and have a family. He still lives with his family in London when he is not roaming the world. He has worked as a surveyor in many, many countries.

Alan enjoys playing Squash. He is warm hearted and kind to everyone. I have never heard him speak unkindly to or about anyone in camp, including Fred. He loves hard rock music. Funny, I would have thought that it would have been classical.

May 29th Thursday – When items that were retrieved from the Land Rover this morning, I had mail! My Guinean I.D. card arrived. Thank you, Mr. Lampietti! There was also a letter from Sue Ryan. She had received the copy of *How to Prepare Common Wild Foods* that I had Mom send her and was enjoying looking at the recipes. Sue said she particularly liked the cover.

I spent a good part of the day napping. Last night it had stormed. I had gotten up to go to the Bog and got completely soaked on the way back to my tent. I didn't have anything dry to put on, since the rain had seeped into the tent soaking everything. I shivered through the night, with only the damp bedspread for covering. I don't know how Jean Charlot managed to live in this tent. I had felt a surge of warmth at the thought of him now in charge of the Sultan House!

It has continued to rain all day. Bill, who is looking much better this morning, David, Raynor, Alan, Wayde and I crowded around the kitchen table drinking instant coffee or sweet tea and playing card games. Fred has sequestered himself in his payotte, amid his hoarded supplies, to work on reports.

There was enough food from yesterday to have leftovers today. Alan had carried a large ripe papaya on his lap all the way from Kissidougou and presented it to me. I shared most of it with the camp members, keeping a sizable sliver for myself.

By late evening the rain had ceased. Everyone had retired but Alan. He had told me privately that he was going to sit in the dark kitchen all night to see if he could catch the thief who had been stealing food from the storage payotte. Since he and Bill had brought several cases of food from the Kissidougou warehouse, Alan figured a theft may occur tonight. If not, he would continue his vigilance tomorrow night.

A couple of hours later I heard Alan at my tent's doorway, awaking me from a deep sleep.

"I caught the thief," he announced.

I hastily dressed, imagining a distressed worker from one of the camps, tied to a support post.

There stood Wayde, dressed only in his underwear, his face streaked with tears. He had entered the back of the storage payotte by wiggling through a small space that he had worked loose from the wall to be secured back into place upon leaving. Raynor had heard rustling within the structure and quietly approached. A group of Guinean children took off as soon as they spotted Raynor. Raynor stood where the children had been, and here came Wayde, wiggling out with a handful of canned tuna.

"You have no business doing what you have done! This is not your food. Have you any understanding of the hardships that you have created in camp by your thieving!" Alan scolded Wayde.

By now, there were other members of the camp witnessing Wayde's disgrace. Tears were streaming down his face. "They are my friends. They need food. I know it was wrong to take the food. But it doesn't make me a bad person."

Wayde then ran to his payotte, his face still streaked with tears.

Bill looked at me and said, "Let me go talk to him, I think that you are a little too upset to do that now."

May 30th Friday – There was some excitement early this morning. One of the payottes in the workers' camp burned down. Luckily, Momodu was returning from a late-night hunt and saw the flames in time to get everyone out. After the emotions of earlier this morning, I had slept through the excitement.

After doing some laundry for Fred and Raynor, I went to Kérouané with Alan, Latiff, a homologue, and some workers, who were to repair some of the road to the village. Dennis was also riding with us.

Bill fired Dennis this morning. Bill has long suspected that Dennis had been pilfering things from Bill's tent when he was away. When he returned from Conakry a couple of days ago, his compass was missing. While Dennis was cooking breakfast for the camp, Bill walked down to Dennis's payotte and found the compass sitting on a shelf.

Bill also had learned that Dennis was responsible for stirring up trouble among the Guinean workers, against our camp members. Dennis makes bold claims that he has special African powers and can cast spells when he is displeased, so the Guinean workers fear him and do his bidding.

Upon being fired, Dennis threatened Bill with unleashing his voodoo powers, but Bill laughed at that and told Dennis, "You're fired, Cunt! Get your things together and get out."

Dennis begged Bill for mercy, claiming he would never steal again or raise trouble among the workers. When Bill flatly refused to relent, Dennis let out an evil hiss and returned to his payotte. An hour later he was calmly standing by the Land Rover with his backpack and bedroll, ready to leave.

The trip to Kérouané went smoothly, we only got stuck once. We let the homologue and workers off at a particularly challenging set of potholes to repair.

In the village, Latiff got the tractor part repaired. Momodu sold 7,000 sylis worth of powdered eggs and tomato paste. Alan and I did the fresh food shopping. Afterward, Alan treated me to a Coca Cola at a little slot of a shop that had a small kerosine refrigerator and a few bottles of soda. Civilization at its best! Well, when compared to camp, it is.

On the way back to camp, we picked up the workers who had spent the day doing road repair. Just a couple of kilometers further, the right, rear wheel fell off the Land Rover. We had to walk 15 kilometers back to camp in the dark, the workers carrying our purchases on their heads – safari style. We arrived at camp around 10:30, tired and hungry after the long trek through the dark jungle with only occasional moonlight lighting up clearings.

Meat had been purchased in Kérouané, so I fixed a late-night dinner of brochettes, insisting that the workers join us. They had, after all, carried our various purchases nine miles on their heads. We ate fresh bananas for dessert. While enjoying brochettes and bananas, Alan and I gloated over the cold cola we had enjoyed. Each Coca Cola had cost the equivalent of seven U.S. dollars. Fred commented that he could not possibly drink a seven-dollar cola; it would literally make him ill! The table erupted into laughter at the remark.

Bill is leaving in the morning to go to Kissidougou to drop off a group of workers. He made the difficult decision to downsize. With the difficulty of acquiring enough fuel and food for the workers to keep the mining exploration functioning at capacity, some of the pits were being closed until next year. Bill would be overnighting at the guest house and wondered if he could take Wayde. He thought that Wayde might enjoy spending some time with Jean Paul's children. I agreed. It was a good idea.

May 31st Saturday – Bill Davis died in the Sonamba River at the Madina crossing around 1:30 this afternoon. His body was recovered by Alan Kingston and David McDonald at 3:00 P.M.

The Madena crossing dugout canoe was being loaded with gear to be transported to the Land Rover waiting on the opposite shore. Bill decided to swim across the river and plunged in. He was not seen again. None of the workers witnessed Bill go under, so both sides of the banks were searched for him. One of the Madina natives volunteered to run up the trail to the village to see if he had swum the river and walked up to the village.

Meanwhile a runner headed across the six kilometers to camp, meeting David and Ebrahem eating lunch.

“Mr. Bill partis dans leau!” “Mr. Bill partis dans leau!”

David jumped in a Land Rover and headed for Madena crossing. Ebrahem raced to the workers’ camp where Raynor, Alan and I were waiting for Momodu to gather his gear. The four of us were heading to Banancora for a couple of days.

Ebrahem’s message was unclear. He was saying “Mr. Bill partis dans leau! Mr. Bill partis dans leau!”

It wasn’t until he collapsed beside the road weeping hysterically that we became concerned. Raynor, Alan, and I jumped in the Land Rover and headed for Madina crossing, passing Fred and Latiff loading water barrels into the tractor for cooling the jumper drill.

Raynor shouted, "There has been some sort of accident at the Madina crossing."

Fred called back that he would follow in the tractor.

What had happened! Where was my son! Did Bill decide to try to drive the Land Rover across the river and it bogged down or…tipped over? I began to shake violently. I have never experienced such terror! Where was Wayde? Had my son entered the river, too? Both Raynor and Alan tried to be reassuring, attempting to keep me calm during the seemingly endless drive to the river.

When we reached the crossing, I jumped out of the Land Rover and ran to the edge of the river. There, on the opposite shore, stood my son, barefooted and wearing his khaki shorts. I will never forget my feelings at that moment, my eyes clouded with tears of relief.

We stood waiting for the slow-moving dugout canoe to reach us. When we reached the other side, I grabbed Wayde and hugged him tightly, my heart still beating frantically at the thought of what might have happened to him.

Wayde pulled away from me and stood solemn but composed. David and seven or eight locals were diving in the river. Raynor asked Wayde what had happened and was told that Bill had decided to swim across since the dugout was fully loaded, and he didn't want to wait for it to unload and return.

Wayde pointed to the widest and calmest part of the backwash and said, "He came up there. Just once. Then went back under. He never came back up."

Then Wayde broke down and sobbed in my arms. Finally, one of the Malinke women from Madina, gently took his arm and led him toward the village.

It was hard to believe that Bill would have gone under there; so calm and so close to shore. More than thirty minutes had passed since Bill had disappeared.

Finally, one of the local men swam out into the backwash, dove down, surfaced with a frightened yell, and wildly thrashed to shore. Alan swam to the spot and came up with Bill's body. David swam out and helped bring Bill to shore. A sand bar was only four or five feet from where Bill had been located. The workers had been preparing to cross in the dugout not more than twenty feet away. No one had heard a cry for help.

Now there were thirty or forty Malinke from Madina, lined up along the river's bank, plus the workers. As Bill's body was lifted from the water they clapped in unison. Two claps. Clap…clap.

The Malinke recognize nyama as a wild energy, the pulsating force in nature. It is present in rocks, trees, animals, people – all that inhabit the Earth. It is like our Western concept of the soul, only more complex. Nyama controls nature, the stars, the moon, the motions of the sea. Its existence is independent of its material form.

Clap. Clap. Bill's niyama was released and is now one with the wind.

The wailing followed, deep, mournful, primeval. Bill was gone. I didn't want to believe it. But I was weeping, too, because I could see that it was so. He had been in the water for nearly an hour and was tinged blue from his waist up and his body had begun to stiffen. Someone handed me a cloth and I covered his body.

Fred and Latiff showed up with the tractor. From the opposite shore Fred saw the still form beneath the cloth. He yelled across to us to start artificial respiration. We who had witnessed Bill being lifted from the water knew that it was too late.

Fred jumped into the river and swam across, then rushed to Bill and flung away the covering to begin artificial respiration. I must hand it to Fred, that took a lot of guts. When Fred began to tire, Alan took over. Then Fred worked on Bill, again. David tried to take over when Fred became exhausted, but David became physically ill. I stood numbly by, glad that Wayde had been taken to Madina before Bill's body had been recovered. Another thirty minutes had passed.

Finally, David and Alan physically lifted Fred from Bill. Fred broke down and wept.

Bill's body was carried to the shade, and we spent the next six hours wetting down his corpse. A Land Rover had to go to Kérouané to bring back the officials. At 7:00 P.M. they arrived – the governor, a doctor, the chief of police, and several PDG officials.

After Bill's body was examined, it was discussed that he could be buried near Madina. Most agreed, but Alan Kingston and I did not. Bill had recently become engaged to Margaret. He had a mother in Wales that he had been extremely close to. I also knew that his family were members of the Church of Wales. Bill needed to go home to be buried there.

Alan volunteered to take Bill to the small airport in Kissidougou, where his body could be flown to Conakry. To save time he would take the rugged back way, that which Latiff and I had traveled after losing track of Tony. Brian Loyd, also from Wales, was at the Saltan House in Conakry. Alan would radio him from Jean Paul's, so that Brian could make arrangements to get Bill the remainder of the way to Wales.

Raynor, now acting camp boss, granted Alan the use of the Land Rover. Bill's bloating body was loaded in the back. Alan requested from me "a kiss and a hug for luck". Alan and I clung to each other and sobbed. Ebrahem had volunteered to accompany Alan. I gave Ebrahem a big hug, too. This was not going to be an easy journey for them.

The night was lit by nearly a full moon, its light shimmering across the water flowing peacefully beneath it, as though no tragedy had taken place in its depths. I walked up the moonlit trail to Madina to get Wayde and thank the woman who had taken him to the village, where he'd been playing with local children.

We all returned to camp. At the kitchen table we sat in quiet with heavy hearts, exhausted from the long stressful day. No one was hungry, but I opened cans of tuna and set out some soggy Pringles. The meager offering got nibbled on. The big question was, "What happened?"

The homologues, who had joined us in sorrow, said that it had been Dennis's curse that struck Bill down. They said that most of the workers, as well as most of the men from Madena, were hunting him.

According to regional Malinke belief, one of the greatest threats to an individual comes from witches or sorcerers – men and women endowed with the power, unconsciously or voluntarily, to direct sickness, death, or other misfortunes toward others. Trial by ordeal is an ancient judicial practice by which the guilt or innocence of the accused is determined by subjecting the person to a painful or dangerous experience. Their physical reaction to the process proves their innocence or guilt. However, even rumor or suspicion is frequently sufficient to indict a person for sorcery and suffer the wrath of the community. Bill had been much loved by the people of Madina. News of Dennis's curse had spread through the village. Dennis will disappear, either by escape…or tribal justice.

I was asked what my opinion was. Having seen Bill's exhaustion coming in to camp a couple of nights ago, plus his confrontation with Lampietti, then again with Dennis, combined with his heavy smoking and beer consumption, I believed that Bill had died of a heart attack.

I retired to my cot in the tent. Shortly after everyone else had left the kitchen for the solace of their quarters, Fred came.

"I don't want to be alone tonight," he said.

Neither did I. I followed him to his payotte. We clung to each other and wept ourselves to sleep. I had seen another side of Fred, today. He isn't all arrogance and bluster, after all. I hope that Fred finds someone who can love him unconditionally, because that is what it would take to be with this man. He is a good man in many ways but would make a difficult partner. As the adage goes, he does not play well with others. And I am one of the others.

Section Three
June 1 – June 8

June 1st Sunday – Tony came to camp this morning. He had gotten into Kérouané last night around 11:00. In the morning he had spotted the Land Rover, which had taken the authorities back to Kérouané late last evening. Momodu had driven them to the village and spent the night in the vehicle.

When Tony approached the Land Rover, he spotted Momodu asleep in the vehicle and shook him awake. Momodu, red eyed, told Tony that Bill was dead, then ran off and never came back.

When Tony arrived in camp, the first thing that he asked Raynor was, “Where’s Bill!”

Tony was told that Bill drowned at Madina crossing. Tony broke down. It was difficult for him to accept what had happened. The whole camp was in shock. As with the rest of us, he was grieved that there was no way that we could find out if Alan and Ebrahem had been able to get Bill to the airport and flown home. We were all in the dark. Tony was extremely distressed that there was no way that we could offer condolences to Bill’s family.

Tony’s fresh grief made everyone’s depression deepen, so Fred, Raynor and David took off to Pit #4 to wash gravel, finding six diamonds. With Bill no longer in charge, all the workers refused to work and wanted to go back to their villages. Therefore, Bill’s pit #5, which he had been so determined to finish before season’s end, will not be completed this season. All the rice and corned beef that Bill went all the way to Conakry to bring back to last until season’s end, will not be used.

I stayed in camp and tried to console Tony. He wanted to take off and walk to Aredor – over the mountain to a road and then twenty kilometers further, which was the closest radio to contact Conakry. I managed to talk him out of that, so his next plot was to drive to Kissidougou to make certain that Alan had arrived. Again, I talked him out of that plan. If Alan hadn't gotten to Kissidougou, what would Tony do then? It was a two-day journey one way. Finally, Tony went to his tent and fell asleep. He had been traveling for two days with little or no sleep, and very little food.

Tomorrow we will take a Land Rover to Kérouané, along with the tractor, hoping to meet Alan.

I had just hung up the wash when the wind picked up. I began snatching the laundry from the lines when a torrential rain came. It sheeted down as strong gusts of wind wreaked havoc. Wayde's payotte caved in; my tent collapsed as one of the aluminum poles snapped in half. The wind swept the table clean of bottles and cups. Alan's tent blew about ten feet, coming to rest against a mahogany tree. Everything was soaking wet.

David, Fred and Raynor arrived in the Land Rover as Tony was crawling out of his drenched dwelling. We all rushed around grabbing up things and cramming them into Fred's payotte – the only dwelling beside the kitchen and the storage payotte that hadn't suffered damage.

Everyone scurried around trying to find enough dry wood to start a fire in the kitchen firepit. The rain and wind continue its destruction as we rushed around trying to minimize the damage. We worked in unison, and in relief. It was the first time since Bill's death that we weren't weighted down with a sense of helplessness. Africa's WAWA came to the rescue and gave us a temporary reprieve from our deep despair.

Soon the kitchen payotte resembled a gypsy camp with wet clothing, sleeping bags and bedding dangling from the ceiling and pinned to the walls hoping to have something dry to bundle up in before nightfall.

Once a fire was roaring in the kitchen firepit, and the rain and wind had eased, I prepared a meal of mashed potatoes, corned beef gravy with dumplings and canned corn. Tony had brought chocolate from Socamer for dessert.

Now I sit in my wet, but resurrected tent, feeling lost as sadness reclaims its hold. Bill had written a note to me just a couple of days ago, when I was feeling down – "I, too, have suffered outrageous misfortune. But I have remained me and intend always to do so."

I read this bit of Bill wisdom as we all sat in the kitchen finishing our meal. We decided that this would be an appropriate quote put on Bill's marker to be placed at Madina crossing.

June 2nd Monday – Early in the morning I drove Raynor and Tony to the base line on the flats. I had to maneuver around several trees which had fallen across the road.

Later Tony and I went to Kérouané in the Land Rover in the hopes of meeting Alan. Last night's storm had downed a great many trees, snapping some into two and uprooting others. But the wind had apparently been brisker in Kaya, downing one huge mango tree and several smaller ones. It was difficult to maneuver around, but Tony managed.

We had picked up a severely ill woman and her infant at Kaya. She laid in the back of the Land Rover and was attended to by another Kaya woman. I gave the woman some aspirin to help make the journey easier, but she was in a worse way when we arrived in Kérouané. She was hospitalized in the unsanitary, fly infested facilities that resemble horse stalls.

Tony spotted Jean Paul's Land Rover coming through town and flagged him down. Alan was with him. The Land Rover that Alan had driven to Kissidougou was somewhere between Kissidougou and Kankan. Ebrahem and the other homologue, Sly, were with it. Alan and Jean Paul had waited in Kankan for three hours before proceeding on. Jean Paul will double back on that route in a couple of days if the missing vehicle hasn't returned.

Bill's body arrived in Kissidougou at 6:00 A.M. Sunday morning. Alan had had many problems driving the muddy route and had extreme difficulty crossing the same bridge that Latiff and I had fallen through on May 1st. Another bridge had to be constructed while vehicles waited. It took nine hours.

Once in Kissidougou, Lampietti was contacted in Conakry via radio and immediately chartered an airplane to Kissidougou, He was very distressed and saddened by the news of Bill's death. He has delayed his return to the Paris office until camp is disassembled and we all get out of Guinea safely.

Bill's body accompanied Lampietti to Conakry. Bill's mother and fiancée had not been contacted, yet.

Jean Paul will stay at our camp a couple of days to discuss the quickest method of dismantling camp. He will also begin making our flight arrangements out of the country.

Latiff arrived at Kérouané with the tractor around 6:00 this evening. He had come to bring Alan's rig across the Milo and found Jean Paul's instead. Latiff and the tractor followed our vehicles in case we got stuck. Jean Paul's Land Rover bogged down once but managed to work its way out. The remainder of the trip back to camp went smoothly.

Raynor heated up some rissoles that he'd made for our dinner while I prepared a green salad and sliced fruit from produce purchased at Kissidougou. After washing the dinner dishes, I retired at 10:30, which was early for me.

June 3rd Tuesday – Around 6:00 A.M. Ebrahem and Sly walked into camp, exhausted. The Land Rover had gotten stuck trying to get around the big, downed mango tree. The vehicle had lost its 4-wheel drive. Tony, Alan, and a couple of workers took off to get it unstuck. They also took saws to cut the big tree into sections, hoping the tractor will come along and remove them. However, the tractor hadn't returned. Tony and Alan continued to Kérouané expecting to find Latiff and the tractor. It wasn't found along the way. It must have broken down somewhere in the village.

There are no longer any Guinean camp helpers, so Raynor and I hauled extra water for the shower. Wayde helped me boil water for the Berkeys and scrub the filters.

After cooking and serving breakfast, I began lunch preparation of a hot stew to feed the ten men now in camp. It was again pouring down rain and everyone was soaking wet and would welcome something hot to eat. After lunch, I swept the kitchen clean of leaves and termite dust. Just as I was finishing up, Fred suggested that I organize the contents of the storage payotte.

While I struggled with heavy boxes and shelving, Fred sat at the table and squeezed the camp's remaining limes into a glass to make himself some limeade. Standing at the storage doorway, sipping his drink, Fred began instructing me on how to arrange the contents of the storage room.

I lost my temper! Fred got a good, loud, angry tongue lashing! He had never seen me lose my temper. I think that I had his hair standing on end. He quickly backed away before I started hurling cans of corned beef at him. That man certainly has a lot of nerve!

Fred is not the most popular person in camp today. Despite Lampietti's orders, Fred wants to stay in camp a couple more weeks. The fifty sample holes that he had been required to drill had been completed ten days ago. Yes, he succeeded in being the most productive Camp A employee.

While everyone else in camp worked at bringing in camp supplies and fuel, Fred drilled holes. When members volunteered to take turns to go to Kérouané for fresh produce and meat, Fred drilled holes and washed samples. As everyone now works to disassemble the camp, Fred drills holes. Now Tony and Alan are digging out a bogged down Land Rover and cutting up a large tree blocking the road, what had Fred done? He slept in, then tried to boss me around while drinking the last limes in camp!

Yes, Fred was hired to dig holes. Everyone here was hired to do a specific job – except for me. I was to be here as Fred's wife, with no specific duties. But we all have worked at multiple things to keep this project functional.

To cool my anger, I walked to the creek and sat near the water. As I watched the small, colorful guppy-like fish, the bewilderment regarding Fred began to ease into understanding. I still loved Fred, but not in the way that I once had.

For a time, I had held out hope that somehow things would work out between us. However, these past few weeks changed any prospect of spending my life with Fred. He is brilliant. He is goal driven. These are good things. But he may also accomplish his goals at the detriment of others if need be. He charges toward his goal with blinders on – seeing only his objective, failing to notice or acknowledge those working beside him. He is driven, but without clear vision.

Later, I walked to the forest to pick fiddleheads for our dinner tonight. While there I found mushrooms. They were brown gilled and strongly resembled an edible *Agaricus* that I was familiar with in Idaho forests. I ate a small portion of one. An hour later, I still didn't feel any stomach distress, so I returned to the patch and ate an entire button. If I have no stomach distress or problems by tomorrow morning, I will return and harvest them. I also found some strange-looking fruits growing from the base of a tree. They looked and tasted like figs. There were only three, I stuck them in my pocket to eat later, after I was certain that there would be no reaction to the mushrooms.

Tony and Alan arrived just before dinner. Several bolts had been sheared from the tractor wheel and Latiff had managed to get it back to Kérouané to seek repairs. There was no machinist that had what was needed to do the work, so Latiff slowly drove it back to camp with Tony and Alan following in the Land Rover. Tony can weld it but may have to go to Sierra Leone to find the needed parts. We need the tractor to get us all out of Baoule Flats.

Following dinner and under the scrutiny of the homologues, diamonds gathered from the sample drillings were weighed and classified at the dinner table. No more diamonds will be collected this year. David has already dismantled his pumps and water pipes.

It will now be just a matter of days before I leave here. I really don't want to leave. My love for this place fills my heart. The love for the members of the camp does also! I am at home here. I went to bed with my stomach knotted in sorrow at the loss of Bill, and the upcoming closing of camp.

June 4th Wednesday – It was Tony's birthday, today. When Latiff made the trip to Kérouané with the tractor this morning, to make certain that John Paul and his Land Rover were able to get across the Milo, he was given funds. His instructions were to bring back meat for brochettes and use his connections to source five of the small bottles of Gin, plus some mango juice to make the liquor palatable.

John Paul arrived in camp, but there had been no sign of Latiff.

I began the kitchen and pantry inventory list, then spent the remainder of the day washing clothes. I also went back into the forest to gather the mushrooms that I had discovered yesterday.

For dinner I had made a side dish of sauteed fiddleheads and mushrooms to go with the brochettes. I also made a large fresh fruit salad, as well as an avocado, cucumber, and cheese salad. The cheese was from Jean Paul.

Since Latiff and the tractor still hadn't shown up with meat and Gin, we sat around eating our vegetarian meal and drinking warm beer, while worrying about Latiff and the tractor. Tony will have to go look for it tomorrow morning.

Raynor and I spent some time together as I listened to Raynor read poetry from his book, *The Collected Poems of A. E. Houseman.* Fred was reading in his payotte until around 2:00 A.M. Alan had retired early but couldn't sleep and returned to the kitchen. We had a visit going over the events of the past few days.

Late this evening, it poured down rain. My bed was a sorry mess, but I spent most of the night in it anyway. Water flooded through my tent floor. My biggest worry was that snakes would take refuge on my bed.

June 5th Thursday – Tony and David took off for Kérouané early this morning to track down Latiff and the tractor. They returned by dinnertime. The tractor, one wheel shorn off, remains sitting in the middle of the road. John Paul had taken a barge across the river. He came across Latiff and the tractor five kilometers later, stranded in the middle of the road. He didn't bother to stop, leaving Latiff on foot with the crippled tractor. John Paul never mentioned that he had seen Latiff or the tractor after arriving in camp, even after hearing our concerns around the dinner table.

Members of the camp had not been pleased with Jean Paul's inability to do his job, which included keeping our camp supplied with fuel, food, and parts for machinery maintenance. With this latest development, he was now downright despised.

Tomorrow Tony, David, and Latiff will have to return and attempt to repair the tractor.

It rained some, today. I spent several hours getting things sorted and scrubbed down in the kitchen. We are supposed to be leaving on Sunday or Monday. A trailer will be rented to transport our equipment to Kérouané, and then a rented truck will transfer the equipment to Kissidougou to be stored at PDG warehouse that Jean Paul oversees.

Two out of the four Land Rovers are operating; the other two must be repaired before our departure.

I don't know whether Wayde and I will be leaving Kissidougou for the United States right away. We could stay in Kissidougou for a few days then go into the field with Alan and Howard Bills as camp cook. They have some additional work to do, as a mobile survey camp for DDX. Or, we could go to Freetown with Tony, Raynor and David for a week.

I took the opportunity to catch up on some sleep in the damp tent so that I would be perky enough to fix Tony a special dinner for his belated birthday celebration.

Tony prepared the brochettes, while I made a pot of rice and heated up some canned green beans. Then I surprised him with a mango upside-down birthday cake with a lime glaze. After a few mugs of Gin and mango juice, I wandered off to my tent and fell asleep.

Tony came and woke me and cajoled me to rejoin the party. Tony and Raynor ended up in a lively debate about Jean Paul, which continued until 1:30 A.M. This evening Raynor gave me his highly prized book of A. E. Houseman's poetry. He had inscribed it:

To Darcy,
"What thoughts at heart have you and I
We cannot stop to tell
But dead or living, drunk or dry,
Soldier, I wish you well."

XXII, p. 28.
Raynor Shaw
Baoule' Valley,
West Africa
June 1980

June 6th Friday – Tony, David and Latiff went to attempt to repair the tractor and have yet to return. I had loads of laundry to do since rain had soaked and soured everyone's clothing and bedding, especially Tony's, which consisted of a large duffle bag crammed full.

This afternoon Alan and I walked up the trail leading beyond the Bog and discovered a freshly dug clandestine pit not twenty yards beyond. They must have worked in the dark of night, but I can't understand how they did it so quietly.

The afternoon was spent moving Tony's tent, which was located inside of a very leaky payotte. It was relocated beneath a couple of trees where his bed and flooring may not get so soaking wet.

Dinner consisted of curried canned chicken and rice. We are all weary of eating tinned food, especially meat. Last night's brochettes were so good!

Tony and David returned late tonight with parts to fix the tractor. They had checked on the Madina woman that had been taken to the Kérouané hospital, in case she was well enough to get a ride home and received sad news. The baby had died the evening that they had arrived, and the mother, the following day.

Tony and the Tractor WAWA

June 7th Sunday – I awoke to now familiar sounds. In the distance was the warning call of a Guinea rooster, "Chi-chi-chi", followed by the loud, raucous, and desperate calls of his small flock of hens, "Come back, come back, come back".

This morning, I rode with Tony and a crew of workers to repair the tractor's shorn wheel. Two Land Rovers were taken, Fred driving the second, in case one got stuck in the mud. It took eight men to lift the wheel onto the tractor, and they had to use levers, at that.

On the way, we dropped Frank, the pup, off in Kaya. The chief said that he would take good care of Frank. The only animal left now is Sange, the monkey. David is taking Sange to Conakry.

While in Kérouané, Fred had purchased three small raw diamonds from a local man, paying him with one of the cheap watches that had been purchased in Dakar, and one of the "gold' nuggets acquired from the Dakarian swindler.

Enroute, we passed a large snake lying in the road, that I thought was a boa. Tony and I moved it from the road with a long stick so that it wouldn't get run over by the tractor. The workers wanted to kill the snake and sell it for medicine, but Tony would not let them do it. We finished our business in Kérouané around

5:30 and reached camp a little after 7:00 with beef and Gin to celebrate our last evening here. The tractor had picked up the large trailer which will be used to load the camp's equipment and our personal belongings.

On our way back to camp I spotted the snake, still lying beside the road and asked Tony to stop. I got out of the Land Rover and approached the snake. It had died. I lifted it up by the back of its neck. The snake's skin had a beautiful geometric pattern in white, black, tan, and yellow. I took the snake with me back to camp. I wanted to remove the skin when we reached Kissidougou or Conakry to preserve it.

David McDonald had a copy of Raymond Ditmars' book, *Reptiles of the World*. We found the snake listed in the volume. It is a Gaboon viper. According to the book, Gaboon vipers are solitary and nocturnal. They are most active early in the night around sunset when they emerge from hiding places to search for food. While hunting, they find a spot among the leaf-covered floor of their habitat and lie perfectly still, waiting for prey to approach. This species of viper has a thick body, and a triangle-shaped head, where it stores large venom sacs and fangs. On the tip of the Gaboon's head are a set of extended scales which have the appearance of rhinoceros horns.

Gaboon vipers have an average length of four to six feet and can weigh up to twenty pounds. The one that Tony and I found was a young snake, approximately three and a half feet long. Like all other vipers, it is venomous. It has the longest fangs of any venomous snake – up to two inches in length – and the highest venom yield of any viper. They are considered one of the fastest-striking snakes in the world. However, bites from this species are extremely rare because they are seldom aggressive.

We lingered over our meal of roasted meat, rice, canned corn, and a fruit salad. I left the kitchen around 10:00, having nothing to celebrate. I was leaving camp, and soon I would be leaving Guinea as well. I have great hopes of returning next season. But what if I don't? What if this is the end of my being here?

Down at the workers' camp, a celebration was also taking place – drumming and singing. I could have joined them. Instead, I buried my face in my bedspread and cried. I finally fell asleep to someone in the kitchen repeatedly playing a song on the Waylin and Willie cassette, *If You Can Touch Her at All*.

PART 6 – LEAVING GUINEA

The following includes information taken from edited diary entries dating June 9th to June 20th, 1980.

June 8th Sunday – I rose a little after 5:00 to watch the sun rise. It had rained last night, and droplets glistened. The air was warm and mellow, scented with dampened earth. Standing on the terrace overlooking Baoule Flats, I gazed across the savannah, its tall grasses swaying to soft breeze songs. My heart captured the moment, never to let it slip away.

I dismantled the tent while Tony went down to the worker's camp and blew his whistle, startling the workers into alertness. Then he and I got the rest of the camp members up. I worked all morning packing up the kitchen and food storage, then helped Tony take down his tent, pack up clothing, and spare Land Rover parts that had crowded his dwelling. Then we helped Raynor and Alan pack up.

The workers came into camp riding in the trailer, pulled by the tractor that Latiff was driving. They were singing and beating rhythm on David's vintage trommel from Pit #3. Around 3:00 this afternoon we were on our way – goodbye Camp A. See you next year?

I rode in a Land Rover seated between Tony and Raynor. Wayde rode in the back with Sange, David's monkey. Latiff drove the tractor ahead, pulling the trailer. The rest of us followed in the four Land Rovers with our personal belongings and some of the workers. There were quite a few mud holes and obstacles to overcome, but our caravan made it to the Milo River. The tractor pulled the trailer across to Kérouané, unhooked it, and then towed each of the Land Rovers across.

I had a mishap while crossing the Milo. When water splashed up over the hood, Sange panicked and grabbed my head. One of his claws scratched my right eye, leaving a large painful scratch across the sclera, causing the eye to water constantly. I am concerned because images viewed through that eye are blurred and doubled. There is also a chance that the wound could become infected. David put a black patch over it when we had reached the Syli Guest House in Kérouané, where we would spend the night.

The trailer will be left here for a tractor from the village to pick up. The large truck that had been rented to transport the mining equipment, camp supplies, and our personal belongings was waiting for our arrival. We all worked unloading the trailer and loading the truck. The hiring of the truck had come at a steep price – six drums of gasoil and one drum of lube oil.

At the Syli house most of the camp members set their cots and mosquito netting up in the living-dining area of the guest house. The workers crowded into the large bedroom with their cots. Now, both rooms resembled dormitories, wall-to-wall with folding cots and mosquito nets. I was put in a large private room with a double bed and mosquito net. It was the house's suite.

Before retiring for the night Tony wanted to go for one last drink at the small illicit Kérouané bar. I felt a little self-conscious because of the eye patch but agreed to go. When Tony and I returned a couple of hours later I learned that Alan had made up my bed. Alan is so thoughtful and kind. I am going to miss him very much when I leave Guinea.

June 9th Monday – This morning, as I was packing up my belongings, Latiff came to my room. He wanted to know if I still had the Gaboon viper. He was told that it was on the back seat of Tony's Land Rover.

Latiff retrieved the snake and took it to the local medicine man to trade for medicine for my eye. The eye was all red this morning and the pain hadn't subsided. The vision was still blurred and double.

Everyone was ready to leave by 8:30. Latiff had yet to return, so I waited at the guest house while Tony and Raynor walked to the Kérouané market for fresh fruit and bread. The four Land Rovers were lined up and ready to go. Just as Tony and Raynor returned, Latiff came with a small glass bottle of medicine he had received in trade for the snake. I immediately moisten a corner of my clean shirt with the liquid and squeezed it into my eye. It stung. The black patch was replaced with a fresh one, then the caravan was on its way!

Enroute to Kankan we were hailed to a stop by a PDG Aredor Land Rover with a flat tire. They were transporting diamonds to Conakry and had no spare. We offered one of ours if they stay with our caravan, since we had only two spares among our four vehicles. Even though the agreement had been made, at one point when the caravan stopped, the Aredor Land Rover pulled out of formation and tried to take off. David saw the attempted escape and quickly maneuvered in front of the vehicle. Alan pulled alongside and Fred brought up the rear, sandwiching the vehicle in place. The errant vehicle pulled back into line.

Approximately thirty kilometers later, a tire on David's Land Rover went flat, and we discovered that our remaining spare had a broken valve and wouldn't hold air. The loaned spare tire had to come off the Aredor vehicle which caused angry words and threats from the driver of the now stranded Land Rover. The Aredor driver, his three passengers, and all their luggage were crammed into our vehicles and transported to Kankan. Since they were on official PDG business, they had the right to commandeer one of our vehicles.

However, when the Kankan PDG official came to select which vehicle the Aredor driver could take, he sadly shook his head and pronounced that none of DDX's vehicles were in good enough condition to transport the diamonds and denied Aredor's request.

None of our Land Rovers started on their own. They had to be pushed to start. Every vehicle leaked steady streams of gas through numerous punctures in the gas tanks. Only two of the vehicles had working headlights – one each. The Land Rover that was in the best shape was Fred's. However, he did have intermittent fires flare up behind his dashboard, so carried extra water to douse them when they began.

The PDG official required that one of our Land Rovers take the three men and their gear to the airport. Fred's vehicle was chosen, but enroute, his vehicle got a flat tire. The ungrateful human cargo grabbed their baggage, and all stormed off in a huff.

Meanwhile, the rest of us went to Kankan's Texico yard where we met up with Dee and JoAnn, again! They had returned from the trip to Florida and had been transferred from Conakry to Kankan. We were given cold beer, soft drinks, sandwiches made with real ham, and all the cheese that we could eat! What luxury – especially considering that we had only enough sylis among us to purchase the equivalent of four loaves of bread.

Fred hadn't returned, so Tony took off with one of the two tires that he was able to source from Texico and found Fred stranded but knowing that help would arrive. Tony handed him a ham sandwich with cheese and a cold soda to enjoy while Tony changed the tire.

David gave the monkey to one of the Frenchmen employed at Texico. Speaking of the monkey, I have repeatedly used the liquid Latiff brought me and my eyesight has greatly improved, and it doesn't hurt nearly as much!

The remainder of the trip to Kissidougou was on better roads. The only excitement that our caravan of worn-down Land Rovers had was Fred's panel fires when the procession had to pause periodically to douse canteens of water on his instrument panel.

At the guest house in Kissidougou, Jean Paul gave each of us two warm beers and some peanuts for dinner. Quite a let-down after the royal treatment we had received at the Kankan Texico. None of us had enough sylis left to purchase brochettes from the street venders. The DDX crew commented that they were obviously working for the wrong company.

The guest house already had three occupants from Camp B and C. Fred claimed the one small private room. The rest of us set up folding cots in close quarters. I was kind of sandwiched between Tony and Raynor. Wayde had lost his mosquito net. The Land Rovers were turned inside out in search of it. Alan offered Wayde his, but Wayde refused the offer, burrowing under the covers in the hot, humid room instead, to avoid mosquito bites. We all visited awhile before retiring.

June 10th Tuesday – Roses appeared at the foot of my bed this morning. They weren't from Fred; nor Alan – I had asked. Raynor was still asleep. Tony? I learned that he had left for the mechanic shop early this morning.

Wayde's mosquito net turned up where none of us had looked but should have. It was hanging above Fred's bed, while the large one that had hung over the double bed in our camp payotte lay crumpled on the floor. When questioned, Fred claimed that the large one was too big for the small bed and too difficult to put up. Fred stood mutely by as I jerked the net from his bed and returned it to Wayde. Surprisingly, I wasn't angry with Fred. I had become accustomed to his behavior.

Fred and I went to the Niandan River where Fred washed buckets of gravel he had yet to process. I washed clothes, amid local women doing the same. This is the same Kissidougou river where we had filled up Jean Paul's water barrels in March, after we had left Conakry enroute to camp. I felt the bite of deja vu, and sadness followed. This was it…I was leaving.

After the bucket of gravel had been washed, barren of diamonds, Fred came over to me and wanted to talk. He said that he was sorry to have lost me and began to cry. I, too, felt sad and the tears flowed. Fred said that he wanted to learn how to love – that he needed to continue seeing me when we reached the United States. He begged for another chance as we clung to one another weeping. We were being stared at by the native women. But that didn't matter in the moment of sorrow and connection. Could our love be salvaged? My emotions were heavy with the sadness of our lost love. I was willing to try…but that weakness was short lived.

Fred pulled one of the white handkerchiefs, that he had requested I bring with me from the United States, out of his pocket and blew his nose. He held me at arm's length and smiled broadly, took a deep breath, and said, "Wasn't that experience beautiful! I loved it! I live for moments like this."

Then he happily jogged back to the Land Rover for another bucket of gravel.

Beautiful? No, it was sad. Heartbreaking. And he had me going again, hoping. I could not teach him how to love, especially unconditionally. I had yet to achieve that myself.

Lampietti had arrived by the time that we had returned to the guest house, leaving a message with Jean Paul that Fred, David, Raynor, Pip, Wayde and I would be leaving for Conakry in the morning. Wayde and I were to return directly home. I was disappointed with the news. However, Fred met with Lampietti later and arranged that Wayde and I stay another week. Raynor and Tony will be staying, too. Only Pip and David will be leaving for Conakry immediately. David was scheduled to take a plane from Conakry to a tropical disease center in Paris.

It poured down rain, so the picnic that Tony had planned and paid for with wages from his cashed paycheck was moved inside one of the PDG buildings. There was plenty of beer and wine, a quarter of a beef, sliced tomatoes, cucumbers, rice, and bread. All PDG employees were invited, and all attended except for David Salsby (who had flown home a couple of weeks ago), Simon (still in Bounoudou), Tys (resigned) and Bill.

Fred was exceptionally attentive this evening. He drank too much beer and I had to help him to his cot in the guest house.

June 11th Wednesday – This morning I had to decide whether to go to Bounoudou for five days on a DDX assignment with Raynor and Alan; stay in Kissidougou with Fred to continue washing samples; or go with Tony to Freetown.

Tony would ride to Conakry in the rented truck towing the crippled Mercedes. Then from Conakry, he would attempt to tow the Mercedes, with one of the Land Rovers, to Freetown to be repaired. If going to Sierra Leone, Wayde and I would be returning alone to Conakry on the bus. I would be back at the Sultan House in time to see Fred and Raynor before Wayde and I left for Idaho.

But if I went to Seirra Leone, I wouldn't see Alan again and he was unhappy over that possibility. This would be goodbye. I was conflicted. However, we talked about it and Alan says that he may come to Idaho for a visit in August if his work here has been completed. Raynor was not happy with the possibility of me going to Sierra Leone, but said it was out of selfishness. He told me that I should go. That after all that I had done for camp, I deserved a vacation, and he would see me back in Conakry afterwards.

So, I decided to go with Tony. Wayde was ecstatic. I really wanted to experience Freetown. But I also wanted to experience it with Tony. My heart was always light when in his company. And Tony was unattached – there was no woman waiting for him to return from Africa. I was ready for a romantic fling if that were to happen. A fling with no future expectation or involvement.

I packed Wayde's and my things. Together Tony and I prepared our order of mission, as illegal as hell, but there wasn't time to go through the regular channels. Tony had swiped some official paper, and using a past order of mission, I copied the style and typed it out on the official paper. Tony had a stamp with his personal coat of arms, which when inked and applied to the paper, then smeared slightly, looked very official! Our dummy document would save us a couple of days' wait. Tony traveled to and from Sierra Leone frequently and many of the guards recognized him and waved him through. The paper was something to flash should one of the guards not recognize him.

Before we left, Tony had peeked into John Paul's warehouse, which had normally been locked, but someone had failed to do so. There was all our missing food! Stacks of canned ham, tuna, chicken, pork and beans, canned vegetables, and fruit. Cases and cases of soda pop and beer. Condiments, pickles, salt, mayonnaise. Plus, large bags of rice and cases of corned beef for the workers! There were food items that we hadn't seen since the beginning of the season. Items that we had ordered from the main store house in Conakry, but never received. We had blamed Tys for not sending the supplies, even though he claimed to have done so. John Paul must be the one selling the supplies to merchants – the items that we have seen in Kérouané and Kissidougou. Tony will be speaking with Lampietti about the problem and Jean Paul will likely not be back next year.

There were several mini WAWAs, so we didn't leave Kissidougou until 7:00 P.M. After the crippled Mercedes had been hooked to the rented truck, I said goodbye to Alan, and we headed off. Wayde rode in the Land Rover with Latiff. Tony and I rode with the driver in the rented truck.

We got as far as Farina, where we tied our mosquito nets to the door handles of the Land Rover and set up our cots beneath. Wayde decided to sleep on the backseat of the Land Rover. It had rained earlier, but now the sky was crystal clear, stars sparkling against the night's blackness. Tony and I shared a bottle of Gin, passing it back and forth. Then Tony reached over and took my hand in his.

June 12th Thursday – We were up at sunrise. Tony woke me just as the large orange ball materialized on the horizon. He had already packed up his cot and rolled up the mosquito net and was eager to get going.

The driver of the large truck picked up his daughter in Farina to take her to Conakry. Wayde and Tony went in the truck while I rode in the Land Rover with Latiff. Unlike our initial adventure going from Kissidougou to camp, losing Tony along the way and overcoming one WAWA after another, Latiff was talkative. He told me a lot about Africa and its culture. Latiff's father is Nigerian and his mother, Sierra Leonian. His parents reside in Nigeria.

One of Latiff's wives was going to the University of Ohio, to get a degree in economics. However, Latiff received word that she isn't going to return to Africa. She had fallen in love with one of her professors and has settled in Texas.

Latiff said, "I must forget her now. I cannot go to America and make her come home."

We saw groups of villagers walking with shovels and hoes. Latiff explained that it is planting season, and growing food is a community endeavor. The villagers go to each farm to hoe and plant. The owner of the farm feeds them, then joins the group in their journey to the next farm where the community planting continues.

It took us sixteen hours to reach Conakry. When darkness came, more barriers between the villages went up. It was stop and start; stop and start, for the last few hours of our journey. At the last barrier, Tony left the truck to check the security of the chains between the Mercedes and the Land Rover. Sitting in the Land Rover, a silly grin on my face, I scrutinized the worn-out shoe, paper bag and a bundle of chicken feet dangling from the barrel.

A passenger vehicle tried to squeeze past the barrier by passing on the wrong side of the road, using the Mercedes as a partial shield.

Suddenly there was the chatter of rapid gunfire as a guard emptied an AK47 into the windshield of the car, spraying glass everywhere. Tony was standing beside the Mercedes when the shooting occurred and was fortunate that he didn't get hurt from the flying glass and bullets! The occupants of the car were dragged from the vehicle and appeared to be dead. I realized how one should respect a barrier regardless of its ramshackle appearance…and have the proper paperwork.

It was with relief that we reached the Sultan House in Conakry with Tys gone and Jean Charlot in his place. Jean Charlot will work at getting a visa for me to enter Sierra Leone. David and Pip were enroute to Paris.

There are not enough company funds to advance Fred for Wayde's and my ticket home…plus I have no official visa for exiting. I will have to work on resolving these issues when I return from Freetown.

I prepared Tony and Wayde some dinner. Tony and I visited and read the latest available Times Magazine, May 12th. Then I showered and retired for the night in Fred's and my previous room.

June 13th Friday – What WAWAs will I face today. For starts, Latiff came to the Saltan House this morning and requested to speak with me. We went to the screened in room and sat at the small table there. Latiff told me that he loved me, then without another word, left.

I was shocked and confused. I didn't know enough about African customs or the Muslim religion to know how to respond to Latiff in the least hurtful way. How seriously should I take his disclosure? How do I avoid hurting his African pride? How many wives does he have? Does he have in mind replacing the one he lost to America with me?

Tony and Jean Paul have secured my visa to enter Sierra Leone! We will be leaving tomorrow, and I can hardly wait. Wayde stayed at the Sultan House reacquainting himself with the monkey while Tony took me to the large open market in Conakry. It was totally different from the crowded, stinky one that Fred took me to. We shopped for fresh produce for tonight's dinner, then walked around town. Tony purchased four leopard claws at a small shop, and I bought a small sterling silver filagree payotte for my charm bracelet. I had a wonderful time.

For dinner I prepared a hot pepper and lime marinade for chicken, which Tony broiled outdoors on the barbeque. I also made salad, baked potatoes, garlic bread and fried plantains. As I was preparing dinner, Tony came up behind me and gave me an affectionate hug. It caused a flutter of desire in me. Was I ready for this?

Jean Charlot put the table on the porch, and we wined and dined with the ocean in the background.

June 14th Saturday – It took until 2:00 this afternoon to get our exit visas, travel papers, and the vehicles ready to leave for Sierra Leone. I think that we were a ridiculous sight, heading down the road with the huge Mercedes truck being towed by the Land Rover. The way was difficult, and the going was slow. Latiff had to apply the Mercedes' brakes frequently so that it wouldn't smash into the Land Rover.

Toward evening, as we reached the border, Tony discovered that we couldn't legally tow the Mercedes into Sierra Leone with the Land Rover. We had to leave the Mercedes at the border and proceed onto Freetown. I must admit that here in Sierra Leone there are fewer wrecked and burned-out cars. Tony had had concerns about getting through the barriers with the Land Rover leaking a trail of gas, sporting a smashed-in front end and missing one headlight. Tony says that he has many friends in Sierra Leone. He will send Latiff back to the border with a borrowed vehicle to tow the Mercedes across the border and into Freetown.

We reached Freetown at 10:30 this evening and went directly to the PDG guest house. It is luxurious! My room has a queen-sized bed with tub, shower and a balcony which looks down on the lights of the city and out across the Atlantic Ocean. There is even air conditioning. Tony's room is smaller, but next to mine. Tony settled Wayde into the small room, where Wayde fell into an exhausted sleep.

After I had cleaned up and changed clothes, Tony took me to the Atlantic Club. It is right on the beach and very elegant. One side is open to the ocean, with tables set in a garden under the open sky; the other side has the backdrop of rolling waves accented with lights. Tony introduced me to some friends there. One of his friends asked me to dance. We disco danced until 4:00 in the morning. Tony and I were exhausted when he returned me to my room. He hesitated at my door. I opened the door wider, and he entered. I quickly went to check on Wayde. He was still sound asleep. Latiff was stretched out on the couch, also asleep, but woke as I was leaving a note for Wayde on a notepad by the phone. Our eyes met. Latiff nodded an understanding, then rolled to his side, his back to me. I returned to my room. Tony and I undressed and curled up together, falling into an exhausted sleep.

June 15th Sunday – Tony and I were up by 9:00 and ready to have breakfast and explore Freetown. We ate at a little place down the street and the food was so fresh and good! Wayde asked for a second breakfast. Tony was happy to oblige.

Freetown is a very large city, complete with banks, supermarkets, gas stations, casinos, night clubs and shops. We took a taxi around and visited a beach at one of the large hotel nightclubs with an ocean front and watched Wayde play with a couple of Sierra Leone children while we enjoyed Samosas. When we returned to the guest house, we changed clothes before going to Latiff's brother's home for a meal of rice and meat sauce. We dined in the small entrance of the brother's photo studio. The meal was very good.

Latiff joined us when we left to visit a Lebanese family that Tony had known for years. Most of the larger businesses in Freetown are Lebanese owned and operated. The family was large, with aunts, uncles, married children, grandchildren, great grandchildren – all living under the same roof. People drifted in and out all afternoon and evening. Eighteen people live in the home.

We left at 8:00 P.M. and returned to the guest house where we met an employee of DDX, who works out of Sierra Leone. He came with Tony, Wayde and me to the Duncans, Tony's friends who live in one of the nicer homes here. Mrs. Duncan is half Lebanese and half Nigerian. She was once a well-known diamond buyer. Her husband is an Englishman. They have several children and asked us to bring Wayde back again tomorrow. I will be going shopping in the morning with Anita, the Duncan's fourteen-year-old daughter.

At 11:30 this evening Tony took me to the Atlantic again and we stayed until 2:00 A.M. Tony stayed with me again tonight. We have become lovers.

June 16th Monday – I met Anita at her parent's house around 10:00. We took a taxi to town, then walked to various shops. I bought a few gifts to take home and a dress for myself. The dress is a long, black sleeveless one with side slits and embroidered trim.

At 2:00, I returned to the guest house. Tony arrived shortly afterward from the office of Mr. Gooding, the PDG payroll person. Tony had been working out the details for the Sierra Leonian worker's pay.

Tony was in a playful mood. He chased me around the room tickling me until tears of laughter ran down my face. Then he hugged me and told me that he was really going to miss me. I will miss Tony, too. We have shared many wonderful and heartfelt times in Africa.

Tony returned to Mr. Gooding's office. Latiff came to see me, and we had an easy, pleasant conversation. He asked that I send him a letter when I return home, and I said that I would. He also said that he won't forget me and that he looks forward to my return to Guinea. He promised that I would be returning next season; that he will use his African powers to bring me back.

Wayde had spent the day at the Duncans', playing with their two boys, Alan, and Robert. Mrs. Duncan brought Wayde home and asked if he could spend the night with them. Unfortunately, we must be at the bus station at 7:30 A.M. to pick up our reserved tickets. Mrs. Duncan said that Wayde was a very polite and bright boy. She and her family are personal friends of Mr. Lampietti and knew that I had applied for a job next season and that Wayde would not be allowed at camp. She indicated that should I return next season that we might be able to work out something where Wayde could stay with her family in Freetown and have schooling along with her children. That way, two weeks out of every six, I could visit my son.

I fixed my hair and put on my new dress. Tony and I are going to the Atlantic Club for dinner. At the Atlantic, we sat at a candlelit table and had hummus as an appetizer. Then we ordered dinner. Tony had steak and potatoes and I ordered Lobster Thermador with mushrooms. The meal was delicious.

We later sat at the bar drinking Star beer and visiting. As we were preparing to leave, the bar tender bought us a round. We had nearly finished when another round arrived from two gentlemen seated across the bar from us. Then they purchased two more rounds. Tony suggested that I go thank them, which I did. They both said that they wanted to dance with me, but since we had been ready to leave, I hesitated. Tony, who didn't care for dancing himself, loved to watch people dance.

I danced until I have blisters on my toes! One of the gentlemen, a Lebanese, managed the 7-Up bottling plant in Freetown. The other man is from Holland and is a refrigerator technician. He travels all over the world and will be in Polynesia next week. He says that he owns a large guest villa in Holland. He gave me his address saying that my son and I are invited to spend a week or two as his guests at the villa. All that I would need to do is give him advanced notice of my arrival so that he can have his staff prepare for our visit should he be out of the country. Perhaps when I return to Guinea, Wayde and I will get to see Holland in the springtime during one of my 2-week vacations.

Tony and I returned home around 3:00 A.M. Latiff had spent the evening with Wayde and was asleep on the couch in Tony's room. After checking on Wayde, Tony and I went to my room and slept wrapped in each other's arms.

June 17th Tuesday – I was up at 6:30 this morning and ready to leave by 7:00. Tony had gotten up early but fell back to sleep after getting dressed. Latiff and I stood on the balcony watching the ocean and the early morning sky.

"A journey is like the sea," Latiff told me, "It goes away, but then it returns."

When Latiff went to fetch a taxi, I woke Tony.

"I don't like you leaving like this, Sweetheart", he told me.

I hugged Tony and felt as though I was going to cry – but I didn't.

Latiff and Tony rode with us to the bus station and I kissed Tony goodbye as I boarded the bus. I wanted to hug Latiff goodbye but felt that it may not have been within his customs, so I shook his hand.

Wayde and I sat at the back of the bus. It didn't depart until ten, but was loaded by 8:00, as is the custom here. Tony and Latiff hovered around the outside of my bus window. It wasn't one that opened, so I couldn't speak to them. Latiff disappeared, then returned with bread, cheese and chocolate for our journey and passengers passed it, hand over hand, until it reached Wayde and me. I was touched by Tony and Latiff's thoughtfulness and felt like I was going to cry. There was a lump in my throat at the thought that I may never see them again. I flashed them a watery smile and wished that they would go away. Finally, they did.

When the bus departed, everyone was packed tight. We were so crammed together that should the bus roll over, none of us would be displaced. The Africans immediately adopted Wayde and me, looking after us the entire journey. A white woman and her child riding a native bus is rare. I love the African people. Why can't my race be as gracious? I feel safer and more welcomed in this bus of caring strangers that I would in a bus in the United States.

When we stopped for lunch, I needed to use the bathroom, which turned out to be a pile of rocks behind a blind, used by both men and women. As I crouched to relieve myself, my mind flashed back to the Conakry market where I had felt very uncomfortable. Now, I realize that I have, during my time in Guinea, lost the fear of appearing immodest. No one here feels embarrassed by the daily function of "passing water".
Lunch consisted of boiled rice and a fowl-smelling meat sauce. Wayde and I didn't partake. My traveling companions worried and fretted over us not eating lunch, even bringing bowls of the

vile stuff to us, and coaxing us like little children to eat. I would have liked to ease their minds and have lunch, but I was very worried about what would happen if we did. We had the food that Latiff and Tony had given us, so I had Wayde go to the bus and get it. Little bits of bread and cheese were handed to every passenger. I confess, the chocolate had been hidden away.

The bouncing, careening bus resembled an amusement park ride designed to create butterflies in the stomach, only there were no seat belts or safety tracks. The trip lasted three hundred miles. And I loved every bit of it!

We arrived in Conakry around 5:30. I didn't have the address to the Sultan House – errant of me not to have remembered to get it from Tony. I worried that I would have difficulty finding my way, but the bus had stopped at the market not more than four blocks from the house.

Jean Charlot greeted us as we entered the Sultan house. Since he doesn't speak English, and I, no French, our conversation was short.

"Freetown, c'est bien?"
"Oui."
"Autobus c'est bien?"
"Oui.Très bien."

Then we bobbed our heads and grinned. I took a nap and woke long enough to eat a little food Jean Charlot had fixed, bob my head, grin, and return to my room. Aside from Jean Charlot, I was the only one at the Sultan House. I am missing Tony. Tomorrow, Fred, Raynor and Simon arrive. I am looking forward to seeing them. I am not looking forward to leaving Guinea. But I know that Wayde and I must.

June 18th Wednesday – I got up late and decided to go shopping at the large market downtown. Tony had given me one hundred sylis as Wayde and I were leaving. Franklin, a Sierra Leonian, was waiting to accompany Simon to Sierra Leone and asked if he could come along. I was delighted to have him since he spoke English and could help me communicate at the market. The taxi that took us to the market wouldn't accept payment. Nor would the one that transported us back to the Sultan House.

The generosity of the Guinean people amazed me. I knew that not all African countries were like Guinea and Sierra Leone. The people from Dakar had not made me feel comfortable or welcomed. But, here in this closed-off country, where food and commodities were scarce, the people were quick to share what they had with strangers. I felt grateful just to be among them. They are happy and loving people.

Franklin followed me around for three hours. He seemed to enjoy bartering for fabric and a tailor's labor. I had decided to have a dress made. It was promised to be completed at 5:00 this afternoon and Franklin said that he would return to pick it up since I was expected to cook dinner for Fred, Raynor and Simon. I asked Franklin to join us, as well.

Franklin didn't return until 7:00. It had taken the tailor longer to finish the dress. I put on the dress and sought his approval. He smiled and nodded. When Fred, Raynor and Simon arrived thirty minutes later, they also approved.

But the big hit was the fried chicken, mashed potatoes and gravy, fresh peas with pearl onions, stuffed eggs, and a pear crisp.

Raynor and Simon were exhausted and retired early. Fred and I visited for a while. He wanted to know if we could try and get back together in the United States. I thought not.

June 19th Thursday – I woke up and began to become concerned as to how I was going to manage to get home. Our tickets have been booked from Dakar to New York, but I am going to be on my own from there with not enough money for plane or bus fare to get across the country to Idaho. Plus, an exit visa is needed to leave Guinea, having not had an official visa when entering the country. Even though Jean Charlot had been to the PDG office to get one for me, his efforts had failed.

An exit visa just about didn't happen, which would have meant at least another week in Conakry. I went to the PDG office and attempted to explain my situation. The gentleman at the desk could understand most of what I was saying but had no idea as to what paperwork I needed to get out of the country. I was directed to another office, where that person was able to find the paperwork that I had signed upon my arrival. He shuffled through it with a puzzled look on his face. Eventually, he stuffed it all back in the file and shrugged his shoulders. However, he pointed to yet another office, indicating that was the person responsible for issuing permission for Guineans leaving the country.

The person that I had been directed to was a very large man, who obviously ate well. He glanced up at the clock and seemed as though he were about to leave for the day. It was getting a bit late, and my stomach was knotting up. He spoke to me in English, asking why I had come to his office.

I explained that my son and I needed to leave Conakry tomorrow morning to head back to the United States. He wanted to know why I needed to leave his beautiful country. I was honest when I told him that I didn't want to leave. To which he replied that I should stay, then.

Obviously, I was getting nowhere. And time was running out.

"I must return home," I stated once again.

To which he asked, "Why?"

Think fast. Think fast.

"Because" I told him," there is no money here. I have money in America, to bring back."

He stared at me in silence, then smiled.

"I wish you to meet my mother when you come back".

"Yes! I will love meeting your mother!"

And with that, he pulled out an official looking form and stamped it, then added his signature, a mere five minutes before the office closed.

"Small bills, no big moneys," he said, as I gave him one last smile before rushing out of the office.

Later, I went to the market with Raynor to help him select material for a dress for Janis and introduced him to the tailor that had made my dress. The dress turned out beautiful! She will love it.

Fred gave me one hundred dollars to help me get home. Raynor loaned me another hundred dollars and gave me his taped play, *The Importance of Being Earnest*.

We had a nice lunch of stew at 2:30 then I packed and changed my clothes. Before I knew it, Wayde and I were waiting at the airport with Fred, Raynor and Jean Charlot to see us off. Simon had already left for Sierra Leone. I gave each of the men a goodbye kiss and boarded the plane. My emotions weren't about the excitement of heading home; my emotions were about the grief I was feeling leaving Guinea. My stomach felt as though I were falling from a ten-story building. Soon I was sitting in the Dakar-Yoff International Airport. Our plane leaves for New York at 1:30 A.M. It is 5:00 P.M. now. I am sitting here wondering if there will be one last WAWA or will all go well during the wait in this crowded, noisy airport.

June 20th Friday – Well, I nearly did have a WAWA, and a major one at that! As hard as I had tried to stay awake in the stiff, uncomfortable airport chair, I fell asleep. Wayde was to be my "right hand man" and shake me if I began to nod off. He was my "right hand man" alright, sound asleep beside me. I hastily woke him up and asked him to check at the desk to see what time it was. It was 1:25 and the plane had been boarded and was taxiing down the runway! It would be another week before another flight from Dakar to the United States!

While the ticket agent radioed the airplane, two men rushed out from behind the ticket booth. One man grabbed my guitar and backpack, while the other hoisted Wayde and his backpack. I grabbed my suitcase and the three of us ran toward the plane, now rolling to a stop. Two other men rushed along behind us, pushing the heavy, awkward wheeled stairway. It was a long dash to the plane, and we all arrived out of breath.

The stairs were rolled into position. Wayde and I scurried up, lugging our belongings. We made our way down the aisle, between rows of disgruntled passengers, to the back seats. We were seated next to a twenty-four-year-old Nigerian flying to Cleveland, Ohio to finish his training as a surgeon. I slept some on the plane. Wayde and I arrived at the New York Kennedy Airport, at 5:00 A.M. New York time.

There wasn't enough money to get to Boise, Idaho. Our expired Apex tickets had a partial refund due. However, it would take three weeks to process. As we dragged our luggage, backpacks, and guitar around the airport, I was dazed with exhaustion.

Wayde was hungry, so first things first. We went to one of the kiosks and purchased a loaf of bread and a jar of peanut butter. I snagged a plastic knife from one of the little airport cafes and started to sit down. Then, I had an idea.

I went to one of the ticket counters and asked who issued the refunds. I had to ask around a few times to get the name and location of the office which processed them. It was at the top mezzanine, six doors down. We hoisted our stuff to the elevator, then lugged it down the hallway and opened the door. It was a nice, cozy office with a small leather sofa facing a long counter. A man was seated behind, sorting paperwork.

I stacked our possessions by the door, and we took a seat on the sofa before making sandwiches.
The man gave us a quizzical look. "May I help you?"

"Would you like a sandwich?" I asked.

"No thank you. How may I help you?"

I stood and approached the desk, showed him our expired tickets, and explained our situation. Ten minutes later, we walked away with two tickets to Boise, via Chicago. I phoned my mother collect, and told her that we would be arriving in Boise at 3:30 P.M. She and Dad would drive the hundred miles from McCall to meet us and drive home.

The flight between Chicago and Boise carried Steve Symms and Senator Frank Church. I talked politics with Steve Symms for quite a while, which made the trip seem shorter.

Mom and Dad picked us up at the airport and we visited on the way home. As we passed familiar mountains and rivers, I felt my love for Idaho and the familiarity of home. But my heart was still in Africa with Tony, David, Alan, Raynor, Fred, Latiff, Jean Charlot…and Bill. Africa was now a long distance away. I felt dazed and heavy in the heart. Will I ever see Guinea again? Or the friends I left behind?

AFTERWORDS

I had written this diary about my bookselling trip with Fred and the time we had spent in Guinea, West Africa. When I returned to Idaho, I wrapped the diary in a silk scarf and tucked it away. It hadn't been opened and read until 2023. One of my apprentices was writing a personal history and wanted to include something about me in her book. I handed her the diary.

When she had finished reading it, she said, "This needs to be a book."

So, forty-four years later, I opened and read my diary. It is difficult to express the emotions felt in revisiting that time and place – the beauty and spirit of Guinea in 1980, the longing, the tears, the sadness that I had felt when leaving her.

I had received a letter from Lampietti, written June 24th.,1980, requesting that I call in mid-July to discuss my situation and my suggestions for the 1981 season. With heavy heart, I made the call and withdrew my application.

Had I done the wrong thing by not returning, as planned? By settling for something that I did not want, but felt that it was the best thing for me to do?

I had been conflicted about leaving Wayde in Freetown for six weeks at a time, seeing him only during two weeks' vacation…and knowing that WAWAs were bound to happen, so I couldn't guarantee seeing him even then. Wayde had begun to "act out" when he realized that he wouldn't be returning to camp with me.

A friend, John, whose mother had introduced me to Fred, had recently divorced. He proposed that we marry, saying that he could provide a male role model for my son. He had a son Wayde's age, Johnny. The two boys had spent time together in the past and got along well. I told him that, although we had been friends for more than six years, I did not love him. He accepted that.

I agreed to the marriage. It lasted a little over two years. In the end, Wayde's stepfather walked away, saying he couldn't cope with my son and his actions.

One of my great sadnesses is that I don't know what became of the friends that I had made in Guinea. I failed to keep in touch. Yet, while writing from my diary they were brought back to life. I laughed. I worried. I loved. I wept …it all seemed to have happened such a short time ago. But the years and the mirror tell me differently.

I do know that Raynor Shaw wrote *Three Gorges of the Yangtze River: Chongqing to Wuhan*, and *Hong Kong Landscapes: Shaping the Barren Rock* while working as a geologist in Hong Kong. They are beautiful books, but I have been unable to contact Raynor.

When I was fifty, a man entered my life – Robert Sweetgall, a fifty-two-year-old bachelor, and Cooper Union chemical engineer graduate. He had walked across America seven times to promote his message of walking and wellness. In the movie, *Forrest Gump*, Forrest's walk across America had been added to the script after the screen writer had met Robert Sweetgall on the Brooklyn Bridge after his first walk across America and back.

I wasn't looking for a husband, but he saw in me something special. After a two-year courtship, we married. I had been married before, but I had never had a husband...a man who treated me with unconditional love, kindness, and respect. We shared eighteen years before his passing.

It was Guinea that taught me how to untangle my life when it became hung up on a pile of debris. A good life requires three basic things – love, food, and shelter. All else is incidental.

The people of Guinea taught me kindness, as well as empathy. And that a smile can open a heart.

The members of camp showed me gratitude and the importance of working as a team. In later years this inspired me to begin a work and learn apprentice program in the study of regional medicinal plants. One hundred and thirty apprentices took me up on my offer and most continue to do amazing work.

But it was Robert's unconditional love that freed me from the turbulent eddies of my life – and led me to open water.

Other books by the author:

How to Prepare Common Wild Foods

School at Home, an Alternative to the Public School System

Mountain Men of Idaho

River Tales of Idaho

Basque Cooking and Lore

*McCall's Historic Shore Lodge (*with Marlee Wilcomb*)*

The Rocky Mountain Wild Foods Cookbook

Salmon River Legends and Campfire Cuisine with Steven Shepherd

*Cooking with Spirit, Native American Food and Fact (*with Lisa Railsback)

Wild Foods of the Desert

Healing Plants of the Rocky Mountains

Medicinal Plants of the Northwest: 130 Monographs

Volume 2 Medicinal Plants of the Northwest another 130 Monographs

Fabulous Wild Fungi ~ Wildly Creative Cuisine

Medicinal Camino ~ Plant First Aid Along "The Way"

Plant First Aid Along the Salmon River (Main and Middle Fork)

The Medicinal Mushroom Beverage Book (with Brent Davy and Kevin Ryan)

Sisters of a Different Dawn (Novel)

Made in the USA
Middletown, DE
11 April 2024

52827152R00166